MW01038285

Germany's Defeat
in the First World War

Germany's Defeat in the First World War

The Lost Battles and Reckless Gambles That Brought Down the Second Reich

Mark D. Karau

 PRAEGER™

An Imprint of ABC-CLIO, LLC

Santa Barbara, California • Denver, Colorado

Library of Congress Cataloging-in-Publication Data

Karau, Mark D., 1969-
    Germany's defeat in the First World War : the lost battles and reckless gambles that brought down the Second Reich / Mark D. Karau.
  pages cm
  Includes bibliographical references and index.
   ISBN 978-0-313-39619-9 (hard copy : alk. paper)–ISBN 978-0-313-39620-5 (ebook)
   1. World War, 1914-1918–Campaigns. 2. World War, 1914-1918–Germany. 3. Command of troops–History–20th century. I. Title.
D531.K35   2015
940.4'0943–dc23   2015004932

ISBN: 978–0–313–39619–9
EISBN: 978–0–313–39620–5

19 18 17 16 15   1 2 3 4 5

This book is also available on the World Wide Web as an eBook.
Visit www.abc-clio.com for details.

Praeger
An Imprint of ABC-CLIO, LLC

ABC-CLIO, LLC
130 Cremona Drive, P.O. Box 1911
Santa Barbara, California 93116-1911

This book is printed on acid-free paper ∞

Manufactured in the United States of America

For Katie

Contents

Introduction

On November 11, 1918, the guns fell silent around Europe. The First World War was over. The armistice that took effect that day was an admission of defeat by a German nation that had seen its allies collapse over the previous eight weeks. Yet, when the armistice was signed German armies still stood on foreign soil in France, Belgium, and on much of the area that had once belonged to the tsars of Russia. Just eight months earlier, the Germans had launched an offensive that at first seemed likely to carry them to victory, yet now a new German government was admitting defeat. For many Germans this turn of events was inexplicable. How could Germany, after all the sacrifices, have actually been beaten? The immediate response in some circles of German society was to argue that the German armies had been stabbed in the back by the collapse and revolution at home. This became known as the "stab in the back" legend, or the *Dolchstoss Legende*, and it poisoned German politics for two decades, helping to create an environment in which the Nazis were able to come to power. In the decades since the Second World War historians have taken pains to debunk the *Dolchstoss Legende* and to demonstrate that the German army indeed *was* finally beaten in the late summer and fall of 1918 and that it was only the German high command's call for an armistice that kept Allied forces out of Germany. The current explanation for German defeat concentrates on the tactical, operational, and technological changes that were made by the Entente's forces over the course of the war and that finally allowed them to break the German defenses and defeat the German army. The question of why the Germans lost the First World War is not, however, a simple one. The defeat on the battlefield was only one element in a complex picture. There were also massive problems on the German home front caused largely by declining supplies of food and fuel. The shortages reduced the standard of living of most Germans and eroded their support for the war. The German army itself, which was slowly being worn down by its enemies with their larger reserves of both manpower and materiel, also suffered from these shortages; therefore these reasons need to be accounted for in any explanation of German defeat. Since Germany's defeat in the First World War set the stage for much of the history of the next 70 years, the reasons for that defeat need to be reexamined. This work is an attempt to begin that reexamination.

Factors and Decisions

There were a number of factors that played a role in Germany's defeat. Some of these factors were obviously of a military nature: the changes in technology over the course of the war that Germany was unable to keep pace with (i.e., the tank); defeats on the battlefield, both of German armies and of Germany's allies; the failures of the German navy; and so on. Yet these military factors by themselves did not bring about Germany's defeat. There were a number of other, nonmilitary factors that also came into play. Social factors, most importantly the collapse of social cohesion on the home fronts of the Central Powers, played a key role as well. Economics certainly mattered; the British blockade of German trade was especially important. All of these factors need to be examined and explained if we are to truly understand why the Central Powers lost the First World War.

Some scholars have argued that German defeat was simply inevitable; that the military and economic forces arrayed against the Central Powers were too much to overcome, especially after the United States entered the war.[1] Although the simplicity of this argument is appealing on the surface it is not really much of an explanation. Few things are actually inevitable in history. Human factors and chance always play a role. In particular, the inevitability argument does not take into account the critical decisions that were made by Germany's political and military leaders both before and during the war nor does it address why some battles were won and others lost and why those that were lost proved to be so much more important.

In order to adequately explain Germany's defeat it is necessary but not sufficient to examine the underlying balance of economic and material factors that could lead one to conclude that the war was hopeless from the start. A full explanation though must also examine the critical decisions that were made by the German high command and government at key moments in the war. I will argue in these pages that the outcome of this war was far from inevitable and that the Germans had opportunities for victory[2] that were missed. I have selected what I consider to be the most significant events and decisions leading to Germany's defeat and in the chapters that follow I will examine each of these in turn. They are, in chronological order[3]: the failure of the Schlieffen-Moltke Plan[4]; the institution of the British blockade and the effect it had on both German society and the German economy; the utter failure of the High Seas Fleet and the corresponding turn to submarine warfare in 1915 and, disastrously, again in 1917; the disastrous Western Front battles of 1916 (Verdun and the Somme); and the failure of the 1918 offensives. All of these events, decisions, and factors played into Germany's final defeat.

Germany's first problem was that it took on a coalition whose material resources dwarfed its own and the most important member of which, Great Britain, was largely invulnerable to German pressure, at least until technology briefly changed that equation. Furthermore, once Great Britain entered the war, the Royal Navy implemented a blockade of German trade that caused the Germans to make some difficult immediate choices (such as whether to use nitrates for munitions or for fertilizer) and which slowly began to strangle the German economy, especially the food supply.

However, none of this came as a surprise to the German high command. Germans were aware of the overall economic inferiority of their alliance and concluded, in the years before the war, that Germany needed to win a quick victory over one of its opponents in the early part of the war. The German scheme to win that quick victory is popularly known as the Schlieffen Plan. Designed to win a rapid victory over France by destroying the French army in a great encirclement battle modeled on Hannibal's victory at Cannae, the plan was seriously flawed from the start and when the German armies were turned back in the west, first at the Marne and then at Ypres, the plan failed. There would be no quick victory. Rather the war would be a long and difficult struggle.

Great Britain's control of the seas was critically important to the Entente's victory in the war. In the years before the war, American naval historian Alfred Thayer Mahan had written a major work, *The Influence of Seapower on History*, which argued that control of the seas was a critical component in Great Britain's victory over France during the Napoleonic Wars. In the First World War, control of the seas was just as important, if not even more so. The Germans had spent many of those prewar years building a battle fleet that could challenge that of Great Britain but when the test of war came the German High Seas Fleet was a complete failure. The British wisely opted for a distant blockade of German harbors rather than a close blockade, which would have exposed them to German attacks, and, by virtue of geography, they were able to close the exits from the North Sea without having to endanger their fleet in German waters. The failures of the High Seas Fleet led the German high command, out of desperation, to embrace a new weapon, the submarine.

Also of critical importance to Germany's defeat were what the Germans called the *Materialschlachten*, the battles of Verdun and the Somme. These cataclysmic confrontations are familiar as disasters for the French and British armies but they were just as disastrous, if not more so, for the Germans. The outcome of those battles convinced the German high command that the war could not be won on the continent and that the German navy would have to unleash its submarines in an unrestricted war against commercial shipping. That decision brought the United States into the war and ultimately sealed Germany's defeat.

Finally, the Germans were given a brief reprieve and a last opportunity to avoid defeat when the Bolsheviks took Russia out of the war and signed the Treaty of Brest-Litovsk. This gave the Germans an opportunity to demonstrate exactly what a German peace for Europe would look like. The extremely exploitative treaty that was eventually forced on the Russians did just that, disastrously. It not only required the Germans to leave substantial forces in the east but also stiffened resistance in the west by making clear to the rest of the Entente that a "German peace" would involve extensive losses of territory on the part of both France and Belgium and would leave Germany in control of the continent. Had the Germans instead granted the Russians a more generous peace, not only they might have freed up additional forces for the Western Front, but they might also have been able to propose a generous peace program as they launched their final western offensives. Without a corresponding diplomatic offensive the Germans faced an extremely difficult task in the spring of 1918 and it was unlikely from the beginning that their last desperate offensives would succeed. When they failed it was the army, not the home front, that cracked and demanded peace.

All of these events/factors and the decisions that were taken in response to them helped to seal the fate of Germany and its allies. In the end Germany's defeat was not inevitable, but it was likely. It was the decisions taken by Germany's leaders in response to the crises and hardships created by the war, combined with the difficult conditions under which the war was waged, that led to Germany's ultimate defeat.

Scope of the Work

This is not a product of new archival research, nor is it intended to be. What I have set out to do here is to survey the existing literature on the war in an effort to explain to my students why the Germans were defeated. The idea for the study stemmed from the courses I teach. Many years ago now I was teaching the First World War in a course on twentieth century world history and when we reached the end of the discussion of the war one student asked the deceptively simple question, just why did the Germans lose? An interesting discussion followed and at the end of that discussion I went looking for a short volume, written for undergraduates, which addressed his question. Finding none I began working on this project. As I mentioned above each chapter examines an event(s) or a factor that led to Germany's defeat. In the years since, a number of fine works dealing with the end of the war have appeared, most notably David Stevenson's *With Our Backs to the Wall*. This book does not pretend to be as comprehensive as Stevenson's. It is rather my hope that this book will serve as an introduction to the reasons behind Germany's defeat. I also hope that the work may be provocative enough to start a more detailed discussion of the reasons why the Central Powers eventually went down to defeat. I see this work as the first step in a larger conversation, not the final word. As a result established scholars will likely find little here that is new other than, perhaps, the interpretation but it is my sincere hope that those beginning their study of the war will find the book engaging and enlightening.

Lastly there are many people without whose efforts this work would never have seen the light of day. First and foremost are the numerous students I have taught over the years; if I have inspired any of you as much as you have inspired me, then I have achieved my goal. Second, Jeff Ellair and the library staff at the University of Wisconsin – Sheboygan deserve great credit for putting up with my endless interlibrary loan requests and more than a few overdue notices. My colleagues in the University of Wisconsin Colleges Department of History have been a great source of inspiration over the years. Every time we meet I feel the need to step up my game. My colleagues at the University of Wisconsin – Sheboygan have also been extremely helpful; in particular Dr. Valerie Murrenus-Pilmaier with whom I team teach a course on the First World War and the literature of the First World War. My family deserves thanks as well: my parents, Donald and Karen Karau, for their continued support; my children Alex and Katie who have put up with a great many days when I have had my head buried in books or glued to the computer; and, especially, my wife Jacqui, without whom none of this would have ever come about. Last and certainly not the least, a special thank you to Andrew Martin. If you had not asked the right question that day Andy, this book would not exist.

CHAPTER 1

The Economic and Military Balance in 1914

When the heir to the Austrian throne, Archduke Franz Ferdinand, was assassinated in Sarajevo on June 28, 1914, a crisis was set off that would eventually lead all of the major powers of Europe into a cataclysmic war— a war that would eventually drag in even non-European powers, most notably the United States. The war was largely the result of a calculated risk that was taken by the German and Austro-Hungarian governments.[1]

Though Gavrilo Princip, the actual assassin, was from Bosnia (and was therefore a subject of the Habsburg Monarchy), he was ethnically Serbian, and the Austro-Hungarian government suspected, and later confirmed, that the Serbian terrorist organization the Black Hand had been involved in the assassination. Since the early 1900s, Serbia had been a center of anti-Austrian propaganda as the Serbian government sought to emulate what Piedmont and Prussia had accomplished in the middle of the nineteenth century and create a unified South Slavic state out of territories currently controlled by the Austro-Hungarian Empire. The Black Hand was the result of an intensified struggle between the two countries that had been going on since 1908, when Austria-Hungary had openly annexed Bosnia, a former Ottoman Turk possession that Austria had been governing since the 1870s. Since 1908 there had been a series of crises in the relations between Austria-Hungary and Serbia, crises that eventually culminated in the assassination. In the aftermath of the assassination, the Austro-Hungarian government determined that the time had come to deal with Serbia militarily. However, since Serbia was supported by Russia, for both geopolitical and ethnic reasons, strong Austrian action could very well bring about a crisis, or a possible war, with Russia. To protect themselves, the Austrians made certain, before they acted, that they would have support from their German ally should war with Serbia lead to war with Russia.

Decades earlier, the German chancellor Otto von Bismarck had built a new German state on a series of victorious wars, the last of which was against France. In the aftermath of those wars, Bismarck constructed an elaborate alliance system to protect Germany from a resurgent France. The centerpiece of that system was a defensive alliance with Austria-Hungary, the Dual Alliance. This alliance pledged the two states to come to each other's aid if either was attacked by Russia. Though most of Bismarck's other alliances had fallen apart in the years since his forced retirement, the Dual Alliance remained, linking the two Central European German monarchies in a defensive pact. Bismarck had also forged links with Russia, the most significant of which was the Reinsurance Treaty, a treaty that pledged Germany and Russia to neutrality in a future war should either be attacked by Austria-Hungary or France. When Bismarck was removed from office and the German government moved closer to Austria-Hungary, the Reinsurance Treaty was allowed to lapse; it seemed to conflict with the Dual Alliance. Left without any ties to Germany, Russia moved to join in an alliance with France and in 1894 the Franco-Russian Alliance was signed, splitting Europe into two camps, with France and Russia on one side and Germany, Austria-Hungary, and supposedly Italy on the other. By 1914 Great Britain and the British Empire had joined in a loose agreement, known as the Triple Entente, with Russia and France to contain German expansion. This was largely the result of a series of international crises that took place between 1904 and 1914 as well as the fact that the German government embarked on a massive naval building program over those same years. As a result, by 1914 both Germany and Austria-Hungary felt themselves to be surrounded by enemies. Seeing no way to break this "encirclement" other than war and fearing that, if Austria-Hungary failed to take strong action against Serbia, the Dual Monarchy would cease to be a great power, the German government gave the Austro-Hungarian government a famous "blank check" to deal with Serbia in whatever way it felt was best. If it led to war with Russia, Germany would stand by its ally's side.

The German government clearly expected Austria-Hungary to launch a military strike against Serbia. It pressed the Austro-Hungarians numerous times in July 1914 to take strong and decisive action against Serbia. It also clearly expected that if war resulted from the assassination crisis, it would be localized and that, when push came to shove, Russia would not risk war against Germany on behalf of Serbia. If they proved wrong in their prediction, however, they were willing to accept the consequences —a European-wide war. In 1912 the Russians had embarked on a major campaign to expand and reform not only their army but also their railroad network, in particular the portion of the rail system that was located in Russian Poland.[2] Those reforms would be completed around 1916–17, and therefore, if war with Russia had to come, it would be better for it to come in 1914 while Germany and Austria-Hungary still possessed the military advantage. Such a conflict would quickly become a European-wide war because of Russia's alliance with France. The German General Staff, the body that was responsible for war planning in Germany, was prepared for just such a war and believed it had a plan to win it. Therefore there was little trepidation on the part of the Kaiser, the German chancellor, or any of the military planners regarding a possible European-wide war, at least not initially. In the immediate aftermath of the assassination, the key German decision makers were convinced that Great Britain would not get involved in a war over Serbia. As long as the British remained out of the war, the Germans were confident they would win the resulting war. The first question to be addressed here is, was their confidence justified?

Did the Germans and Austro-Hungarians possess a military advantage in 1914? To determine this we will examine the military and economic balance of 1914, *for the war the Germans thought they were going to fight*, from six different angles. We will look at population statistics and the size of the respective military forces; the industrial base of the involved nations; the role played by geography; and, finally, the forces within each state that served to either strengthen or weaken the social cohesion of the respective states. Then we will repeat the process *for the war the Germans actually ended up fighting*, a war that involved not only France and Russia but also Great Britain. We will examine the same factors with an eye to assessing the influence that British entry into the war had on the conflict as a whole.

Population and Military Establishments

In terms of raw population figures, the Franco-Russian Alliance had a significant advantage over the Dual Alliance.

As Table 1.1 shows, the combined populations of Russia, France, and Serbia amounted to 204.6 million compared to only 118.0 million for the Central Powers. Of course though, this type of raw number does not

Table 1.1   Population of France and Russia versus the Central
Powers (millions)[3]

Russia	164.0
France	36.6
Serbia	4.0
Germany	67.0
Austria-Hungary	51.0

Germany and Austria-Hungary are the Central
Powers.

tell the full story. Of greater interest are the number of men of military
age in each country and how many of those men were trained for military
service. Table 1.2 shows these figures, defining men of military age as men
from 15 to 49.

Even from this perspective, the Central Powers were clearly outnumbered by their opponents, both in terms of trained personnel and in terms
of potential trained personnel. Comparing the numbers of men trained
for military service one can see that the Franco-Russian Alliance could
field over 11 million men compared to just under 8 million for the Central Powers. However, in terms of potential manpower the numbers are
much worse, with the Franco-Russian Alliance having access to over
30 million men of military age to only about 16 million for the Central
Powers. If one keeps in mind that the French could also draw manpower
from their colonial empire of 57.7 million people,[4] things look dark
indeed for the Central Powers.

Looking at the size of each nation's military establishment confirms the
superiority of the Franco-Russian Alliance. Since each of the four major
powers we are examining practiced at least theoretical universal military
service and relied on a mass army of recruits, the peacetime establish-

Table 1.2   Men of Military Age and Trained Manpower[5]

Nation	Men of Military Age	Number Trained
Russia	21,520,000	6,000,000
France	9,998,000	5,067,000
Serbia	440,000	NA
Germany	9,750,000	4,900,000
Austria-Hungary	6,120,000	3,000,000

Table 1.3 Military Strength of the European States

Nation	Peacetime Military Establishment	Fully Mobilized Wartime Establishment[6]
Russia	1,300,000[7]	5,971,000
France	910,000[8]	4,017,000
Serbia	52,000[9]	200,000
Germany	891,000[10]	4,500,000
Austria-Hungary	444,000[11]	3,000,000

ment, which consisted only of the currently active classes, was considerably smaller than the wartime establishment, which included several different categories of reservists, depending on which country one is discussing.[12] Table 1.3 shows this difference.

In terms of the peacetime establishments, the Central Powers found themselves outnumbered by nearly 2.2 million to roughly 1.3 million. When the reserves are included, those numbers shift to roughly 10 million opposing 7.5 million. In terms of sheer military manpower, the Franco-Russian Alliance was clearly and significantly superior to the Dual Alliance, which begs the question, why were the Germans confident that they could win despite this overwhelming disadvantage?

The answer to that question reveals the reasons for the now or never mentality of the German government in 1914. The Germans possessed several distinct advantages over their foes, the most important of which was their industrial strength. It was precisely this advantage that would lessen over time as the Russians expanded their army, industry, and railways in the coming years. Simply put, Germany was the economic and industrial powerhouse of Europe. The German generals believed that German industrial might and, most importantly, the German transportation network would offset the Franco-Russian advantages in manpower if they were utilized properly.

The Industrial Strength of the Opposing Alliances

By 1914 Germany had taken Britain's traditional place as Europe's greatest industrial power. By the time war came, German industry was outperforming British industry in most categories. The powerful German economy trailed only that of the United States in terms of its productive capacity, and it was far more industrially powerful than either France or Russia. Tables 1.4, 1.5, and 1.6 give some indication of this differential.

Table 1.4   Coal, Iron, and Steel Production of the Powers (metric tons)

Nation	Coal Production[13]	Iron Production[14]	Steel Output[15]
Russia	36,000,000	9,537,000	4,918,000
France	40,800,000	21,918,000	4,687,000
Germany	277,200,000	28,608,000	17,609,000
Austria-Hungary	43,900,000	3,039,000	2,611,000

German industry produced far more coal and steel than Russia and France combined. The latter combined produced more iron than Germany but the French iron fields were located along its borders with Germany and Belgium, in precisely the locations where the fighting would likely take place if Germany and France went to war. The loss of those deposits would cause French production to plummet. The most significant of these figures is that for steel production since steel was vital to the war industry for all the nations. Here German industry produced more than twice the combined output of its enemies. Further statistics (Tables 1.5 and 1.6) confirm this German dominance.

Yet again, German output equals that of its two rivals. The peacetime figures are clear; the Germans had a very significant edge in industrial production. It was largely fear that this edge would slip away in the future and that Russia would become dominant not only in population but also in industrial might that convinced many of the German leaders that it would be better to fight Russia in 1914 rather than at some future date.

Another area in which the Germans had a very significant advantage was in their transportation network. Germany was covered with railroads, providing excellent connections across the country. These connections allowed the German military to move quickly from one end of the coun-

Table 1.5   Energy Use of the Powers

Nation	Energy Consumption in Metric Tons of Coal [16]	Output of Electricity (gigawatt hours)[17]
Russia	54,000,000	2.04
France	62,500,000	1.80
Germany	187,000,000	8.00
Austria-Hungary	49,400,000	NA

Table 1.6   Percentage Shares of World Manufacturing Output of the Powers[18]

Russia	8.2
France	6.1
Germany	14.8
Austria-Hungary	4.4

try to the other in response to a crisis. In 1913 Germany was covered by 63,378 kilometers of railroad compared to 40,770 kilometers in France and 70,156 kilometers in Russia.[19] Although at first glance the Russian number seems impressive, the Trans-Siberian railroad consumed a large percentage of it. The Russians had few railways serving the vital areas of Russian Poland, where any war with the Central Powers would be fought.

This advantage in their transportation network was a major factor in German war planning. Given that all of these nations had to mobilize large numbers of reserves in the event of war, having a dense transportation network gave the Germans the advantage of speed. German soldiers could be gathered quickly from the corners of the empire and rapidly armed and prepared for battle. German military planners, most famously Alfred von Schlieffen, used this in their military planning. The famous plan that bears Schlieffen's name was based on the speed with which Germany could mobilize its army. Though the German army would be significantly outnumbered if it had to fight both France and Russia at the same time on two widely separated fronts, Schlieffen and his successor Helmuth von Moltke (commonly called Moltke the Younger to separate him from his famous uncle, who led the Prussian armies in the wars of German unification) were convinced that Germany could use its superior railroad net to quickly mobilize in the west, defeat France in a campaign of roughly six weeks, and then transfer its army to the east to face the Russians before the latter could become a serious threat. Hence, Germany would be able to use its industrial and railroad strength to offset its disadvantage in numbers and turn defeat into victory. However, if the Russians expanded their own railroad net as they planned to do, the Germans would lose this advantage; hence it was better to face war in 1914 than in 1916 or 1917.

Once the industrial might of both sides is taken into account, the overwhelming advantage in numbers for the Franco-Russian Alliance becomes less significant and the German confidence in victory becomes more understandable.

EUROPE, 1914

Geography as a Military Factor

Geography served as both an aid and a hindrance to both sides. From the German perspective, Germans occupied a central position between their two most likely enemies. This meant on the one hand that, given Germany's excellent transportation system, they should be able to react fairly quickly to any moves by their opponents. A Russian offensive could be met by shifting troops from the French front and vice versa. However, this also meant, by definition, that the Germans were faced with a two-front war, a situation that could prove to be disastrous should France and Russia were able to coordinate their military maneuvers. The ability of the Germans to quickly move reinforcements from a quiet front to a threatened one would largely be negated should the Russians and French launch simultaneous offensives. It was difficult for the Russians and French to do so, of course, given the communications technology of the period but it is precisely what happened in 1916 and it did indeed create major problems for the Germans.

These geographic considerations also played a role in the creation of the German war plan and in the July Crisis itself. The pressure of a potential two-front war and the need to avoid such a conflict was another of the imperatives driving the Schlieffen-Moltke Plan. The General Staff hoped that by using the German railroad system and their geographic advantage they could quickly strike the French army a crippling blow and then, with the war in the west won, turn to the east to deal with the larger Russian threat. In other words, geography, as well as technology and industrial power, was to help the Germans offset their numerical disadvantages.

Domestic Factors

A final factor that needs to be considered as we assess the strengths and weaknesses of the opposing alliance blocs in the summer of 1914 is the forces within each nation making for greater or lesser social cohesion. In other words, how stable was each of these nations and what factors affected that stability?

The alliances were symmetrical in that each alliance consisted of one coherent nation-state (France and Germany) and one multiethnic, basically dynastic, state (Austria-Hungary and Russia).

Austria-Hungary was riven by bitter interethnic conflicts as the German and Magyar populations ruled over large numbers of Poles, Czechs, Serbs, Croats, Slovenes, and Rumanians. According to one set of figures, 12 million Germans and 10 million Magyars ruled over 8.5 million Czechs and Slovaks, 4 million Ukrainians, 3.3 million Rumanians, 3 million Croats, 2.7 million Serbs, 1.4 million Slovenes, and 800,000 Italians.[20] Moreover, it is something of a misnomer to imply that Austria-Hungary was a single state; it was not. It actually consisted of two separate states joined together in the person of the monarch, who served at one and the same time as emperor of Austria and king of Hungary. There were also some common institutions, such as the army, but each state maintained its own administration. (Even in the military sphere they maintained their own forces, separate from the main *Kaiserliche und Königliche Armee*, the joint army that both Austria and Hungary contributed to. In effect there was one large joint army and navy, supplemented by what amounted to two state militias.)

In both the Austrian and the Hungarian halves of the monarchy, campaigns of either Germanization or Magyarization had been carried out in the years prior to the war. These campaigns forced the minorities to assimilate into the dominant culture of their half of the empire. The campaigns were enforced to a greater or lesser extent, depending on the conditions in any given province. In most areas these campaigns created resentment against the state and agitation for greater autonomy. In some regions, such as Galicia, greater autonomy was granted to one group, in this case Poles, at the expense of another group, Ukrainians. This was not a new problem for the Habsburgs; they had been dealing with it since the early nineteenth century. In 1848 there had been nationalist revolutions in Hungary and Bohemia as well as what were at that point Habsburg possessions in Italy. In the 1860s the Habsburgs lost those Italian possessions to the new state of Italy, and in 1866 in a war with Prussia, they found themselves excluded from the new Germany. Now, in the early 1910s, the greatest threat came from the South Slav population of the empire, some of whom wanted to create an autonomous South Slav state while remaining within the monarchy, others of whom wanted to separate from the monarchy completely and join with Serbia in a Yugoslav state. The assassin of Franz Ferdinand was one of the latter. It was to defuse this threat that the monarchy opted for war in 1914; however, it was taking into that war a nation that was bitterly divided below the surface. There were significant reserves of loyalty to the current Kaiser, Franz Joseph, who had been on the throne since those revolutions in 1848, but the loyalty did not run much deeper. There was no real sense of Austro-Hungarian nationalism for the government to draw on, and when the war turned out not to be a quick, victorious campaign, the state began to come apart at the seams.

Germany on the other hand proved to be remarkably stable. The achievements of the Bismarckian state since 1871, as well as its progressive social policies, had inspired a tremendous amount of nationalism. Germany was thriving not only economically but also culturally, with many of the major scientists and thinkers of the late nineteenth and early twentieth centuries working at German universities. The German people saw themselves as a bulwark of Western civilization standing against an Asiatic civilization that was represented in the popular mind by the backward and despotic tsarist monarchy of Russia. Of course there were potential problems here as well, the largest of which was political.

The state that Bismarck created was a constitutional monarchy but one in which most of the power remained in the hands of the monarch. The Kaiser appointed his own ministers; they were not responsible to the popularly elected assembly, the Reichstag. The Reichstag itself was elected on the basis of universal manhood suffrage, granted by Bismarck when he wrote the constitution because he was convinced that the majority of the population was generally conservative. As a result Germany had one of the most progressive franchises in all of Europe but it was tied to an organization that had little concrete power. For example, the Reichstag could not make laws though it did have control over the budget and therefore could not simply be ignored by the administration. The law-making body of the government was the upper house of the legislature, the Bundesrat, which was made up of representatives chosen by the individual state governments, such as Bavaria and Prussia. This body was dominated by Prussia, which did not employ universal male suffrage but rather used an archaic three-tier voting system that gave more weight to the votes of the landed nobility, the Junkers. While the system hardly deserves the label of autocratic that was thrown at it during the war, it was also not a truly representative system and this created some political resentment, particularly among the supporters of the largest political party in Germany, the Social Democrats (SPD). The SPD was the largest and most powerful Socialist party in Europe and the imperial administration was concerned about what it might do in the event of war. The official Socialist platform called for pacifism, blaming wars on capitalist greed and imperialism. Given the significant backing that the Socialists had in German politics, they could prove to be a potentially disruptive force in any war. It was concern over the stance that the SPD would take that led the German Chancellor, Theobald von Bethmann-Hollweg, to take pains during the July Crisis to make Russia appear to be the aggressor in the crisis. In the end his efforts paid off as the SPD pledged its support to the state and voted for the increased military budget that was proposed in early August 1914. Over the entire course of the war, the SPD and its deputies proved to be strong supporters of the German state, rather than a threat to its stability. The fears of the prewar government were shown in the end to be groundless and Germany proved to be remarkably, given the conditions the German people were forced to endure during the war, stable. The conditions of the Central Powers were reflected in their opponents.

France in many ways resembled Germany. It was an established nation-state with a strong record of cultural and scientific achievement, having been of course the center of the Enlightenment. As with Germany it appeared, on the surface, that France had serious political problems. France worked under a democratic constitution that required the government to be responsible to the French parliament, the Chamber of Deputies. Prime ministers and their cabinets came from the party or parties that dominated the Chamber and if they lost control of the Chamber they also lost control of the government. This led to instability and frequent changes of government that created an impression of weakness. Another similarity between Germany and France was the existence of a powerful Socialist party in France. Led by the charismatic Jean Jaures, the French Socialists were second only to the German Socialists in their prominent antiwar stance, and there was concern in French government circles, as there was in Germany, that the Socialists would oppose any war. In the end of course, as was the case in Germany, the French Socialists went along with the war. Jaures was assassinated in the days leading up to the war, and when the German invasion was launched, the French Socialists joined the famous *Union Sacrée*, which mirrored the *Burgfrieden* that was proclaimed in Germany. French society would prove to be remarkably resilient over the course of the war as well, as the French people suffered tremendously high casualties as well as the destruction of many of the most productive areas of their nation and yet remained determined to see the nation through to victory.

Russia, on the other hand, was a dynastic state that resembled the Austro-Hungarian Empire in many key ways. As was the case with Austria-Hungary, Russia was a multiethnic state with its roots in the prenationalist past. The Great Russian population centered in the region running from St. Petersburg on the Baltic through Moscow and on to the Don and Volga valleys and dominated the country. The tsar and most of the powerful noble families were of Great Russian descent, and they often pursued policies of Russification that were designed to force the other nationalities to assimilate to Great Russian rule. Among those other nationalities could be found White Russians, Ukrainians, Poles, Georgians, Armenians, Kazakhs, Uzbekhs, and numerous other small groups. Many of these groups did not have developed national consciousness but some did, most notably the Poles and the Ukrainians, both of whom were restless under the Great Russian rule. The nationality issue was not as divisive in Russia as it was in Austria-Hungary but it existed. Here as in Austria-Hungary there was no clear sense of Russian nationalism; it was not clear what it really meant to be "Russian" as opposed to being a subject of the Romanov dynasty.

Russia also suffered from three other significant problems. First of all, Russia was in the early stages of the Industrial Revolution. Working and living conditions for the working class in Russia were among the worst on the continent and little had been done by the state to alleviate those conditions. In many ways the Russian working class was in a situation analogous to that of the British working class in the earliest stages of the Industrial Revolution in Great Britain. This created significant unrest among the working class, which, however, remained small in comparison to the rural population, which had issues of its own with the tsarist state.

Russia had emerged from serfdom late. It was only in the 1860s that Tsar Alexander II abolished serfdom and granted land to the Russian peasantry. However, that land came with a cost that, frankly, was not understood by most Russian peasants. The monarchy reimbursed the noble landowners for the land that was being granted to the peasants and then charged the peasants a yearly fee for "restitution." For many Russian peasants this was seen as the monarchy intervening to charge them for something that had traditionally been theirs free and clear. The reality of their former serfdom mattered less than the perception that the state was abusing them and as a result there was a revolutionary current in the countryside led by a group that called itself the Socialist Revolutionaries. By the turn of the century, this group was agitating for land for the peasants. Little was done, even after the Revolution of 1905, to address its demands and unrest continued to simmer below the surface of the countryside in the years leading up to the war.

Lastly the Russian state was also plagued by political dissension. The long-term social problems of the state had combined with military defeat at the hands of Japan in 1905 to trigger a series of protests that quickly ballooned into a revolution. The Russian Revolution of 1905 eventually culminated in the creation of a parliament for Russia, the Duma, and the institution of a limited constitutional monarchy. In reality though, the Duma had very limited powers and the state remained essentially autocratic. Reforms were enacted, in particular in the countryside under Pyotr Stolypin, but there was a strong current of dissatisfaction with the system present in the politically articulate professional classes. Unlike

France and Germany there was not a strong Socialist party in Russia, at least not in the western European sense. The strongest opposition "party" was the Socialist Revolutionaries, but in 1914, they were not a serious threat to the tsarist regime. On the surface Russia was stable and powerful, but, as was the case with Austria-Hungary, trouble lurked below the surface, trouble that could easily become manifest once again in the event of future Russian military defeats. The Russian colossus was riven with cracks.

When the domestic conditions of each alliance are taken into consideration, the greater social cohesion presents another advantage for Germany, certainly against Russia if not against France. If the Germans could inflict serious enough defeats on the Russian army perhaps the dissent that rose to the surface in 1905 would appear once more, and if Russia were to leave the war the Franco-Russian advantage in numbers would leave with it.

Therefore despite the fact that the Franco-Russian Alliance had a significant advantage in numbers, that advantage was more than offset by Germany's industrial strength and, in particular, by the strength of the German transportation system. It seems very likely that, had the Germans been able to fight the war they expected to fight in 1914, they would have won it. The problem of course is that they were not able to limit the war to just France and Russia. Great Britain, the other major industrial power of Europe, intervened and one need look no further than that intervention to find the first reason for Germany's defeat. Britain's entry into the war completely altered the economic and military balance, against Germany.

The British Impact

Despite what some members of the German government, most notably the Kaiser, allowed themselves to think, by 1914 it was highly unlikely that Great Britain would remain neutral in a war between France and Germany. Though Britain and France were not formally allied, they had developed increasingly close relations over the decade since the Entente Cordiale was signed in 1904.[21] Over the course of that decade, the two nations had engaged in extensive staff talks and military planning. Those plans eventually led to the small British army taking a position on the far left wing of the French army. Despite British Foreign Minister Edward Grey's continual claims that these talks did not in any way limit Great Britain's freedom of action in the event of a Franco-German war, the staff talks and the military planning had slowly created a situation where many men on both sides of the English Channel felt that Great Britain had taken on an obligation to France. Grey himself seems to have felt this obligation though he was always obliged to press home to his domestic critics that nothing had been done that would obligate Great Britain to intervene in a European war. In other words, on the surface the Entente Cordiale remained a nonbinding agreement that simply ended the colonial rivalries between Britain and France, a fact that was not materially changed when Russia adhered to the agreement in 1907, creating the Triple Entente. The reality however was quite different. By 1914 the Entente had effectively become an alliance. While it is true, as Grey stated, that there was no obligation on the part of Great Britain to come to France's aid, it was all but certain that it would do so. There were some members of the Asquith cabinet who were firmly opposed to war in 1914 but they were in the minority. When war came what Grey needed to do was find a way to win over enough of those members of the cabinet to keep the government intact. The Germans solved that problem for him.

The German war plan, the Schlieffen-Moltke Plan, was created to take advantage of the extensive German railway system and the speed with which the Germans could mobilize their army. The objective of the plan was to overwhelm the French army in roughly six weeks, which would then allow the German army to turn east in force to face the Russians, in the process negating the Franco-Russian advantage in manpower. However, the French had built extensive fortifications along their border with Germany in the years since the Franco-Prussian War and both Schlieffen and his successor Moltke were convinced that it would take too long for the German army to batter its way through those fortifications. The only way to defeat France quickly then was to bypass those fortifications. This meant attacking France along its northern border with Belgium, which was largely unfortified. This of course would mean that the German army would have to violate Belgian neutrality, which had been guaranteed by all the major powers in an 1839 treaty. When war came in 1914 and the Germans demanded passage through Belgium, the Belgians refused and resisted. For Edward Grey and the interventionists in Britain this was a godsend. The invasion of Belgium allowed some members of the antiwar bloc to ease their consciences and support intervention because Britain could be seen as coming to the aid of a small nation that had been unjustly assaulted and as a result Grey was able to persuade the cabinet to support intervention with only two members dissenting, and eventually resigning.[22] Accordingly the British government

Table 1.7   Populations of the Entente and the Dual Alliance (millions)

Dual Alliance	118
Russia and France	200
Great Britain[23]	46
British Empire	434

sent an ultimatum to Germany on August 3, ordering the Germans to evacuate Belgium or face war with Great Britain. When the Germans did not accede to those demands, Great Britain declared war on Germany on August 4, in the process completely changing the balance of power in the war.

Great Britain brought to the conflict another large population base, especially when the Dominions are included, as well as a powerful industrial economy. Furthermore it was, for the most part, internally stable, though the British did have their own minority problem in Ireland, which was slowly transitioning toward Home Rule in 1914. The British political system was built on solid foundations; it was representative of most Britons and was strongly supported. British nationalism was built on a foundation of imperial success going back to the victories over Napoleon and was strengthened by the glories of the Pax Britannica. Even socialism was seen as less of a threat in Britain where the increasingly powerful Labour Party was a party of reform, not of revolution. A few statistics help to demonstrate the material advantages that Great Britain brought to the Entente (see Table 1.7).

The numbers in Table 1.7 clearly drive home the point that Great Britain, in particular the British Empire, brought with it a truly vast population. However, the numbers for the British Empire can be somewhat misleading since many of those 434 million were Indians who were not likely to be brought to war in Europe. A more useful number is the population for the Dominions, which amounted to roughly 20 million.[24] The story is similar when we look at men of military age (Table 1.8) that were available to each power.

Two things are immediately apparent from the numbers in Table 1.8; the first is the large number of men that were available for military service in Britain. The second is the incredibly small size of the standing army. Britain, unlike the continental powers, did not have a conscript army. The British government preferred to rely on a small, long-serving professional army and a large powerful navy for its security. The British navy employed over twice as many men as the British army did, with a standing

Table 1.8   Men of Military Age[25]

Nations	Men of Military Age	Number Trained
Central Powers	15,870,000	7,900,000
France and Russia	31,518,000	11,067,000
Great Britain	10,445,000	248,000

strength of 532,000.[26] What this meant in the immediate context of 1914 was that the potential significance of the British army was underestimated by German military planners, with Moltke derisively claiming the German army would "arrest them" on its way into France. The Germans could hope that if the Schlieffen-Moltke Plan worked and France could be defeated quickly, the British army would not matter; however, if that plan failed and the war became a long and drawn out affair, the large pool of potential British manpower might well become decisive. In fact, when war came, the British army, like the other armies, did expand upon mobilization, to 975,000 men,[27] and it played a critical role in the events of August and September 1914.

The British and Imperial manpower reserves added to the already existing advantages that the Franco-Russian Alliance possessed in terms of manpower. Of even greater significance were the naval and industrial strengths that the British brought to the alliance (see Tables 1.9–1.12).

The numbers in Tables 1.9–1.12 make something else very clear; the accession of the British to the side of France and Russia not only negated the Germans' industrial advantage, but also shifted it decisively in the favor of the Entente. In truth, however, the most significant of all of these numbers is that for naval tonnage. Britain's naval superiority was such that, combined with its geographic advantages, it was able to cut the Central Powers off from most contact with the outside world. The British cut the cables linking Germany with the United States and took control not only of German overseas trade via a naval blockade but also over

Table 1.9   Naval Strengths of the Powers[28]

Nations	Warship Tonnage
Central Powers	1,677,000
France and Russia	1,579,000
Great Britain	2,714,000

Table 1.10   Coal, Iron, and Steel Production of the Powers (metric tons)[29]

Nations	Coal Production	Iron Production	Steel Output
Central Powers	321,100,000	31,647,000	20,220,000
France and Russia	76,800,000	31,455,000	9,605,000
Great Britain	292,000,000	16,254,000	7,787,000

what news was released from Europe to the outside world. This meant that they were able to present the war to the neutral nations, most importantly the United States, in the way they chose. This also proved to be a significant advantage. British naval dominance also meant that the Entente had access to overseas sources of supplies, again, most importantly from the United States, and the Central Powers did not. This would become critical as the war went on. In the end, British control of the seas turned the Central Powers into a fortress under siege.

British entry into the war shifted the economic balance so thoroughly against the Central Powers that some historians have argued that the defeat of the Central Powers became inevitable and that, in effect, the economics of the situation were so stacked against them that they could not possibly succeed.[30] At first glance it is a compelling argument. The numbers certainly do not show much reason for optimism on the part of the Central Powers, yet in 1918, the Germans stood deep in enemy territory on all fronts and were able to launch an offensive that left some on the Entente side wondering if they were not going to lose the war after all. In the end war is about more than just numbers of men and amounts of materiel; as Richard Overy has pointed out in his excellent work on the Second World War, *Why the Allies Won*, governments still need to put those masses of men and materiel to use and the side that does so best usually prevails. Furthermore, the economic interpretation does not take into account that victory does not necessarily require the total

Table 1.11   Energy Use of the Powers

Nations	Energy Consumption in Metric Tons of Coal[31]	Output of Electricity (gigawatt hours)[32]
Central Powers	236,400,000	8.00
France and Russia	116,500,000	3.84
Great Britain	195,000,000	2.5

Table 1.12   Percentage Shares of World Manufacturing Output[33]

Central Powers	19.2
France and Russia	14.3
Great Britain	13.6

destruction of your enemy; it only requires that your enemy be willing to accede to your demands. In other words, victory can be achieved by breaking the will of your enemy to continue the fight and by convincing him that peace on your terms is a more amenable result than continued death and destruction. That human factor can never be removed from the equation and it means that the outcome of any conflict is rarely inevitable. Certainly Britain joining the war on the side of France and Russia made it more likely that the Entente would emerge victorious, but it did not guarantee it.

In the end Britain's greatest contribution to the Entente cause was geographical and naval. The addition of the Royal Navy to the Entente cause negated the German navy, which, though far more powerful than the combined navies of France and Russia, was numerically weaker than the British navy. Furthermore, given Britain's geographical position athwart the exits from the North Sea, it was relatively easy for the Royal Navy to cut Germany off from the outside world. The British also controlled the entrances to the Mediterranean Sea at Gibraltar and the Suez Canal, thereby allowing them to cut Germany's ally Austria-Hungary off from access to the outside world as well. This geographical and naval advantage would eventually prove to be decisive in the outcome of the war.

CHAPTER 2

The Schlieffen-Moltke Plan and the Battle of the Marne

When the then Prussian army fought the wars of German unification in the 1860s and 1870s, it fought under favorable diplomatic circumstances thanks to the efforts of Otto von Bismarck. In the 1866 war with Austria, Prussia was joined by Italy and Austria was isolated. In the Franco-Prussian War of 1870–71, the Prussians fought an isolated France. In the intervening years Bismarck created an elaborate series of alliances to protect Germany's dominant position in Europe, but, due to a series of diplomatic failures dating from the time the "Iron Chancellor" was forced out of power in 1890, by 1914 the German army found itself facing a war not against an isolated foe but against a powerful Franco-Russian coalition. This left the German army in an unfavorable position. The German General Staff estimated that Germany and Austria-Hungary combined could field a force of just over 3.5 million men and that their enemies could field over 5 million French, Russian, and Serbian forces.[1] Modern estimates of the opposing sides' strengths vary but all of them retain the basic ratio of forces: the Dual Alliance of Germany and Austria-Hungary was outnumbered and surrounded. From 1894 to 1914 the heads of the German General Staff, Alfred von Schlieffen and Helmuth von Moltke, had to wrestle with this problem. The answer that they eventually devised is now known as the Schlieffen-Moltke Plan.[2]

The Evolution of the Schlieffen-Moltke Plan

The fundamental problem the Central Powers faced was the potentially overwhelming number of men their enemies could mobilize. Fully mobilized the Russian army was capable of fielding nearly 6 million men while the French could field an army of 4 million. In comparison a fully mobilized Germany could field 4.5 million men and Austria-Hungary, 3 million.[3] It was necessary therefore for the Germans to find a way to defeat one of their opponents before the other could bring its full military might to bear. Fortunately for the Germans they had the most developed transportation infrastructure in all of Europe, and by using the extensive German railway system, they could quickly transfer forces from one end of Germany to the other. This allowed them to make use of their interior lines on a strategic level and meant that the German army, if it could mobilize its forces more quickly than its enemies, could send the bulk of its forces to one front, win a decisive victory there, and then transfer those forces back to the other front before the other enemy state was fully prepared. That left two questions, which front to strike at and how to win that decisive victory?

In assessing their two potential foes the German General Staff was concerned with two primary issues: the speed with which their enemies could mobilize their forces and the likelihood of those enemy forces being forced to stand and fight a decisive battle against superior German forces. Over the course of the 1880s the Germans prepared and gamed a number of battle plans, some with a focus on the west against France and others on the east, but starting in 1892 the new head of the General Staff, Alfred von Schlieffen, began focusing his planning on France.[4] The reasoning was simple: the Russian rail net was not fully developed and therefore, given the size of Russia and the relative paucity of railroads in particular in Russian Poland, it would take several weeks before the Russians would be able to strike effectively against Germany or Austria-Hungary. Theoretically therefore the German army could force the French army into a decisive battle while the Russians were still in the process of calling up their reserves. Yet fighting France posed its own problems. Most importantly the French had a very strongly fortified eastern border, which meant that, if they chose not to fight an immediate battle and instead retreated behind their fortresses, they could simply wait for their Russian allies to mobilize while the Germans were unable to do anything other than bombard those forts. Under those circumstances it would be impossible for the Germans to force the French army into a decisive battle and Germany would eventually be overrun by the combined forces of her enemies. In order to prevent that, the Germans had to find another way into France and this led Schlieffen to begin considering an invasion of the Low Countries, Belgium and the Netherlands, as a means of bypassing the French fortresses.

In 1905, with the Russians embroiled in a losing war with Japan and facing tumult and unrest at home, Schlieffen devised the plan that would bear his name. What he proposed was a massive invasion of Belgium and the Netherlands by the bulk of the German army in an effort to turn the flank of the French fortress line. The Germans would place the bulk of their forces along their right wing, leaving only a token force in eastern Germany to harass the Russians while they mobilized and another, only slightly stronger, force to protect the Franco-German border. This powerful right wing would drive through Belgium and the Netherlands and sweep into northern France, making a great wheel around Paris, sweeping the French army before it and eventually driving the French army against its own fortifications, recreating on an operational level the Battle of Cannae, where, in the Second Punic War, a Carthaginian force surrounded and completely destroyed a Roman army (though Carthage went on to lose the war, largely due to Roman naval power, a lesson evidently lost on Schlieffen).[5] Within six or seven weeks the French army would be defeated and this great victory would then allow the Germans to transfer the bulk of their forces east to face the Russians. Whether this was an actual plan that Schlieffen intended to implement in the event of war, as has traditionally been asserted, or whether it was more of an intellectual exercise that was never meant to be a war plan, the general concept came to be adopted and embraced by Schlieffen's successor, Helmuth von Moltke.[6]

Von Moltke kept the fundamental Schlieffen concept but modified it in significant ways. First and foremost, whereas Schlieffen was willing to see the French attack the German positions in Alsace and Lorraine and even possibly move into German territory directly, Moltke was unwilling to abandon any German territory to the enemy. Therefore he strengthened the German left wing on the Franco-German frontier, moving troops from the offensive right wing and stationing two German armies on that frontier. This dramatically altered the ratio of German forces. In the original Schlieffen concept the ratio of strength between the right and left wings was 7:1. After Moltke's modification that was changed to 3:1, significantly weakening the main offensive force. An additional change was a result of the worsening relations between Germany and Great Britain in the decade before the war. In 1905 Schlieffen could reasonably reckon on at least the possibility of British neutrality in a Franco-German war; by 1914 it was far more likely that Britain would intervene in such a war. Therefore Moltke detached an additional corps from the German right wing and sent it to the northern frontier to defend the provinces of Schleswig-Holstein and to guard against a possible British invasion of the German coast.[7] Yet another change was to incorporate the use of reserves with the frontline troops, partly to carry out rear area duties such as screening fortresses and garrisoning towns and partly to supplement the field army, which had been starved for funds since the passage of the Second German Naval Law and the creation of the High Seas Fleet; consequently the field army was not as large as either Moltke or Schlieffen thought it needed to be. A final, and extremely significant, change was that Moltke, wisely, dropped the invasion of the Netherlands. His reasoning was that the Netherlands, as a neutral, would provide a "windpipe" through which Germany could bring in necessary supplies if the British entered the war and instituted a naval blockade of Germany's ports. He argued "As long as Holland remained neutral, imports would be possible via that country under the American flag. It is hardly to be expected that England would not respect that flag."[8] In the event this proved to be a wise political move but in the short term it greatly complicated matters for the German army because it meant that the entire German right wing had to move through the narrow neck of the Belgian-German border, a border dominated by the fortress of Liege. This would require the Germans to seize Liege very quickly once war was declared, before it could be fully garrisoned by the Belgian army. Failure to do so would risk disaster for the entire operation.

Moltke also discontinued German war planning for an offensive against Russia instead of France, for two reasons. First of all he was convinced that, regardless of how and where war broke out, France would always align itself with Germany's enemies; therefore it was unnecessary to have plans for an offensive against anyone else. Second, he also believed that it would be impossible for Germany to win a quick and decisive victory against Russia because Russia, unlike France, had the luxury of size. The Russians could retreat from the German army and avoid battle, as they did in the war against Napoleon in 1812. The French however would have to stand and fight. By 1914 therefore the German General Staff possessed only one plan for military operations, the Schlieffen-Moltke Plan.

The plan however had several serious flaws, which combined to make it, instead of a recipe for victory, a gigantic gamble. First were the simple logistical needs of the plan. According to Herwig the plan required 20,800 trains of 50 cars each and 118,000 horses to transport nearly 400,000 tons of material in order to supply an army of over 2 million men. The trains could get the army to its jumping off points but from there the army would be largely dependent on horse-drawn transport until the captured Belgian railroads could be repaired.[9] Nor was there any effort to coordinate with the High Seas Fleet, which could have been used to try and prevent the transport of British forces to the continent, forces that Moltke confidently expected to "sweep up" as the Germans moved through Belgium but which would, in the actual fighting, prove critical to the defeat of the German plan. In addition the plan required prodigious, nearly superhuman efforts from the German soldiers. They were expected to march roughly 25 miles every day while also engaging in battles, a feat nearly impossible without motorized transport. The plan also depended for its success on units that did not exist when the plan was created. While the Germans did strengthen the army in 1912 and 1913 they went to war with a force that was barely adequate for all of its tasks. Furthermore, the plan was also dependent, for any hope of success, on a slow Russian mobilization, but over the very years when the Germans were fine-tuning this plan the Russians were engaged in a railroad-building program that would allow them to mobilize their army much more quickly than the Germans anticipated. In the actual event the Russians would invade Germany within four weeks of their initial mobilization. Last and most significant, the plan all but guaranteed that Great Britain would join the war against Germany. Moltke believed this to be all but certain anyway and he was likely right but it was the invasion of Belgium that allowed Edward Grey, the British foreign minister, to persuade his colleagues in the Cabinet that Britain needed to go to war against Germany. That in turn made it less likely that the French would quickly seek peace even if their army was decisively defeated in the early battles. Furthermore, when the crisis over the assassination of Franz Ferdinand began moving toward a military clash after July 28, the fact that the Germans possessed only this one war plan drastically limited the options of the German chancellor, Theobald von Bethmann-Hollweg. In effect the existence of a war plan that was so dependent on timing for any hope of success meant that once one of Germany's enemies began mobilizing their army Germany would have to either back down or go immediately to war. In sum the plan was a gigantic gamble. The plan deprived Germany's leaders of flexibility in the crisis of 1914 and meant that that any war between Germany and the Franco-Russian alliance would almost certainly involve Great Britain, putting Germany in a very difficult position in any war that was not ended quickly. Essentially the Schlieffen-Moltke Plan all but ensured that if they could not win the war quickly they could not win it at all.

The Disposition of Forces

The German army went to war in 1914 with just over 2.1 million men.[10] The Schlieffen-Moltke Plan divided those men into eight armies. One of these, the largest with 500,000 men, was stationed in East Prussia to harass the Russians and defend, as best it could, the easternmost German territories. The remainder faced the French and Belgian frontier. The weakest of the armies, the Seventh, with only 125,000 men, was stationed furthest south and covered the region between Strasbourg and the Swiss border. To the north was the Sixth Army, consisting of nearly 220,000 men. Together these two armies were to hold the German left, in Alsace and Lorraine. Ideally they would pin the French forces opposite them in place and prevent them from moving to the French left wing. The Fifth Army, with 200,000 men, was based on the fortress city of Metz and would serve as the hinge of the German left and right wings. This would require it to make a small push toward the French fortress of Verdun. The southernmost of the right wing armies was the Fourth, which was tasked with occupying Luxembourg and moving toward Sedan. It also had 200,000 men. The slightly smaller Third Army of 180,000 men was to move through the Ardennes forest and toward Dinant and Givet. The hammers of the German force were the First and Second Armies. Combined they wielded a force of nearly 600,000 men (320,000 in the First Army and 260,000 in the Second Army). They were to invade Belgium; seize Liege, Brussels, Namur, and Antwerp; and then drive into France. Including ancillary and reserve forces the Germans conducted their great gamble with just over 1.6 million men.[11]

Those German forces were opposed by nearly 2 million French soldiers. The French had an offensive war plan of their own, known as Plan XVII. According to this plan the heart of the French army was to strike into Alsace-Lorraine in an attempt to retake the so-called lost provinces and to prevent the Germans from sending significant forces east to face the Russians. The French commander, General Joseph Joffre, arrayed his forces in five armies with his strongest, the First and Second Armies, based in the south and tasked with carrying out the invasion of German territory. The hinge of the French line, the Third Army, was based around Verdun and was to attack the German fortress of Metz. The Fifth Army was the leftmost army and it was supposed to deal with any German strike into Luxembourg. The Fourth Army was held in reserve behind Verdun to either exploit success in the south or move to the north if the Germans invaded Belgium.[12]

Joffre and the French General Staff did anticipate that the Germans might invade Belgium and they were determined, for political reasons, to ensure that French forces did not enter Belgium first. Joffre feared that an early French move into Belgium would make it less likely that Britain would join France whereas a German invasion would make such intervention far more likely. Joffre showed here far more political acumen than his German counterparts. What Joffre did not expect was the extent of the German invasion and the size of the German right wing, and as a result, he remained committed to his offensive into Alsace-Lorraine.

The campaign began on August 3 when the Germans issued an ultimatum to the Belgian government, stating that if the Belgians did not resist the German invasion the German government would ensure the restoration of Belgium's independence when the war was over. They were to be disappointed. The Belgians did resist and added their small but determined army to that of the French. The Belgian army consisted mainly of garrison troops, 200,000 of them, and a small field army of just over 100,000 men. Small as it was this force would play a key role in the coming campaign, at both Liege and Antwerp, and would help to defeat the German plan.

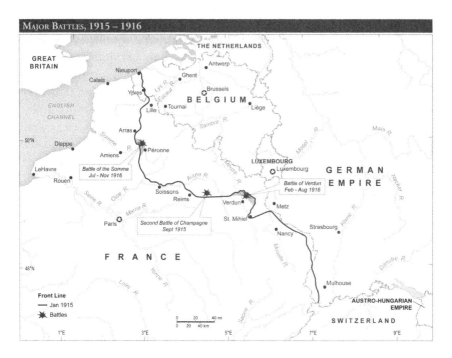

The final force the Germans faced in their western invasion was the small but highly professional British Expeditionary Force (BEF). This force of roughly 100,000 men was deployed on the far left of the French line, around the city of Maubeuge. Moltke and the German planners paid little heed to what the Kaiser famously called a "contemptible little army," but this small force consisted of some of the best trained and equipped soldiers in all of Europe and they too would play a key role in the events to come.[13]

The Initial Battles

The crisis that led to war in 1914 began with the assassination of Archduke Franz Ferdinand, the heir to the Austro-Hungarian throne, by a group of Bosnian Serbs who had been aided by the Black Hand, a terrorist organization run by Dragutin Dimitrijevic, the head of Serbian military intelligence. The assassination took place on June 28 but the crisis that led to war did not begin until July 23, when the Austro-Hungarian government sent a harsh ultimatum to the Serbian government, demanding, among other things, that the Serbs allow Austro-Hungarian officials to enter Serbia to investigate the assassination. The Serbian government accepted every other demand on July 25. Unsatisfied because it wanted war, the Austro-Hungarian government first broke off diplomatic relations and then declared war on Serbia on July 28. By doing so they risked the outbreak of a much larger war. The Serbians were supported by the Russian government, which, driven partly by Pan-Slavism and partly by a desire to dominate the Balkans, decided to mobilize its army on July 30. By mobilizing the Russians started the clock on the Schlieffen-Moltke Plan. The German government, which had earlier promised its complete support for any Austro-Hungarian measure, now had to decide whether to go to war or to allow its ally to face Russia and Serbia alone. According to the Schlieffen-Moltke Plan the mobilization of the German army would also bring about a quick occupation of Luxembourg and a strike to seize control of the forts around Liege. Failure to rapidly seize those forts would create a massive bottleneck that would destroy the German hopes for victory immediately. Therefore, on July 30, Moltke began pressuring Kaiser Wilhelm II and Chancellor Bethmann-Hollweg to order German mobilization. Those two men responded by sending an ultimatum to the Russians on July 31. They demanded that Russia cease its mobilization or face war with Germany. The Russians did not respond to the ultimatum and on the following day, August 1, the Germans ordered general mobilization and declared war on Russia. The Schlieffen-Moltke Plan went into operation.

The next day German forces occupied Luxembourg. That same day an ultimatum was sent to the French government, insisting that they turn their border fortifications over to German control or face war with Germany. The French did not respond and on August 3 Germany declared war on France while German forces began entering the eastern portions of Belgium. Belgium too now received their ultimatum, which they rejected, and on the next day the fighting in the west began when German forces launched their assault on Liege. The only diplomatic response came from Great Britain, which sent the Germans an ultimatum to leave Belgium or face war with Britain. The Germans did not respond and that evening the British declared war on Germany. The First World War had begun.[14]

The initial German assault on Liege did not go according to plan. Over the course of the next few days, August 4–6, the German Second Army launched a series of infantry assaults on the Liege forts. These assaults accomplished little and resulted in heavy German losses. On August 7, German forces led by Erich Ludendorff did manage to seize the citadel in the center of Liege but the forts continued to hold out, slowing down the onset of the full German offensive. It was only on August 12, when the Germans were able to bring up their heaviest guns, 305 mm and 420 mm siege guns, that they were able to begin battering the forts into submission. Over the course of the next four days these massive guns pulverized the remaining forts. On the 16th the last of the Liege forts surrendered. However, the stubborn resistance of the forts was sufficient to throw the heavily regimented Schlieffen-Moltke Plan off schedule by two days. It was the first of numerous events that should have reminded all concerned of the Elder Moltke's dictum that "no plan survives first contact with the enemy."

While the German right wing was held up by the Liege forts the French implemented their plan, simply called Plan XVII. It called for French forces to invade Alsace and Lorraine and drive the Germans from the "lost provinces." Accordingly French forces crossed the German border on August 8, taking the southern German town of Mulhouse. German forces were able to rally and counterattack, retaking Mulhouse on August 13, but these early skirmishes were replaced by a full-scale French invasion on August 14. As the German right wing began pushing west between Brussels and Namur in Belgium the French right wing began driving into Alsace and Lorraine. The French learned here the same thing the Germans learned at Liege, that infantry assaults against well-prepared defensive positions were deadly. They too suffered heavy casualties in the fighting from August 14 to 16. French forces did capture the city of Sarrebourg on the 17th, but by that point Joffre was becoming aware of the large German force to his left and he halted the invasion in order to shift some forces north for a strike into the Ardennes. That shifting of forces allowed the Germans to regroup and on the 20th, they counterattacked, recapturing Sarrebourg and driving the French back to their starting positions. Plan XVII, though it failed to capture Alsace and Lorraine, did have one significant impact: the French threat to his left led Moltke to transfer six replacement divisions to the south. In the plan these divisions were meant to occupy Belgian territory and provide security for the main army, which would now be forced to detach some of its own forces to perform those duties.

Meanwhile, on August 15 the first German and French forces clashed in Belgium, around the city of Dinant. At this point Joffre was working under the assumption that the German strike into Belgium was limited to southern Belgium and that the main German force was moving through the Ardennes forest toward Sedan. As a result he ordered the French Fifth Army to hold the area between the Meuse and Sambre

Rivers while the reinforced French Third and Fourth Armies prepared to strike through the Ardennes in the direction of Liege, in the hopes of cutting off the German forces moving into Belgium. It was left to the small Belgian army and the equally small BEF to hold the rest of Belgium. Those Belgian forces chose not to face the German army in the field, wisely, and instead retreated to the fortress of Antwerp, which they reached on August 20, the same day that German forces entered the Belgian capital of Brussels. The Germans were capturing large stretches of Belgian territory but to this point, now over two weeks into the six-week Schlieffen-Moltke window, they had not yet won any decisive victories. In fact the decisive right wing was instead being slowly weakened; not only had Moltke shifted six divisions south but with the Belgians retreating to Antwerp the commander of the German First Army, Alexander von Kluck, was now forced to detach a corps to besiege the Belgian army.

On August 21, German forces reached the northern bank of the Sambre River and the large siege guns were sent into action against the fortress of Namur. On the same day Joffre launched his offensive into the Ardennes. The French Fourth and Fifth Armies marched into the hinge of the German line, the German Fourth and Fifth Armies. The battle in the Ardennes raged for two days before the French were driven back and forced to retreat behind the Meuse. The French lost over 26,000 men and the Germans lost nearly 38,000 in the course of two days.[15] At the same time the German Second Army struck at the French Fifth Army along the Sambre River and the German First Army encountered the BEF at Mons. In two days of heavy fighting the Germans were able to cross the Sambre and drive the French Fifth, along with the Third and Fourth Armies, into retreat. At Mons the First Army ran into much tougher resistance than it expected from the small British force. Over the course of the 23rd of August the British II corps, employing rapid, massed, and disciplined rifle fire, was able to stop the German IX corps cold. The weight of German numbers however soon forced the British to retreat as well.

The German victories of the 21st to the 23rd seemed to indicate that the German plan was succeeding. The Belgians had retreated to their fortresses, the BEF and the French armies were in retreat, and the German forces were pushing continually west. However, the Germans were taking very heavy casualties in the process, and their strength was slowly being eroded. It was at this point that the Schlieffen-Moltke Plan encountered another unforeseen difficulty: the Russians launched a two-pronged invasion of East Prussia, much sooner than the Germans had expected. The Russian First Army invaded from the east while the Russian Second Army pushed north out of Russian Poland. The two armies hoped to encircle and destroy the German Eighth Army and thereby open the road to Berlin. Concerned by the invasion and by the pleas of the commander of the Eighth Army for aid, Moltke sent two corps that were originally intended for the right wing in France to East Prussia instead, further eroding the power of the main German strike force. Moltke also appointed a new commander for the Eastern Front, General Paul von Hindenburg who was aided by Erich Ludendorff. Upon arriving in East Prussia the two German commanders quickly realized that the Russian First Army, which was invading from the east, was moving very slowly and cautiously and was not in a position to threaten either the German Eighth Army or the major city of Konigsberg. Therefore they decided to attack, sending the entire Eighth Army against the Russian Second Army, which was invading from Russian Poland to the south. In the ensuing battle, Battle of Tannenberg, that Russian force was almost completely destroyed. The battle made Hindenburg a war hero and saved East Prussia. Ironically the two corps that Moltke sent from the west did not arrive until after the battle had been won. They played no meaningful role in the east and were sorely missed in the west in the coming weeks.

In the meantime the German push to the west and now south continued. On the 26th, the Germans defeated the British II corps in the Battle of Le Cateau, forcing the BEF to retreat behind the Oise River. The British commander, Sir John French, began a lengthy and continuous retreat that repeatedly exposed the flank of the French Fifth Army. French seemed to have lost his nerve. Joffre sent numerous requests in the final days of August trying to convince French to halt his retreat and hold his ground, all to no effect. Joffre even ordered the French Fifth Army to launch an assault on the German Second Army on August 29 in an effort to bolster British morale. This attack, as with the other French attacks, failed. On August 30, the Germans counterattacked, driving the French Fifth Army further back. By the end of August the Germans had effectively won what became known as the Battle of the Frontiers. The French and British were in retreat in the north though the lines had stabilized in the south. The Entente forces had suffered roughly 260,000 casualties and had lost significant French territory, territory that comprised 83 percent of France's iron ore deposits and that provided 60 percent of France's steel production.[16] German forces were within 60 kilometers of Paris. However, the Germans had lost roughly 260,000 men of their own from the decisive First and Second Armies. Most of these were battle losses but some men fell from the sheer exhaustion of having to march and fight every single day for several weeks. By the end of August, the German First Army had already marched 500 kilometers from its starting point; in the process it had also outrun its supply lines. In addition, as we have seen, forces that had been earmarked for the right wing had been shifted, some to the east, others to the south, and still others to the north to watch the Belgian army in Antwerp. The decisive arm of the German push had been significantly weakened by these decisions. All of these factors led Moltke to abandon the sweep around Paris, probably wisely, and to order the German right wing to concentrate on pushing southeast instead. The objective remained the same, to force the French army into a decisive battle in which it would be destroyed.

At this point Joffre reevaluated the Entente's situation. It was now clear that the main German effort was coming through Belgium and against the French left wing. As a result he concluded that the time had come to go over to a defensive posture. The French left was pulled back to a line running from Maubeuge to Verdun and Joffre began transferring forces from the right wing to the left. In addition a new army, the Sixth, began to assemble in and around Paris.

Over the course of the next two days the German forces continued their push to the southeast. By doing so though the German First Army exposed its flank to Paris and the newly created French Sixth Army. The commander of the French Sixth Army, General Joseph Gallieni, asked Joffre for permission to attack that flank. Joffre agreed, and on September 4, he ordered his left wing armies to cease retreating and prepare to join in a counterattack on the German right wing. Moltke came to realize the danger to his First Army as well and he accordingly issued new orders of his own. On September 4, he ordered the First and Second Armies to cease their advance and hold their ground. Moltke expected a French counterattack and accordingly he ordered the two German armies to support one another when that attack came. In the interim it would now be the Fourth and Fifth German armies, in the center, who were to take over the brunt of the attack. They were to continue pushing southeast and the Sixth and Seventh Armies in the south were also to attack in order to keep as many French forces as possible in the south. The Third Army would support either the defending First and Second Armies or the attacking Fourth and Fifth Armies as circumstances warranted. These orders were not well received in the headquarters of the First Army where General Kluck was convinced that the French were on the run before him. His failure to follow these orders would result in the creation of a gap between the First and Second Armies, which would endanger the flanks of both of them. The stage was set for what would be the most decisive battle of the entire war, the Battle of the Marne.

The Battle of the Marne

By September 4, the main lines on the Western Front stretched from just outside of Paris to the Swiss border. On the northern end of that front, three Entente armies—the French Sixth Army in Paris, the remaining forces of the BEF, and part of the French Fifth Army—faced the German First and Second Armies. The French Fifth faced the left flank of the German First Army and the right flank of the German Second Army. The BEF was to their west with the French Sixth on the end of the line. Further east another newly created French army, the Ninth, faced part of the German Second and the entire German Third Army. The Germans were outnumbered in both men and guns; just over 260 German battalions faced more than 350 Entente battalions and roughly 1,600 German artillery pieces were opposed by nearly 2,000 Entente

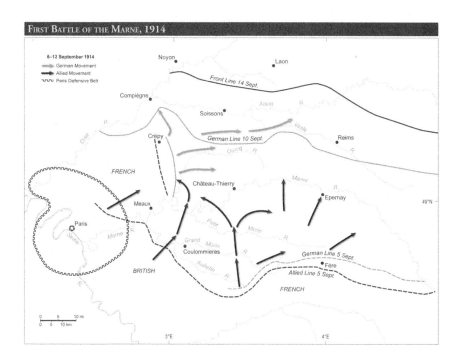

FIRST BATTLE OF THE MARNE, 1914

pieces. These outnumbered forces would fight the climactic battle that would determine the success or failure of the Schlieffen-Moltke Plan. It was time to roll the iron dice.

The Battle of the Marne really began on September 5. On that day the French Sixth Army advanced out of Paris against the German First Army. General Gallieni planned to strike the right flank of the Germans and begin turning the German line. The French force, numbering roughly 150,000 men, engaged a small screen of German forces and drove it back 10 kilometers. General Kluck then turned the First Army to the right to meet this new enemy and made plans to counterattack. To do so he shifted two corps from his own left flank, where those corps were maintaining contact with General von Bülow's Second Army. This move opened a 50-kilometer gap between the two German forces—a gap that was covered by only a weak cavalry screen. This presented Joffre with a major opportunity. If the Sixth Army could hold and the BEF, with portions of the Fifth Army, could push into and through the gap, the Entente forces could encircle and destroy the entire German First Army, in the process crushing the German offensive in the west and opening the door to a major Entente counterattack along the front. Accordingly Joffre ordered a major counterattack of his own for the next day. The Fifth and Sixth Armies, joined by the BEF, would attack the both the First and Second German armies.

That attack took place on September 6. Over 1 million Entente soldiers from all three armies attacked 750,000 Germans. As part of that counterattack the BEF began cautiously moving against the German cavalry screen in the gap. The British faced only minimal resistance but moved forward very slowly and cautiously. Nonetheless the advance and the precarious position of his First Army led General von Moltke to panic, a panic aggravated by his lack of control over the battle.

Unlike Joffre who seemed to be everywhere in these critical days as he traveled from army to army, Moltke was content to maintain his position in Imperial Headquarters, 400 kilometers to the rear in Luxembourg.[17] To a degree this was the result of the nature of the two systems. The French army was highly centralized and Joffre's role was vital whereas the German army functioned in a more decentralized fashion, with greater responsibility and authority given to Moltke's subordinate commanders. In the German system the General Staff created the operational plan and each army group commander was assigned his mission; how he achieved that mission was then left to him. The army group commander in turn gives each of his subordinate army commanders their particular portion of the overall mission. This system had great strengths, mainly that the men on the fighting front who had the most immediate information of what was going on in their sector could react quickly without having to communicate with Imperial Headquarters on every decision. However, none of those on the scene had knowledge of the events in other sectors of the front, events that often would directly impact their own position. Only the overall commander was privy to that information through reports sent to him from his commanders. However, the limitations of the communication technology of 1914 often left Moltke in the dark regarding just what was going on. Furthermore, even when he had adequate and accurate information he had a difficult time disseminating that information back down the chain of command. Another problem reared its head at the Marne: there was no overall army group commander on the right wing, and each army commander was subordinated directly to Moltke, who, however, was based well behind the lines. If those front commanders did not communicate and work with one another Moltke was too far away to enforce that kind of cooperation. The latter problem, exacerbated by petty jealousy between Kluck and Bülow, proved critical.

Over the course of September 6th as both Kluck's First Army and Bülow's Second Army came under heavy attack, the two commanders reacted very differently. Kluck, who had now turned his army to face the French Sixth Army, was heavily engaged all day but his army held its ground. As a result he became convinced that he could defeat the French Sixth Army on the following day and destroy the French flank. He expected Bülow to hold his ground while he did so. However in the early morning hours of September 7, Bülow decided to retreat his army behind the Petit Morin River. He did not inform Kluck of this decision, a decision that widened the gap between the two armies. Evidently Bülow anticipated that Kluck would withdraw to the east to close the gap but Kluck was determined instead to continue his battle with the Sixth Army, in the hope that it could be defeated before the BEF's penetration of the gap could pose a critical problem. As the fighting continued on the 7th Kluck was unable to defeat the Sixth Army and the BEF continued its slow penetration of the gap. Due to pressure from the Entente forces Bülow decided early on the 8th to shift his right flank forces back another 10 kilometers, widening the gap between the First and Second Armies to 65 kilometers. By noon on the 8th the BEF had reached the Petit Morin River, a 40-kilometer advance into the German lines. Kluck still gave no sign that he intended to fall back and close the gap. Instead he planned to renew his attacks on the Sixth Army. The forces he had pulled from his left flank arrived on his right by the evening of the 8th and he intended to throw them against the Sixth Army on the following day. At this critical juncture, with the fate of the entire German line at stake, Moltke finally intervened.

On the 8th Moltke sent Lieutenant Colonel Richard Hentsch to visit the armies on the center and right wing and ascertain the real conditions at the front. Hentsch began his visit with the central armies— the Third, Fourth, and Fifth—and determined that the situation was satisfactory on those sectors; however when he arrived at the headquarters of the Second Army he was informed by Bülow that the situation was extremely serious and that Entente forces were about to break completely through the gap between the First and Second Armies. The nervous Bülow feared that his army had reached its breaking point. On the morning of the 9th, before Hentsch left to visit First Army, Bülow ordered yet another retreat. When Hentsch arrived at First Army headquarters later that morning he received a very favorable report from Kluck's staff, stating that the French Sixth Army was nearly beaten. There was little concern over the gap. Despite this report Hentsch, using power he may or may not have been given,[18] informed Kluck and his staff that the time had come for a general retreat along the front. Hentsch ordered the First Army to break off its battle with the Sixth Army and retreat in the direction of Soissons while the Second Army would fall back to the east bank of the Marne, Third Army would fall back northeast of Chalons, and the Fourth and Fifth in the direction of the Argonne. Kluck was unable to dissuade Hentsch and the retreat began. Hentsch was in all likelihood correct. There were no fresh forces available to stop the BEF from completely severing the links between the First and Second Armies. If Kluck had been allowed to continue his assault on the French Sixth Army it is quite likely that the First Army would have been cut off from the rest of the German force. The Germans had simply suffered too many losses from both battle and fatigue to continue the momentum of their advance. Joffre's and Gallieni's decisive actions had stopped the German advance at the Marne River. It was clear that the Germans had been defeated and it became clear later that the defeat was decisive. Hentsch and Moltke hoped to regroup once the retreat was over and then renew the assault but it was clear that even if they managed to do so they would not be able to win a decisive victory before they would have to actively engage the Russians on the Eastern Front. The great German gamble on victory had failed. The Schlieffen-Moltke Plan would not succeed.

When the Germans began their retreat, the French forces went on a full offensive. The French Sixth Army now switched roles with the German First and attempted to turn the latter's flank. However the French had suffered too many casualties of their own to press the Germans back very far. The Germans did fall back behind Aisne River but from those positions they were able to defeat the French counterattack over the course of the 10th to the 14th of September. Eventually the line stabilized as both armies were forced to stop from utter exhaustion. In the weeks to come both sides would move fresh forces to the front and the fighting would resume in what would come to be known as the "Race to the Sea," with each army attempting to turn their enemy's flank. During that march the Germans would finally take Antwerp though the Belgian army would manage to escape to the French and British lines and would remain in the war until 1918. In the end neither army would succeed in its goal and this march would eventually push both armies all the way to the coast of the English Channel, which is where the fighting would stalemate and both sides would begin digging in, eventually creating a line of trenches that ran from the coastline all the way to the border of Switzerland. The latter campaigns of 1914 however were anti-climactic; none of them held much real promise of victory. The French and British victory at the Marne had saved the French army.

The Aftermath

The scope of these battles was immense. Over 3 million men were engaged in the west from mid-August to mid-September 1914. Never before had armies of this size engaged one another and never before had losses of this size been dealt. Of those 3 million men over 700,000 became casualties. These were the bloodiest days of the entire war. They were also the most decisive. The Entente victory at the Marne meant that Germans' great hope to offset their disadvantage in numbers had failed. They would have to face a two-front war. Moltke could not withstand the failure of his plan. In the course of the last days of the battle he suffered a nervous breakdown and was replaced as chief of the General Staff by the war minister, Erich von Falkenhayn. Moltke would not live to see the end of the war or its aftermath, in which he was resoundingly blamed for Germany's defeat by supporters of Schlieffen, who argued that if only Moltke had not modified the plan it would have led to certain victory. This was nonsense. The Schlieffen-Moltke Plan was never a recipe for victory. At best it was a desperate gamble to try and deal militarily with a very difficult political situation, having both Russia and France as enemies. Moltke certainly could have done many things differently but the plan he inherited from Schlieffen was unlikely to succeed in any form.

On the other side Joffre became a French hero and the victory quickly came to be called the "Miracle on the Marne." In truth there was little miraculous about it. Joffre simply kept his head and maneuvered his armies well. He realized where the decisive sector of the line was and was willing to surrender French territory if necessary to put his reserves where they needed to be. He also managed, through enormous effort, to persuade a reluctant Sir John French, the British commander, to commit his own worn-out men to the decisive sector of the counterattack. Joffre was able to make use of interior lines to quickly and effectively transfer his forces and by doing so was able to concentrate sufficient force in the critical sector at the critical time. However, though the French army had been saved from defeat at the Marne and the Germans' hopes for ultimate victory had been dealt a devastating blow, the Germans were left in occupation of nearly all of Belgium and most of the richest provinces of France and the war would go on. In fact the occupation of that French territory and the German victories against the Russians in East Prussia and Poland hid the full significance of what had happened at the Marne. Not even most German soldiers or even many of the political and military leaders of the country, much less the civilian population, were ever informed of what had actually happened at the Marne. With bad news from the front being strictly censored most Germans only knew about successes such as Tannenberg. They saw maps with German troops occupying enemy territory and were told that victory was imminent. This led many of them, from industrialists and professors to politicians, to hatch grandiose plans of a German peace that would leave France and Russia prostrate; Belgium, Poland, and vast stretches of the east under German control; and Britain humbled. However, there were some members of the political and military hierarchy, most notably the new Commander General Falkenhayn and Chancellor Theobald von Bethmann-Hollweg, who understood the reality of Germany's position; the German army could no longer win a decisive enough victory to allow for the implementation of a "German peace." The failure of the Schlieffen-Moltke Plan left Germany now facing a massive enemy coalition that possessed vastly greater manpower and wealth than it did. That coalition was powered by Great Britain, the world's preeminent financial and naval power. Germany and its ally Austria-Hungary would soon find themselves cut off from the rest of the world by a British naval blockade. Isolated and forced to rely only on their own resources and those that they could conquer while their enemies had access to their own global empires and to the markets of the neutral world, most importantly those of the United States, the Central Powers were at an extreme disadvantage. The Germans now faced their worst prewar nightmare; they were encircled and isolated by an enemy coalition with vastly more power than they themselves possessed. Their only ally was the weak and poorly managed Austro-Hungarian Empire, which became more of a drain than a support to the German war effort as the war went on. Their hopes for a short and victorious war shattered, the Germans now had to face the reality of a long war.

CHAPTER 3

The British Naval Blockade and the Long War Germany Feared

With the defeat of the German armies in the Battle of the Marne and their ensuing failure to turn the left flank of the Entente armies during the Race to the Sea, the Germans found themselves engaged in a stalemate on the Western Front. The German victories in the east saved Germany from Russian invasion and pulled Russian forces away from the Austro-Hungarian front but were insufficient to truly offset the losses in the west. As a result of those fall 1914 battles, Germany was left a besieged fortress. The Germans had staked their hopes for a rapid victory on the Schlieffen-Moltke Plan and the failure of the plan meant that the German people would have to face the reality of a long and drawn out war. In such a conflict, the Entente, in particular the British, had enormous advantages, mainly due to the power of the Royal Navy, which quickly demonstrated that power by instituting a blockade of Germany in the fall of 1914. In the end, that blockade and the German failure to effectively deal with it would prove fatal to the German war effort.

German Industry and the Food Supply before the War

The German munitions industry was one of the world's strongest in the years before the war and it had built not only the most powerful army in the world but one of the most powerful navies as well. This industry consisted of both privately and publicly owned companies with some of the larger German states, most significantly Prussia, owning their own munitions plants. Overall the German munitions industry employed roughly 16,000 people in the years before the war and it was able to supply the majority of Germany's military needs.[1] Though Germany had plentiful deposits of coal and iron (though their iron was not of a particularly high grade), there were several materials that were vital to modern industry that Germany did not possess in sufficient quantities. Therefore the productivity of German industry was dependent on the importation of these key goods from other nations. For example, the Germans were heavily reliant on the importation of Chilean nitrates not only for the creation of munitions but also for the creation of fertilizer. In 1913 the Germans imported 747,000 tons of nitrates from Chile. Those were converted into 119,490 tons of nitrogen. At the same time domestic production of nitrogen amounted only to 14,000 tons.[2] Nitrates were one prominent import; rubber was another. The Germans even imported iron ore from Sweden.

It was not only German industry that was dependent on imports; so was German agriculture. For example, German farmers imported roughly 30 percent of all the fodder for their livestock.By importing nitrates for fertilizer and fodder for livestock German farmers could produce 90 percent of their nation's basic food needs, though in practice the Germans actually imported 19 percent of their overall food supply during peacetime, specifically 27 percent of their proteins and 42 percent of all their fats.[3] The numbers are somewhat misleading though since the Germans were among the best fed people in Europe. For example in 1910 Germans

Table 3.1   Agricultural Production and Consumption in 1913

Grain Production in Germany 1913 (thousands of metric tons)[4]						
Wheat	Rye	Barley	Oats	Corn	Potatoes	Beets
5094	12,222	3673	9714	621	54,121	18,540

Livestock in Germany 1913 (thousands)[5]				
Horses	Cows	Pigs	Sheep	Goats
4558	20,994	25,659	5521	3548

Value of German Agricultural Production (millions of marks)[6]			
Cereals/vegetables	Meat	Milk/Eggs	Total value
3540	4593	3607	11740

Consumption of Basic Foods in Germany 1913 (kilograms)[7]							
Meat	Fish	Rye	Wheat	Potatoes	Vegetables	Fruits	Sugar
44.9	9.3	65.2	66	203	63.5	22.6	20

consumed 120 percent of their daily requirements of food. This diet included 51 kilograms of meat every year.[8] In fact, one of the stereotypes of the prewar German, alongside that of the militaristic Prussian, was that of the chubby, heavy-drinking Bavarian. In truth though the overeaters were a small percentage of the population, generally consisting only of the very well-off. Nonetheless, Germans' reliance on imports left their economy vulnerable to economic pressure, specifically from Great Britain. In a war against Great Britain any transatlantic imports would almost certainly be cut off. Imports from across the Baltic could be protected, unless the British navy opted to force its way into the Baltic Sea, which was highly unlikely due to the dangers of mines and torpedoes, but little food was imported from the Scandinavian countries. Table 3.1 summarizes prewar German agricultural production and consumption.

The average prices for these goods ran anywhere from DM 1 to DM 3 for a half kilo of butter, or one dozen eggs, or one kilo of meat. The average family in prewar Berlin spent roughly DM 23 every month on food.[9] The average daily wage for a working man in Germany in 1914 was DM 4.84, meaning the average worker spent roughly five days' wages on food each month.[10]

The war, in particular the British naval blockade, placed great stresses on the German economy, particularly on agriculture. An increasing scarcity of resources, combined with economic mismanagement and a progressively tighter blockade, slowly eroded the agricultural sector of the German economy, leading to food shortages, heavy inflation, and a wearing away of the nation's cultural consensus in favor of war.

Economic Problems Caused by the War

The outbreak of the war led to immediate problems in both the industrial and agricultural sectors of the German economy. In the industrial field the immediate problem was the unexpectedly vast expenditure of ammunition. The Germans had studied the expenditure of munitions by both sides during the Russo-Japanese War and had begun to expand their munitions supply beginning in 1912 but those plans were never fully completed and the Germans, along with the other belligerents, entered the war without sufficient munitions, in particular for their artillery. By October 1914 all of the German munitions reserves had been expended and the Germans were left to rely on current production for their needs.[11] Furthermore, that production was limited by the loss of the Chilean nitrates that German industry was dependent upon. The Germans were fortunate that Fritz Haber had developed, just prior to the war, a process by which nitrogen could be extracted from the air. According to one historian this process "saved the German war effort."[12] However, that process could not provide sufficient nitrates for both industry and agriculture and the munitions plants were given priority, which meant that German agriculture suffered from a lack of fertilizer from the very earliest days of the war.[13]

German agriculture suffered from problems that went well beyond the loss of fertilizers. The loss of imported fodder meant that some of their domestic food production going forward would have to be devoted to the production of fodder for their livestock, or the livestock would have to be slaughtered. In addition roughly 60 percent of all farm labor and large numbers of draft animals were called to military service. This left German farmers desperately short of labor and animal power exactly when they were beginning to bring in the 1914 harvest.[14] The shortage of labor and animal power was aggravated by a preexisting shortage of agricultural machinery. All of these made it difficult to bring in the entire harvest. By early October there were bread shortages in some major cities. Those shortages led the Bundesrat, the upper house of the German legislature and the real lawmaking body in Imperial Germany,[15] to begin regulating the food supply. On October 28, 1914, it ordered that henceforth all wheat and rye bread was to be leavened with 5 percent potato flour in order to stretch the grain supply. Within a matter of months that would rise to 10 percent.[16] The German people soon dubbed this K-Brot and it became a large component of the diet for poorer Germans. Since the law was circumvented from the very beginning, purer bread remained available, but only on what would become a thriving black market. Hence wealthier Germans were still able to purchase wheat bread while the poorer members of German society came to subsist increasingly on K-Brot.

The Bundesrat, recognizing the food problem as critical, quickly acted to expand its control. In November 1914 it created an Imperial Grain Authority, which was empowered to purchase or, if necessary, confiscate stores of grain from German farmers.[17] All German farmers were required to register their grain supplies with the Imperial Grain Authority, which would then buy those stores from the farmers at state-mandated prices. In addition an Imperial Allocation Office was created to handle the distribution of purchased grains to the populace. To prevent farmers from dodging the law by feeding their grains to their livestock, the Bundesrat banned the use of wheat and rye as fodder. Bread rationing was also introduced, initially only in Berlin, but by June 1915 it had been extended to the nation as a whole. Henceforth each German was to be allowed

4.5 pounds of bread each week (roughly 2,000 grams).[18] However, what looked on the surface like a centralized program of food acquisition was in reality a confused mess of different offices and agencies that frequently worked at cross-purposes with one another and with little actual oversight. In fact, the civilian agencies often competed with the German army, which had its own food procurement agencies. The net effect of the regulations was a refusal on the part of German farmers to sell at state-mandated prices, which in turn made it difficult for the state to ensure that the bread ration could actually be provided. That led some private businesses to begin their own efforts to procure food for their employees.[19] The net effect was competition between private businesses, the German army, and the Imperial Grain Authority, and farmers quickly realized that they could play one agency or group off against the others to get better prices for their products than those that the state was mandating. The result was serious inflation.

To deal with that problem the federal and some state and local governments began enforcing price controls. This policy was counterproductive for two reasons. First of all it drove German farmers to focus on the production of goods that did not have price ceilings on them, and second, the largely local nature of the controls created internal chaos as some areas, those with price controls, found themselves suffering from scarcities while those areas that did not implement price controls found themselves with a surplus of goods because farmers from nearby regions would transport their goods to the areas where they could pull in the maximum profit.[20] In effect what was created was a system in which certain groups had privileged access to food while others went short. The wealthy had access to whatever they could afford on the black market and in the early stages the war had only a minimal impact on their way of life. The food shortages also had only a minimal effect on the diet of German farmers in the early years of the war. The remainder of the population was effectively divided into three, with the soldiers having first claim on the food supply, followed by workers in war industry, and then workers in nonessential industries or civilian pursuits.[21]

Industry conditions were also chaotic as separate agencies competed with one another for the acquisition of raw materials and workers. As in agriculture the competition to procure the necessary materials led to inflation. An early attempt was made to get a handle on the distribution, if not the procurement, of raw materials when the *Kriegsrohstoffabteilung* (KRA) was founded by Wichard von Moellendorf and Walther Rathenau in August 1914. Rathenau, a successful German businessman, took the lead. He met with the German War Minister Erich von Falkenhayn on August 9 to discuss the creation of a central authority, which would oversee the supply of raw materials to German industry. Falkenhayn agreed to the idea and appointed Rathenau to lead the organization. On August 13 the KRA was created.[22] The KRA was to determine which businesses and facilities could make the best use of Germany's scarce resources and to ensure that those businesses received what they needed, at the expense of other less efficient or less important businesses. A secondary goal was to oversee the creation of "replacement" or ersatz industries, which would produce substitutes for those goods that were in short supply. K-Brot was one example; it was also known as Ersatz-Brot.[23] The KRA eventually consisted of 25 divisions, each of which was devoted to a single raw material and which oversaw what were known as War Raw Materials Corporations (*Kriegsrohstoffgesellschaften*), private corporations created out of investments from German industry but overseen by committees made up of leading members of industry and government officials. These committees were empowered to buy, store, and distribute raw materials. Eventually the KRA also came to negotiate price ceilings with German businesses. The purpose was both to rationalize the use of Germany's limited raw materials and to increase the profits of the major German industrialists. It succeeded on both counts, at least in the first years of the war.[24]

None of the solutions that the Germans implemented to deal with their economic problems was completely effective but they certainly were not alone on that score. The other belligerents experienced similar problems but the Entente had a priceless asset that the Central Powers could not match; the Entente could augment and relieve shortages with purchases from neutrals, in particular the United States. The Germans and their allies were unable to do so because the Royal Navy controlled the seas and, almost as soon as the war began, implemented a naval blockade of Germany that became increasingly onerous as the war progressed. The story of Germany's internal problems cannot be told effectively without, at the same time, telling the story of what was Britain's greatest contribution to Allied victory and the weapon that ultimately doomed Germany, the naval blockade.

The Institution of the British Naval Blockade

Naval blockades had long been a staple of British warfare, going all the way back to the eighteenth-century Anglo-French wars and most notably the wars against Napoleon. It was no surprise therefore that when war was declared on Germany one of the first measures undertaken by the Royal Navy was the implementation of a naval blockade. However, technological advances in naval weapons since the days of Napoleon, in particular the development of mines and torpedoes, made the traditional method of blockade, stationing ships directly off the enemy coastline to intercept traffic heading for specific ports, far more dangerous. Small, fast, and relatively easy-to-produce ships, called torpedo boats, could rush out of enemy ports to attack blockading capital ships[25] with torpedoes, possibly sinking or heavily damaging ships that were far more powerful, expensive, and difficult to produce. Minefields, which again could be laid by far cheaper ships, could also prove deadly to capital ships. The new technological realities of war at sea in the early twentieth century led to extensive debates in the British Admiralty over the future of the blockade as a weapon. Additional, specific debates concerned the ways in which the Royal Navy could implement an effective blockade of Germany.[26]

The debates came to revolve around the question of whether to implement a traditional, close (off shore) blockade or to find a way to impose a more distant blockade. This question was inextricably linked with the question of neutral trading rights. It was accepted naval law that in order to be legal any blockade had to be "effective," which meant that it had to be capable of actually preventing ships from entering or leaving harbors. A distant blockade, which closes the entrances to the North Sea to German trade, would not fulfill that criteria but would be far less risky than a traditional close blockade.

For their part the Germans fully expected that the British would implement a traditional close blockade. The initial German strategy for the war at sea depended on the British doing precisely that. Knowing that their battle fleet was inferior to that of the British and that it was very unlikely that they could defeat the Royal Navy in battle, the Germans opted for a strategy, which they called kleinkrieg, or little war. The basic idea behind kleinkrieg was that German light forces, submarines, and torpedo boats primarily would carry out a naval guerrilla war of hit-and-run raids on blockading British forces. These raids would slowly whittle the Royal Navy down to a point where the High Seas Fleet could sortie and possibly win a decisive naval engagement.[27]

In the final analysis, military necessity won out over political obligations and the concerns of neutrals. When push finally came to shove the British opted to implement a distant blockade. They used their geographical position, which interposed them between Imperial Germany and the latter's access to global trade, and closed the entrances to the North Sea.

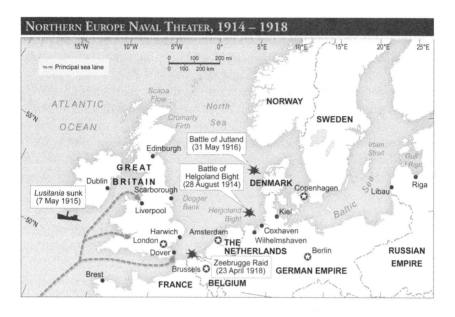

The first steps to implement the blockade were taken within days of the declaration of war. A special command was created at Dover, the Dover Patrol, with the primary task of sealing off the Dover Strait to all commerce. This force initially consisted of four light cruisers, 24 destroyers, 13 submarines, and various auxiliary craft.[28] These forces patrolled the strait and laid and maintained secret minefields that were designed to force merchantmen to come into port for inspection. Only those who did so would be escorted safely through the minefields. At the northern end of the North Sea, the passage between Scotland and Norway was patrolled by another specially created unit, the Tenth Cruiser Squadron. This force initially consisted of eight of the Royal Navy's oldest and most obsolete cruisers, ships that could no longer compete with most of their German rivals in firepower, armor, or speed and therefore were given what was assumed to be less hazardous duty. This squadron was assigned to patrol the waters between Norway and Scotland and was ordered to stop, board, and search all ships attempting to make their way through the passage. Any German warships trying to pass through were to be destroyed if possible. Four of the cruisers were assigned to the Norwegian coastal area (the Norwegian Patrol) and the remainder were assigned to the Shetland Islands area (the Shetland Patrol).[29] In the end the Tenth

Cruiser Squadron had severe problems carrying out its mission not only because of its limited numbers but also because its duties were constantly in flux. For example throughout the remainder of 1914 these cruisers were used to supplement the Grand Fleet (the main British battle fleet) on a number of the latter's sweeps into the North Sea. At times they were also assigned to defend harbors against the possible incursion of German submarines or even sent off to check out reports of German minefields. All of these latter tasks detracted from their most important mission, sealing off the northern entrance to the North Sea. They did receive limited reinforcements to aid in their expanding duties but those were insufficient to offset the increased duties. In October 1914 the northern blockade was dealt another blow when one of the cruisers was sunk by a German submarine. The attack led to the British pulling the blockade line further back, north of the Shetland Islands.[30]

The physical forces used by the Royal Navy were only one part of the complex machinery that comprised the blockade. Two committees were also created to oversee its implementation. The first of these was the Restriction of Enemy Supplies Committee, which studied all of the trade routes leading into Germany and recommended means by which those trade routes could be closed. The other, which turned out to be more significant, was the Contraband Committee. This was created in August 1914 and was tasked with deciding just what would be considered *contraband*, the term that denoted what goods could be seized by blockading nations. Traditionally contraband referred only to military materials or materials of a warlike nature but the industrialization of warfare meant that these terms had become very flexible. In the years before the war numerous international conferences had been held to try and better define the term. No firm decision had ever been reached. The Contraband Committee therefore was tasked with altering the definition of *contraband* in order to help Britain win the war. In practice this committee became the executive body that oversaw the implementation of the entire blockade. It was chaired by Sir Eyre Crowe and had three other members, one each from the Admiralty, the Foreign Office, and the Board of Trade.[31] Early in the war the committee was forced to undertake a delicate dance in which it attempted, as best it could, to tighten the blockade without alienating neutral, in particular American, opinion too much. In the words of Britain's Foreign Secretary Sir Edward Grey, "The object of diplomacy, therefore, was to secure the maximum of blockade that could be enforced without a rupture with the United States."[32]

One of the committee's earliest measures, and one that did elicit protests from the United States, was the reinstatement of the old notion of continuous voyage. According to this idea any good or product that originated in a belligerent nation or was ultimately bound for a belligerent was liable to seizure. For example goods bound for the Netherlands, which would ultimately be reexported to Germany could be seized under this doctrine. Whether these goods were carried in neutral ships or belligerent ships was irrelevant, what mattered was their ultimate destination or point of origin. The United States had traditionally disagreed with this position, arguing instead that "neutral ships made neutral goods" and that neutral nations should be allowed to trade with both sides in any war. Acceptance of this notion would have made a mockery of any blockade, and as a result, the British did not accept the idea. Instead they adopted continuous voyage and began implementing it in September 1914, especially against the Netherlands, which had suspiciously begun increasing its imports of food. The Dutch government was forced to give guarantees to the British that these goods were not going to be reexported to Germany. Only then would these shipments be allowed to proceed. Similar arrangements were reached with the governments of Norway, Denmark, and Sweden, all of whom had increased imports of neutral goods and were correspondingly increasing their exports to Germany. In essence all four neutrals promised not to reexport contraband goods to Germany in exchange for those goods not being seized by the blockading British forces. Problematically for the British they had no way to enforce these agreements.[33]

The British continued to tinker with the blockade machinery over the remainder of 1914. In mid-September they expanded the contraband lists by adding rubber, magnetic iron ore, unwrought copper, and glycerin to the list of conditional contraband, an elastic term that referred to goods that were not specifically designed for military use but that *could* be used for military purposes.[34] In December the list was expanded again, to include all ingredients that could be used to manufacture explosives. A major change took place on November 5, 1914, when the Admiralty declared the entire North Sea a war zone and warned that all vessels entering the area by the northern route did so at their own risk. The idea was to force merchant ships into the Channel where they would be easier to find and stop.

To strengthen the Northern Patrol, the old cruisers making up the Tenth Cruiser Squadron were retired. By December they had been replaced by 23 armed merchant cruisers.[35] This would remain the basic makeup of the Northern Patrol for the remainder of the war. As a result of these reinforcements the British were able to create four patrol lines in the north: one north of the Faeroe Islands, another to the north of the Shetlands, a third west of the Hebrides, and a final one south of the Faeroes.

This first period of the blockade has been labeled the "restricted blockade"[36] because of the limitations that were placed on the British by their need to placate the United States, which was providing the Entente with supplies in growing quantities. Despite the limited nature of the restricted blockade it did have an immediate impact on the Germans. By the end of 1914 the merchant shipping of the Central Powers had been virtually eliminated. A total of 245 German ships had been captured by Entente forces, 221 were lying idle in German ports, and 1,059 were interred in neutral harbors.[37] From this point on, the Central Powers were utterly reliant on neutral shipping for their overseas supplies.

Deepening Problems—Germany in 1915

As 1915 began the problem of economic scarcity continued to worsen in Germany. Numerous goods were in very short supply. Some of these, such as vegetable and mineral oils, were important for cooking and food preparation; others, most notably tobacco, were luxury goods. Still others, rubber for example, were important for the war effort. Most seriously the country was facing a critical shortage of copper and zinc, both of which had to be imported past the blockade. By the fall of 1915 these two metals were in such short supply that the government was forced to begin requisitioning materials that were made of either metal, for example, plating from roofs, downspouts, ornamentation from trains, doorknobs and knockers, bathtubs, church bells, and even pots and pans from individual households. The goods that were requisitioned were then melted down and used for the war effort. By that fall individual Germans had contributed over 1 million tons of scrap metal.[38] The requisitioning efforts provided little that was useful and the shortage eventually had to be dealt with through increased imports through neighboring neutrals such as Denmark and the Netherlands.

The zinc and copper shortage was serious but the major problems continued to be in the agricultural sector where bread rationing was creating both hunger and resentment. Bread was one of the major components of the German diet. In the years before the war most Germans consumed an average of five pounds of bread and seven pounds of potatoes every week. The initial bread ration was set at roughly one-half pound per person per day, reducing bread consumption, theoretically, to three and one-half pounds per person per week.[39] However the ration was only the theoretical amount that the ordinary German was entitled to; it was not necessarily what one received. Acquiring one's daily allotment meant waiting in increasingly long lines. As the war went on it became increasingly likely that those at the back of these lines would reach the front only to discover that all the day's supplies had been sold. In fact fear of diminishing food supplies was already causing trouble in the spring of 1915. By February of that year there were incidents of fighting being reported in bread lines in Berlin as those to the rear of the lines began pushing forward out of fear that all the food would be gone by the time their turn to buy came.[40]

The problems with the food supply were aggravated by the responses of German farmers to the parade of new regulations. When the Reich government responded to the refusal of farmers to sell their goods in areas with price controls by instituting national price controls on wheat and rye in January 1915, many farmers opted to feed those grains to their livestock rather than sell them. There were no price controls on meat so it was far more profitable for the German farmers to use their wheat and rye to fatten their livestock, and then slaughter the livestock and sell the meat. To address that problem the German government made an infamous decision in April 1915; it ordered what would become known as the *Schweinemord*.

By that April the war had gone on much longer than anyone had initially expected and it showed no signs of ending any time soon. Fearing food shortages the Reich government decided that, because livestock were an inefficient form of food production (cattle and pigs consumed more calories in grain than they gave back in meat) and because so many grains were being used as fodder instead of being sold to the state at the mandated price, farmers would be forced to kill much of their livestock, specifically their pigs. Nine million pigs were to be slaughtered.[41] German farmers protested the law, arguing that it was shortsighted because it ignored the importance of meat as a protein and because the timing was poor. The pigs had just come through the winter and were much leaner than they would have been that fall. The protests went for naught and the *Schweinemord* went forward. As a result for a time pork became very cheap and the diet of most Germans improved. However, in the long run this move proved to be disastrous as the slaughter of the livestock helped to cause massive meat shortages in the latter years of the war. Nor did the slaughtering of the livestock solve the grain shortage. Farmers who did not want to sell their goods at government-mandated prices were often able to sell their goods on the black market instead.

As the year wore on, the number of goods in short supply expanded. Supplies of dairy products, in particular milk and butter, ran short. Lard and other cooking oils remained scarce as did coffee and cocoa. In addition by fall the meat glut of the *Schweinemord* was over and meat became scarce. The government responded by declaring that Tuesdays and Fridays were henceforward to be "meatless days," days when no butcher or restaurant would be allowed to sell or serve meat.[42] In October the government set up an Imperial Potato Office to take control of the nation's potato stocks. With the creation of K-Brot and the increasing use of the potato as a replacement food the popular tuber had become an ever more critical part of the German diet, a trend that would continue as the war dragged on. Unfortunately the Imperial Potato Office ran into many of the same problems that plagued the Imperial Grain Authority, primarily the reluctance of German farmers to go along with the decrees of the Imperial administration, which, quite frankly, lacked the necessary bureaucratic apparatus to enforce its decrees.[43] In fact, the only organization in Imperial Germany that had the type of bureaucracy necessary to enforce such decrees was the German army. It was partly for that reason that the German army would come to play an increasingly more prominent role in domestic affairs as the war progressed.

In the short term though what resulted from the failure of the German bureaucracy to enforce these regulations was a thriving black market where those who had the means could acquire nearly anything directly from the farmers. It became common for urban Germans to make trips to the countryside to purchase their supplies directly. Farmers dodged the regulations and held onto food either for themselves or for the black market. Those Germans who lived in the cities and did not have access to either the black market, an employer who purchased goods on the black market, or relatives who could do so were left to deal as best as they could with the shortages. Even those Germans saw the prices of their daily necessities increase as inflation became normal throughout Germany in 1915. For example, by the summer of 1915 Berliners were spending an average of DM 40 on food every month, up from DM 25 every month in peacetime.[44] Those who worked in vital war industries had wages that nearly kept up with the increasing costs of food; those who did not and instead worked in civilian industries saw their living standards decline. All told, over the course of the war prices in Germany rose 200 percent while the pay of armaments workers increased 142 percent and the pay of those in civilian industries only increased 68 percent. White collar workers were hit just as hard as those in civilian industries with their real income decreasing by roughly 30 percent over the course of the war.[45] By the fall of 1915 the constant shortages and the clearly unequal way in which the burdens of the war were being borne began to lead to protests and to a slow erosion of the cultural consensus in favor of the war. The social fabric of the nation began to weaken as the relationship between consumers on the one hand and merchants and producers on the other became increasingly adversarial. For the hungry members of the German public, the merchants and farmers came to be seen as war profiteers, putting their own interests ahead of those of the nation.

As 1915 dragged on and the hardships continued with no end to the war in sight the mood of the nation began grew worse. From October 14 to 17, 1915, a small series of butter protests took place in Berlin, and the Berlin police noted that, for the first time, some of the protesters were speaking out against the war.[46] That Christmas, the second of the war, the *Berliner Tageblatt* ran a commentary by Walther Rathenau, head of AEG (Allgemeine Electricitäts Gesellschaft) and founder of the KRA, stating that "Privation has welded us together, love has tied us with one another. We know the justice of our cause and believe in its victory, whether near or far."[47] Rathenau was expressing the new mood of the nation, which was no longer one of jubilant expectation of imminent victory but one of grim determination to see the conflict through to eventual victory. By that point in the war over three quarters of a million Germans had been killed and it was clear that the war was heading into a second long winter.[48]

The political mood also began to change. Though the Reichstag and the German political parties continued to support the war there was one ominous sign for the future. Late in 1915 the left wing members of the Social Democratic Party (SPD), led by Karl Liebknecht, began demanding a Reichstag investigation into Germany's war aims as well as an examination of the events that led to the outbreak of war in 1914. Party discipline held and the SPD remained united behind the war effort but the cracks that would eventually lead to the splintering of the party and the creation of the Independent Social Democratic Party were beginning to show.[49]

Aware of the worsening mood of the nation the Reich government took steps to raise support for the war. They first turned to culture to promote the war. Publishing houses were commissioned to begin turning out novels that glamorized the fighting and played up the heroism of the frontline soldiers. Pictures of great national heroes, especially Paul von Hindenburg, began to appear not only on postcards but on products as diverse as playing cards, ashtrays, and lampshades. In addition the government collected materials from the war and put them on exhibition at home. Particularly prominent were sketches and paintings made by soldiers that, once again, were designed to play up the heroism of the military and the heroic nature of the struggle. School children were encouraged to draw pictures of the front and to write to local soldiers. Even the trenches themselves were used to try and garner support for the war. Dioramas of the front and of great battles from Germany's past were created and placed on exhibition around the country. These dioramas took care to play up the secure and homelike nature of the trenches and dugouts. This was taken to an extreme in the summer of 1915 when a full scale replica of a Western Front trench was constructed in Berlin, complete with concrete bunkers that were equipped with electric power and small garden patches behind the lines where the soldiers grew their own food. One can only speculate on what soldiers returning from the front thought when they saw this romantic depiction of their conditions.[50]

By far the most famous example of early war propaganda in Germany, and possibly the most famous of the entire war, was the creation of the so-called Iron Hindenburg in Berlin. On August 28, 1915, a 19-foot-high wooden statue of the famous Eastern Front commander was built outside of the Reichstag building in Berlin. Its purpose was to both honor Hindenburg and those who had fallen in battle. Berliners were encouraged to help create an "Iron Hindenburg" by first purchasing a nail (gold, silver, and iron were all available, for differing prices)[51] and then hammering the nail into the wooden statue. The proceeds from the sale of the nails were used to assist the widows and families of those who had died in battle. The project was an enormous success as thousands of nails were sold. Similar statues were erected in other cities around Germany as part of the same effort. The propaganda succeeded in helping to maintain generally strong support for the war all the way through 1915 and on into 1916. It took several additional developments before that support really began to erode. It was the events of 1916, from the disastrous *Materialsschlachten* on the Western Front to the horrific Turnip Winter of 1916–17 that really began to erode the support for the war.

Germany's internal problems were caused by a number of factors, from the increasing shortages to the ineffectiveness of the government's responses to those shortages and there can be little doubt that the

German government's actions at times did more harm than good but it is also necessary to point out that most of those problems could have been alleviated had the Germans been able, as their opponents in Britain and France were, to freely access foreign supplies of grain, potatoes, meat, and raw materials. That they could not do so was directly attributable to the existence of the British blockade, which became increasingly effective over the course of 1915 and 1916.

The Development of the Naval Blockade

As 1915 began the British blockade lines ran from the Hebrides Islands northwest to Iceland, between the Orkneys and the Faeroes, from the Shetlands to Norway and north of the Faeroes. With these lines and the blockade lines in the south around the English Channel, the Royal Navy was able to stop and examine most of the mercantile traffic bound for Europe.[52] Between January and June 1915, 2,466 vessels entered the North Sea and the Royal Navy stopped and inspected 2,132 of those ships. Most were stopped in the Channel area, roughly 12 per day there compared to 2 per day in the Northern Approaches.[53] Only a few of these ships were detained however, out of fear of angering the United States, which had responded to the war by dramatically expanding its exports to Europe. In February 1914 American businesses exported roughly $150 million worth of goods to Europe; one year later, in February 1915, they were exporting $268 million worth.[54] A significant portion of these additional exports were going to the Scandinavian countries who then reexported those goods to Germany. For example the value of American exports to Denmark increased from roughly $560,000 to over $7 million between 1914 and 1915. Exports to Sweden increased from $377,000 to $2.9 million, and those to Norway from $477,000 to $2.3 million. In contrast American trade with Germany fell from $32 million to $2.2 million by the end of 1914.[55] What was created was, in effect, a gigantic loophole in the blockade through which Germany was still able to provision itself, albeit at a slower pace it they could in peacetime. Much of the effort of the Royal Navy and the British Foreign Office in 1915 and 1916 was aimed at closing this "neutrals loophole."

The efforts of the British government to tighten the blockade against the neutrals were unintentionally aided by the Germans just as they were beginning. In February 1915 the German government made one of the most costly and momentous decisions of the entire war when they launched a counterblockade of Great Britain using submarines. Basing their legal argument on the fact that the British had declared the North Sea a war zone in November 1914 and claiming that the British blockade was illegal because it was not "effective" the Germans declared a war zone of their own, one that surrounded the British Isles. The German government warned that shipping within this war zone was subject to being sunk by German submarines without warning. This was the first round of what came to be called "unrestricted submarine warfare" and it was deeply offensive to most neutrals, especially the United States. The British blockade inconvenienced the neutrals and in some instances cost them financially. Unrestricted submarine warfare would lead not only to greater financial losses with no chance of compensation but also to the loss of human life. It was seen as a barbarous measure by many neutrals and the Admiralty, led by Winston Churchill, jumped at the opportunity to tighten the blockade in retaliation. Three new measures were implemented.

The first measure taken was a simple extension of the contraband list. On March 11, the Contraband Committee declared that all lubricants, wool, tin, and animal hides were now considered contraband.[56] Adding lubricants to the list forced the Germans to begin using vegetable oils as lubricants, further hurting the German food supply. Cutting off imports of wool led to severe clothing shortages and cutting off imports of leather eventually led to shortages of shoes and boots.

The British also tried to close the "neutrals loophole" with two new measures. The first of these was referred to as bunker control. It was an attempt to use Britain's supplies of coal and, in particular, its control of coaling stations, to regulate neutral trade with Germany. Beginning in May 1915 the British government banned the export of coal to foreign countries. Then, in October 1915, the Admiralty began refusing to let any ship that did not voluntarily enter British ports and submit to inspection to refuel from British coaling stations.[57] Bunker control had its most severe impact on nations such as the Netherlands, which had an extensive colonial empire in the Pacific and whose ships were dependent on British coaling stations for their journeys across the world's oceans. It was in some ways counterproductive, however, since the United States stepped in and offered to export coal to some former British markets.

The British also attempted, without great success, to ration the amount of goods that neutrals could import. The idea was originally proposed by the French in June 1915. They suggested pegging neutral imports of goods to their peacetime levels.[58] Any imports above those peacetime levels would be assumed to be for reexport to Germany. As with every other

British policy during this period this also ran into resistance from the United States. As a direct result of American protests and counterpressure the British raised the neutral quotas above their originally proposed limits, allowing for some additional importation and likely reexportation to Germany. In the end the policy failed. At the very end of 1915 and the start of 1916 they tried yet another measure to close the "neutrals loophole," blacklisting.

In December 1915, the British Parliament instituted the Trading with the Enemy Act, which authorized the British government to ban trade between British companies and foreign companies with "known enemy connections." Such firms were placed on the statutory list, the first of which was issued on February 29, 1916. All ships belonging to companies that were on the list were liable to immediate seizure and detention. The open and public statutory list was supplemented by various secret lists, such as the ships black list, which listed ships that were known to trade with the enemy, or the bankers black list, obviously for bankers who continued to conduct business with enemy firms. Firms that appeared on the statutory list were denied coal for their ships under the bunker control system.[59] The purpose was to convince these firms to voluntarily cease trading with the Central Powers. This system though ran into the same problem as every other British attempt to tighten the blockade, American resistance. For several months American firms that traded with the enemy were exempted from blacklisting; instead a separate system known as navicerting was created and applied primarily to American companies.

Under the navicerting system firms could apply to their local British embassy to assert that their goods were not bound for Germany. If the local embassy officials agreed the company's ships would be granted a navicert, a certificate of navigation, which would allow them to pass through the blockade lines. The potential problems with this system are obvious. As a result it did not work and eventually, by July 1916, even American companies began to appear on the statutory list.

In the summer of 1916 the British made their most effective move to improve the blockade by modifying the rationing system. It was abundantly clear that many neutrals were importing far greater amounts of supplies, especially food, than they had in peacetime and that they were then turning around and selling those goods at premium prices to Germany. The worst offenders in this regard were the Dutch, whose wartime imports were 600 percent higher than their corresponding peacetime imports.[60] As a result, starting in June 1916, all goods in excess of peacetime imports were to be detained in Great Britain. The goods would not be seized outright, once again in deference to American opinion, but they would be held up in British ports long enough to begin causing serious financial losses. At the same time the British began requiring neutrals to sell a portion of their home produce to Britain at a fixed price in an attempt to keep that produce from going to Germany. Since the Germans were almost always willing to pay higher prices than the British were, this policy had to be backed by force. Therefore the British began to blockade trade to neutrals that refused to sign such purchasing agreements. Those that refused to go along with the policy would have their rations reduced by the value of the goods that they refused to sell to the British and their ships would be subject to outright seizure.

In addition to the new trading regulations the British also took measures in 1916 to rationalize the blockade apparatus. On February 23, 1916, they created a new Ministry of Blockade. This combined the numerous committees and departments that were all running various aspects of the blockade into one coherent ministry, run by Lord Robert Cecil.[61] Also that February a new Order in Council placed the burden of proving that their goods were not bound for Germany on the captains of merchant ships. Previously it had been the responsibility of the British authorities to prove that these goods were heading for Germany, which was an extremely difficult task. Now the equally difficult task of proving they were not going to Germany was shifted to the merchant captains. As the year wore on, the contraband list also continued to expand. Taken together these measures did begin to have a discernible effect on the German economy and war effort. Though the "neutrals loophole" was never closed in 1915 or 1916 it did get progressively smaller. The single greatest factor limiting Britain's ability to close that loophole completely was the stance of the United States. Unfortunately for the German government and people, that simple fact was not clearly understood in Berlin.

Feeling the Bite of the War: Germany in 1916

Conditions continued to deteriorate in Germany as the war entered another new year. Most civilian goods either were already in short supply as 1916 began or quickly became scarce as the year continued. At the end of the year many of those shortages, especially those of food, reached crisis levels. Both at home and on the battlefield, 1916 was the year that Germany really began to feel the bite of the war.

For most Germans on the home front the shortage of food remained the most important consequence of the war. By the time 1916 began, bread, butter, beef, and pork were all in extremely short supply. As the year wore on beef and pork would disappear completely from the markets for days at a time. By the summer of 1916 sugar had all but disappeared as well. Eggs were nearly gone and milk was being strictly reserved for young children and the elderly. By that summer the potato had become the staple of the average German's diet and even that was not available in sufficient quantities to meet the needs of both the army and the home front. There were a host of problems in agriculture that aggravated these shortages. Sugar beet production was scaled back in favor of increased production of wheat and rye for bread, thereby helping to cause the sugar shortage. Fodder for cattle was also cut in favor of grains for human consumption, leaving an insufficient supply of food for the dairy herds, thereby leading to lower production of milk. Even the growing of barley was cut back in favor of wheat and rye, leading to a shortage of beer by the end of 1916.[62]

Though the food shortage was extremely serious and the one that most occupied the thoughts of the German people it certainly was not the only one. Due to the war the production of pipes, paints, wood, wires, and other building supplies was greatly reduced. That led, in 1916, to the virtual cessation of housing production and, more significantly, to an inability to maintain and repair existing housing stock, which therefore began to decay as the war continued. Clothing too was scarce. By 1916 Germany's stock of cotton had all but run out. What remained was being requisitioned by the army for the creation of uniforms. Civilians therefore were left without access to new clothing or, often, even the ability to repair the clothing they still had. By November of 1916 clothing, like food, was being rationed and Germans were limited to two sets. Leather for shoes was also scarce. To stretch the existing supply as far as possible the German government turned to the production of ersatz shoes and ersatz clothing. Recycled paper and cardboard along with other cellulose products came to be used for the creation of clothing. This was euphemistically called "natural silk."[63] Shoes were now being made from thin wood and cardboard painted over with varnish. These ersatz products elicited disdain from many Germans.

Other shortages affected basic household goods. German families were limited to one small bar of soap every month[64] and matches were nearly unheard of, but, apart from food and clothing, the most serious shortage by far was that of coal. Germany had massive coal deposits but the production of coal had dropped because of a shortage of labor caused by the war. Furthermore, the coal that was being produced was being consumed at prodigious rates by Germany's munitions industry. What this meant was that there simply was not much coal available for Germany's civilians. As a result of the lack of coal, the production of electricity for Germany's cities was reduced. Streetcar service in many major cities, such as Berlin, was cut back. Curfews were introduced in the winter of 1916, the amount of coal available for the heating of civilian homes was reduced. During the warmer months of 1916 this shortage was less serious than the food shortage but in the winter of 1916–17 it caused tremendous hardship. In the second half of 1916, beginning in the summer, the shortages caused a "marked increase"[65] in food riots, disturbances, and small strikes around Germany. The people and the government tried, in various ways and with varying degrees of success, to deal with these shortages.

One attempt to deal with the shortages undertaken by businesses was the widespread use of substitutes. Vegetable oils, such as sunflower seed oil, came to replace animal-based oils. Rye and even barley were increasingly used as fillers in bread. Roasted barley grains were marketed as ersatz coffee. Various types of plant leaves made their way to German tables as ersatz teas. Blood sausage came to replace the other increasingly scarce sausages. A type of plastic was even devised by the German chemical industry to try and deal with the rubber shortage.[66] Ersatz goods alone however were clearly insufficient and other measures were necessary.

Another step was the creation of communal kitchens to provide food for the German public. These were devised to serve two purposes: first of all to more efficiently distribute what food there was and second to relieve German women from having to spend long hours waiting in lines to try and purchase their daily supplies. Unfortunately the communal kitchens were a failure. They were associated with soup kitchens for the poor and therefore most Germans saw them as demeaning. As a result they actually aggravated the food shortage by being underutilized. They consumed more supplies for the creation of their meals then they actually then distributed. As a result they were shut down after the disastrous winter of 1916–17.[67] Clearly stronger measures were needed and the German government began discussing the creation of a War Food Office early in 1916. Those measures bore fruit in May.

On May 22, the Bundesrat authorized the creation of the *Kriegsernährungsamt*, or KEA. This organization was empowered to take control of the national food supply, thereby limiting the local autonomy that had created such chaos and confusion and had hampered most of the earlier

Table 3.2   Rationing as a Percentage of Peacetime Consumption[68]

Product	July 1916–July 1917	July 1917–July 1918	July 1918–Dec. 1918
Meat	31	20	12
Eggs	18	13	13
Butter	22	21	28
Cheese	3	4	15
Flour	53	47	48
Potatoes	71	94	94
Rice	4	0	0
Vegetable fats	39	41	17

efforts to rationalize that supply. In theory the entire German food supply could now be inventoried and then allocated nationally on the basis of rationing. All Germans were to register with local shops from which they would then purchase their rationed goods. Those shops would report to the KEA the amount of food they would need for their registered customers and the KEA would then proceed to acquire and distribute the necessary food.[69] The first goods subject to national rationing were butter, potatoes, all meats, sugar, eggs, milk, fats, and coal. Under the rationing system each head of household was to pick up ration coupons each week, and someone from the family would take those coupons to their registered store where they would wait in line to purchase their allotment of goods. Those allotments varied. Citizens in larger cities generally received higher allotments than those in smaller towns. Industrial workers received higher allotments than white collar workers, and industrial laborers working in the munitions plants received higher allotments than other industrial laborers. A category was also created for those with "special needs, such as expectant mothers." Despite the plethora of different categories it is possible to come up with average figures for what the German civilian was allotted. On a weekly basis these came to: 3.5 kilograms of potatoes, 160–220 grams of flour, 100–250 grams of meat, 60–75 grams of fats, .7 liters of milk, 200 grams of sugar, 270 grams of jams, one egg, and 120 grams of fish.[70] Table 3.2 lists these as a percentage of the peacetime consumption of these goods.

It is important to understand that these figures represent what the ordinary German was allotted under the rationing plan, not what Germans actually received. There were many problems in the system that prevented it from working as it was designed. First and foremost, the KEA had no authority whatsoever over the German military, which had its own requisition and distribution systems that worked at cross-purposes with those of the KEA. Second, the KEA often ran into the resistance of the deputy commanding generals, who were the ultimate local authorities under the Law of Siege. Under that law the districts of the country were placed under military control and the deputy commanding generals had, in effect, dictatorial powers over their district. Their first duty was to manage the resources of their district for the war effort. This meant acquiring manpower, industrial goods, raw materials, and food for the army from their district. They were only subject to the orders of their military superiors, not to any civilian agency. As a result these officers could not be forced to cooperate with the KEA. Even in instances where the KEA was aided by the deputy commanding generals and did not conflict with the military it still experienced numerous problems. The fundamental problem remained what it had been since the start of the war. The government was insisting on purchasing goods from German farmers at prices that were considerably lower than what those farmers could have obtained on a free market and as a result many resisted selling their crops to the state. The German government was as yet unwilling to simply seize crops and as a result the black market continued to thrive.

Statistics vary but roughly 20–3 percent of the entire German food supply was obtained not by rationing but on the black market.[71] This varied by good, one-eighth of all grains and one-seventh of all potatoes were obtained on the black market but quarter to one-third of all milk, butter, and cheese was only available illegally. One-third to one-half of all egg, meat, and fruit production went to the black market where prices in 1916 were, on average, ten times above their 1913 level.[72] Many of these black market goods were acquired on what were euphemistically called "Sunday excursions" where wealthy Germans would leave the cities and go directly to the countryside to buy directly from German farmers.[73] The existence of the black market meant that, at least for now, Germans who had sufficient wealth could avoid most of the direct hardships of the war. Of course their actions made the suffering worse for their less well-off countrymen, and this would begin, in particular in the winter of 1916–17, to erode the national consensus in favor of war.

Taken together, the existence of the black market, the existence of a separate food agency for the army, and the obstruction of local officials like the deputy commanding generals meant that the stores that took part in the system rarely received the amounts of food they requested, and as a result, many of their customers would often find themselves waiting in line for hours for the chance to purchase their supplies only to discover that when their turn came the supplies were gone. The creation of the KEA ultimately changed nothing. By the summer of 1916 most Germans were surviving on only 40 percent of their peacetime diet. In some working and lower middle class areas it was closer to 33 percent of peacetime norms.[74]

The first noticeable break in the consensus in favor of the war came in April of 1916 when Karl Liebknecht broke with the SDP and formed the Spartacist League, a revolutionary organization opposed to the war and to the monarchy. This led to Liebknecht's arrest in May and to the first major antiwar strike in Germany, in June 1916 in Berlin. That month 55,000 Berlin workers took to the streets to protest Liebknecht's arrest. The protests ran their course and the workers returned to their jobs without the release of Liebknecht.[75] In fact, the following month the Berlin authorities went on to arrest Liebknecht's closest associate, Rosa Luxemburg. These events foreshadowed the larger and more significant breakdown of the SPD that came in the spring of 1917 when Hugo Haase led a group of antiwar socialists to form a new party, the Independent Social Democratic Party or USPD.

In July angry civil servants and metal workers took to the streets to protest the food situation, which was hitting the civil servants particularly hard because of the salaried nature of their positions and the relatively fixed nature of their pay. These protests did not yet turn to strikes and they remained short-lived but they also grew in intensity as the year wore on. By that fall urban Germans were beginning to view their rural countrymen with not just suspicion but enmity as many began to suspect German farmers of withholding food from the markets in order to drive up prices and enrich themselves at the expense of their countrymen. For their part many German farmers saw themselves as being exploited by the urban communities, especially factory workers in the munitions industry who were seeing greater increases in pay than other Germans. In addition everyone was growing angry at the "war profiteer," in particular the factory owners and the elite of German society who still had the wherewithal to purchase what they needed or wanted on the black market and were making enormous profits while other Germans fought and died in the trenches and their families starved at home. The government was also blamed for incompetence in handling the food situation and calls went out for the army, the one branch of the government that most

Germans still retained great faith in, to take over the distribution of food. Berliners began to refer to the daily struggle for food as the "battle of the marketplace";[76] it was a battle that most Germans were losing.

In 1914 the German government had assured the German people that Germany would not run out of food during the war. By the fall of 1916 more and more Germans were beginning to doubt that assurance and a belief was growing that, despite the rationing and hardships, the food supply would ultimately run out. As a direct result some Germans began to urge the government to end the war without annexations or indemnities. Their cries still mostly fell on deaf ears. There were more strikes and protests in 1916 than there had been in 1915 but the strikers were most concerned with economic matters such as wages, working conditions, and food; they were not trying to end the war.[77]

A separate but related issue was an increase in crime, in particular juvenile crime. The absence of parents, with fathers at the front or in factories and mothers often working outside of the home, left young Germans an enormous amount of free time and this resulted in a 50 percent increase in juvenile crime in 1916, mainly among 13- to 14-year-old boys.[78] Most of these crimes were property crimes, especially theft, oftentimes of food or drink. The increase in crime resulted in many local governments instituting curfews and added to the growing disruption of German life, a disruption that became much more severe that fall.

Disaster struck German agriculture in 1916. The autumn of 1916 was exceptionally wet and rainy and the first frosts struck early. The combination of the two events decimated the German potato crop. In 1915 the Germans had produced 50 million tons of potatoes; in 1916 the disastrous weather combined with the decrease in available fertilizer cut that production in half, to only 25 million tons.[79] The grain harvest was affected as well when Rumania entered the war on the side of the Entente in August. That cut the Germans off from one of their major sources of grain, at least until Rumania was overrun later that winter. The loss of Rumanian grain caused the German government to reduce the bread ration to only 7 ounces a day. The loss of grains also caused many breweries to shut down completely. The disaster was so thorough that the government was forced to replace the potato ration with turnips, starting in early December. As a result the winter of 1916–17 came to be known as the Turnip Winter. Food prices jumped to over 800 percent above their 1913 levels due to the extreme shortages and many Germans saw their diets reduced to roughly 800 calories/day, mostly without grains or fats.[80]

The Turnip Winter was not just a winter of near starvation; it was also one of the coldest winters in memory with temperatures reaching record lows in January, February, and March of 1917. At one point the temperature in Berlin reached an unheard of −25 degrees Fahrenheit.[81] The extremely low temperatures coincided with the coal shortage.[82] Many cities shut down their schools because they could not heat them. Most Germans, who relied on coal to heat their homes, were forced to go without as the munitions plants and government offices received their supplies first. Even those buildings, as well as others that had central heating, did not receive sufficient coal and as a result the indoor temperature of these buildings was reduced to around 60 degrees Fahrenheit. This coincided with a shortage of clothing and other textiles, such as blankets, which left many Germans using paper to help insulate themselves from the cold. Unsurprisingly the German people began to experience serious health problems that winter.

That winter German doctors began recording increased cases of disease, most notably tuberculosis and other respiratory ailments but they also noted increases in gastrointestinal diseases from lack of fruits and vegetables as well as from the generally poor nature of the diet overall. Blood problems and skin disorders were also increasing, once again mainly due to the extremely poor diet of most Germans. Fatigue and apathy were frequently noted along with a general sense of lethargy, unsurprising since all are symptoms of malnutrition. In short, the German people were being slowly exhausted physically. Munitions workers and soldiers still ate better than most of their countrymen but even they were suffering increased incidences of disease and were experiencing malnutrition. For the Entente powers the Turnip Winter was a blessing. The strains on Germany were attributed to the growing effectiveness of the blockade and they fed optimism in eventual victory. Entente, in particular British, propaganda played up every story of hardship within Germany and advanced, at every opportunity, including to the Germans in the trenches of the Western Front, the notion that Germany was starving to death. Stories were spread by the British that German bakers had been reduced to using sawdust as filler for bread and that many Germans at home had been reduced to eating grass to survive.[83] These reports provided badly needed boosts to Entente morale since that winter saw immense hardships not only in Germany but also in Russia. In fact, before the winter was over the tsar would be overthrown and a new, revolutionary government installed in Russia.

Allied propaganda may have exaggerated the hardships of the German people but the real hardships were severe enough; they were so severe that the German military and civilian leaders were forced to face something that they would not yet admit to their people, that Germany might lose the war. In top secret meetings in early January 1917 the Kaiser, the chancellor, and the newly appointed commanders of the army, Paul von Hindenburg and Erich Ludendorff, discussed Germany's dire position and concluded that defeat was likely if the war continued for much longer. Serious doubts existed in the minds of all these men as to whether or not the German people could sustain another winter of war. In the end the Kaiser and his advisors concluded that they could not and that the war therefore had to be brought to a victorious conclusion in 1917. That decision led in turn to the ultimately fatal decision to unleash an unrestricted submarine campaign against allied and neutral shipping in February 1917.

CHAPTER 4

Total Defeat: The War at Sea 1914–1916

The Entente victory in the Battle of the Marne and the failure of the Schlieffen-Moltke Plan meant that the war was not going to be decided quickly; instead it was to be a long and drawn-out affair. That in turn meant that British naval power and the ability of the Entente to draw upon the resources of not only the British and French empires but also of the neutral nations would be critical to the outcome of the war. The German defeat at the Marne meant that the war at sea would now take on enormous significance for the outcome of the war. If the Royal Navy could maintain the Entente's control of the seas and deprive Germany of access to the world's oceans through an effective blockade, it would bring enormous economic pressure to bear on Germany and its allies. On the other hand if the German High Seas Fleet could somehow break that control or find a way to blockade the British Isles, it could possibly force the British out of the war and give the German army a new opportunity to enforce a "German peace" on France and Russia.

The Anglo-German Naval Race

The growth of the German navy began in 1898 when the Reichstag passed the First Navy Bill, a piece of legislation that called for Germany, traditionally a land power, to begin constructing a battle fleet. This first law called for a fleet consisting of 19 battleships, 12 heavy cruisers, and 30 light cruisers to be built by 1903.[1] The law, which resulted from the efforts of the new head of the Imperial Navy Office, Alfred Tirpitz, really had its roots in the naval passions of Kaiser Wilhelm II.

Prussia, the state that had created the new Germany through its victories over Austria and France in the wars of 1866 and 1870, had never been a naval power. The new German state of Kaiser Wilhelm I and Otto von Bismarck was content to remain a continental power but when the old emperor and then his son died in quick succession in 1888, his grandson took the throne. The new Kaiser was also a grandson of Queen Victoria on his mother's side and grew up fascinated with the history and power of the Royal Navy. That fascination with all things naval was augmented by Wilhelm's reading of Alfred Thayer Mahan's *The Influence of Seapower upon History*. In his book Mahan argued that naval power and the control of the seas were critical to Britain's victory over France in the Napoleonic Wars and that naval power in general, especially the possession of a large battle fleet, was essential for modern states that wanted to survive in the Social Darwinist world of the late nineteenth century. Mahan's work persuaded many of the leaders of the major industrial powers to push for the construction of large navies. Kaiser Wilhelm II was one of them. Wilhelm became convinced that if Germany was going to remain a great power and reach its fullest potential as a world power then it would need to create a great colonial empire and a strong navy to protect that empire. Germany would have to seek, as he put it, its "place in the sun." He needed only to find an architect who could bring his vision to fruition. He found that man in Alfred Tirpitz.

Alfred Tirpitz entered the small Prussian navy in the 1860s and spent his early career, in the 1870s and 1880s, in the torpedo arm of the fledgling service. In the 1890s he served for a time as chief of staff of the Naval High Command. He shared the Kaiser's views of Germany's future and the belief that if Germany was to remain a great power it would have to seek territorial expansion overseas. This, of necessity, would require Germany to possess a strong navy. He came to the attention of the Kaiser in 1897 and was appointed secretary of the Imperial Naval Office that same year. He was appointed specifically to oversee the creation of a large and powerful German fleet. The Navy Bill of 1898 was his first step toward the construction of that fleet. The fleet that was approved in 1898 would have given Germany a respectable force, more powerful than that of Russia and roughly on par with that of France but nowhere near the size or power of the Royal Navy; as a result this first naval bill did not occasion much comment or concern in Great Britain. That changed significantly with the Second German Navy Bill of 1900. It was this bill, which called for a fleet of 38 battleships, 20 armored cruisers, and 38 light cruisers[2] based in the North Sea and aimed at the Royal Navy, that garnered attention in Britain and triggered a naval arms race between the two nations. The bill was passed in the heat of the anti-British sentiment aroused by the Boer War and was portrayed as being necessary to protect German shipping and commerce against the Royal Navy. Tirpitz, the Kaiser, and the new chancellor after 1900, Bernhard von Bülow, believed that the British would be unable or unwilling to bear the cost of a long and drawn-out arms race and would instead seek an alliance with Germany, an alliance that would be purchased with British concessions overseas. They seriously miscalculated. Instead the British accepted and met the German challenge. The end result was a naval race that would last nearly until the outbreak of war in 1914 and the collapse of the traditional friendship between Great Britain and Germany. In the end this race would lead to Britain joining its traditional rivals Russia and France in war against Germany.

The British responded to the threat of the growing German navy, the German support for the Boers during the Boer War, increasing German belligerence overseas, and growing economic competition from Germany by rapidly building up their own fleet, recalling many of their overseas squadrons and concentrating their forces in the North Sea.[3] They also responded by making diplomatic overtures not to Germany but to France. These negotiations, which began tentatively after the Fashoda Crisis of 1898, came to fruition in 1904 when Britain and France signed the Entente Cordiale, an agreement that ended the most critical colonial disputes between the two nations and eventually led the two governments to agree to cooperate in the event of a European crisis. The Germans promptly provided just such a crisis by sending the Kaiser to Morocco, which the British had agreed should become a French colony. German threats of war resulted in the First Moroccan Crisis and led not to the destruction of the Entente as the Germans had hoped but to closer ties between London and Paris. Those ties now included high-level staff talks between the French and British armies, talks that led to a decision that in the event of a Franco-German war the British Expeditionary Force (BEF) would deploy to France to take up a position on the left flank of the French line. In the ensuing years the naval race accelerated despite some efforts to end it via negotiation and the British continued to pull closer to the French and even to Russia, eventually signing the Triple Entente with the latter in 1907. This was in essence another colonial agreement that ended long-running disputes between the two countries over such territories as Afghanistan. It also brought Great Britain, for all intents and purposes, into the Franco-Russian alliance.

In 1905 the First Sea Lord of the British Admiralty, Sir John (Jackie) Fisher, introduced an entirely new warship, the *Dreadnought*. This ship incorporated a new engine design, replacing reciprocating steam engines with turbines, as well as heavier armor and a main armament of all heavy, 12-inch diameter, guns. The *Dreadnought* immediately made all prior battleships obsolete, including all of those Tirpitz had been building for Germany. It also inaugurated a new stage of the naval arms race as both sides now began building *Dreadnought*-class warships. Britain had three great advantages in this race: first, Fisher had given the British a head start by creating the first *Dreadnought*; second, the British had a far larger and more experienced shipbuilding industry with the proper facilities for the construction of the new ships; and third, the British did not have to devote much of their defense budget to their army. Nonetheless the Germans attempted to meet the challenge until 1912 when, for the first time since 1900, the budgets for new naval construction were cut and spending was redirected toward the German army. By 1914 the naval race had run its course and Britain had won it handily. The Royal Navy in 1914 fielded 21 dreadnought battleships to 13 for the Germans and the British force was quickly augmented at the start of the war when the Royal Navy seized three dreadnoughts that were under construction for other nations, giving the British Grand Fleet, their main battle fleet, a total of 24 dreadnoughts. The British also had a slight preponderance in another new type of warship, the battle cruiser, with four to Germany's three.[4] These latter ships were also inventions of Fisher's. They were heavily armed but light-armored warships that were designed to scout for the enemy battle fleet and to screen their own fleet. They were also able, in theory, to outgun anything they could not outrun and vice versa. In the end the design would prove to have severe flaws but in the short term, these battle cruisers served to buttress British naval superiority.

In the final analysis the Germans did manage to build a large fleet, one that could at least challenge the Royal Navy on paper. However, in doing so they brought about what they most feared, their encirclement by a ring of hostile nations, by driving Great Britain into the arms of France and Russia. What remained to be seen was whether that fleet could prove its worth on the battlefields of the North Sea.

Plans for War

Although Tirpitz built the German navy he did not create its war plans. That responsibility fell on the commanders of the High Seas Fleet (the name that was given to the navy). They studied British operations in earlier wars and concluded that when war came the British would institute a blockade of the German coast and harbors. In their wars with the French in the eighteenth and nineteenth centuries the British had placed frigates (fast sailing ships) off the major harbors of their enemies while keeping their battle fleet ready at sea should their enemy attempt to leave port. From those positions the British warships could stop and search or seize enemy and neutral merchant ships attempting to enter the ports. By doing so they could cut off both enemy and neutral trade and slowly strangle the economy of their foe. However, the changed conditions of war in 1914 as opposed to those of 1815 made this traditional blockade far more difficult to implement. First, the ships of the Napoleonic Wars were sailing ships that only needed to return to harbor for new provisions, not to refuel. By 1914 though nearly all warships were either coal- or, in rare instances, oil-fueled, which meant that they had to expend fuel, getting to and maintaining their blockade stations. This meant that these ships could only remain on station for a limited time and that time was dependent on the distance between the ship's home port and the port they were blockading. If Britain went to war with Germany those enemy ports would be hundreds of kilometers from the nearest British ports, which meant in turn that the blockading ships would have to be relieved very frequently.

A further problem for any blockading fleet was the advent of new weapons such as the mine and the torpedo. The blockaded fleet could lay minefields outside of its ports that would endanger any blockading force. They could also sortie with small craft, called torpedo boats, which could launch torpedoes at the blockading ships. In other words the blockaded fleet could attack the blockading fleet and inflict losses on that fleet without risking its own prime assets, the battleships. The latter problem was made far worse by the development of the first submarines in the years before the war. These small and lightly armed ships could sneak out of blockaded ports to attack the blockading fleet, ostensibly with only minor risk to themselves. All of these factors made a traditional blockade, what was referred to as a close or effective blockade, far more difficult to implement. The Germans built their war plans around that difficulty.

The Germans planned to implement what they referred to as "kleinkrieg," a war of light craft against the blockading royal navy. They would use their torpedo boats and submarines to lay minefields and launch attacks against the blockading British forces in order to whittle away at Britain's naval superiority. It was hoped that the ensuing losses would either force the British to give up the blockade and allow German trade to resume or force the British to send heavy forces to support their

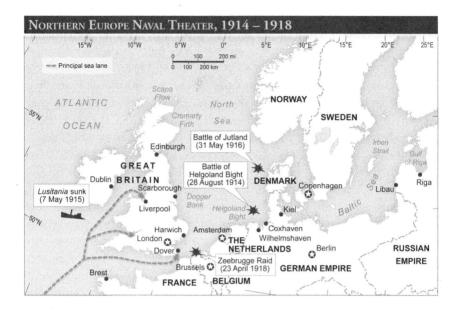

NORTHERN EUROPE NAVAL THEATER, 1914 – 1918

blockading ships. In the latter instance the Germans planned to sortie the High Seas Fleet against these forces and attempt to defeat in detail a segment of the Royal Navy. They hoped that these tactics could eventually reduce Britain's naval superiority to such a state that it would be possible for the High Seas Fleet to seek a decisive battle with the weakened Grand Fleet. The Germans had no answer to what they would do if the British did not arrive as planned.

The British were every bit as aware of these problems as the Germans were and for a time they were unsure of how to deal with them. According to international law a blockade was only legal if it was effective, which meant that it had to be able to actually prevent enemy forces from entering and leaving harbors. This meant that only close blockades were legal but to implement such a blockade of the High Seas Fleet ran the risk of unacceptable losses and the possible destruction of the main British battle fleet. Fortunately for Britain geography provided them with an answer.

As a quick glance of any map of the North Sea shows, the British Isles lie between the main German harbors and their access to the world's oceans. The British, in particular with France as their ally, could control the English Channel and close that waterway with patrols and minefields. This would flip the problem of distance on the Germans. If they wanted to relieve the blockade in the Channel they would have to sortie long distances from their bases to attack the Entente patrols and therefore they would be susceptible to interception and destruction on their way home. The other exit from the North Sea, the waters between Britain and Norway, could be patrolled as well. With both the northern and southern exits of the North Sea closed, Germany would be cut off from all foreign trade without the Royal Navy having to risk the dangers of a close block-ade. A distant blockade would allow German forces to sortie into the North Sea whenever they chose but there was little damage that could re-ally be done by those forces. In the meantime the distant blockade of the North Sea, coupled with Britain's control of the Straits of Gibraltar and the Suez Canal, would allow Britain to completely close the Central Powers off from all access to the outside world. From the perspective of the war at sea the distant blockade was the answer. It would create prob-lems for the British Foreign Office, which would have to deal with the complaints of neutral nations such as the United States, whose shipping would be interfered with by a blockade that was not legal according to the traditional rules of the sea, but in the eyes of the Admiralty that was a small price to pay. Accordingly by the time war came in 1914 the British had switched to the distant blockade.

Upon the outbreak of war the major British units, the battle fleet, now christened the Grand Fleet, moved to a new harbor at Scapa Flow in the Orkney Islands and a squadron of obsolete cruisers was set to patrolling the Northern Passage. The Channel Passage was turned over to smaller units, torpedo boat destroyers, and a few cruisers, which made up the Har-wich Force and the Dover Patrol. With the exits to the North Sea closed the British were able to immediately cut off German trade without greatly endangering their fleet. Unaware of the change the Germans waited for the Royal Navy to arrive off of the Heligoland Bight.

Missed Opportunities: The War at Sea 1914–1915

The Grand Fleet significantly outgunned the High Seas Fleet when the war began and the preponderance of British power would only grow as the war progressed. German armaments manufacturers would be forced to concentrate most heavily on the production of shells and guns for the German army. The production of new warships for the High Seas Fleet became a luxury whereas in Great Britain the new construction of war-ships was deemed essential. At the outset of the war the British possessed 24 dreadnoughts and 4 battle cruisers against Germany's 13 and 5, and over the course of the war the British would add another 11 dreadnoughts while Germany would only add 2.[5] Therefore the Germans had their best opportunities to strike at the British early in the war.

The High Seas Fleet's greatest opportunity to positively impact the war came almost immediately when, on August 12, the British began transporting the BEF to France. Remarkably neither the German army nor the High Seas Fleet had any plans to deal with this. The German army had scant respect for the BEF because the latter consisted of only six divisions whereas the German and French armies possessed hundreds of divisions. In fact Moltke famously remarked that the German army would "arrest" the British as they swept through Belgium. This was a major oversight in German planning. Neither Schlieffen nor Moltke made any provision for the presence of the British army in Belgium or France. Nor did the German fleet plan to sortie to disrupt the crossing. In order to do so it would have needed to penetrate the English Channel and expose itself to battle with the Grand Fleet under unfavorable circumstances; this likely would have resulted in heavy casualties and perhaps the destruction of the High Seas Fleet. With the army confident that it could defeat the British along with the French, there appeared to be no need to risk the fleet to stop the British from arriving on the continent. This would prove to be a critical error in judgment as the small but highly professional BEF played a critical role in first slowing and then defeating the Schlieffen-Moltke Plan at the Marne River. It took the British a week to complete the transfer of the BEF and not one soldier was lost to enemy action. Though the Germans did not realize it at the time this was a critical lost opportunity.

Another came within weeks, in the waters of the Heligoland Bight itself. The bight is the body of water between the island of Heligoland and the German North Sea coasts. It was here that the Germans expected the British to arrive in force and institute their close blockade; it was accordingly here that the Germans planned to implement their kleinkrieg. However, when the British did not arrive in the days immediately following the declaration of war, the Germans allowed their defenses in the bight to become lax. The commander of the High Seas Fleet, Friedrich von Ingenohl, placed Franz von Hipper, the commander of the Scouting Forces, in charge of the defense of the bight. Hipper in turn put together a haphazard series of destroyer patrols supported by light cruisers while the heavy ships of the fleet, the battleships and battle cruisers, remained in Wilhelmshaven and the other German harbors. The battle cruisers were kept theoretically ready to sail in the event that the British would arrive but they were moored in the Jade River estuary and at low tide these large warships would draw too much water to leave the estuary. If an enemy attack came at low tide these powerful ships would be unable to intervene in any resulting action.

Many British officers found the inaction of the first days of the war unpalatable. The expectation of both the service and the British people was that their fleet would engage the German fleet in a climactic battle in the first days of the war and destroy it. When the Germans proved uncooperative and failed to sail out to their destruction both the nation and the service became restless. The commander of the Grand Fleet, John Jellicoe, was determined not to put his fleet into a position where it could be defeated in detail. He was acutely conscious of the fact that he was, as Winston Churchill famously stated, the "only man who could lose the war in an afternoon." In particular Jellicoe feared that the Germans would attempt to draw his forces into a submarine trap where German U-boats could attack and destroy his dreadnoughts, leaving his fleet weak enough to be destroyed by the High Seas Fleet. He was prescient as the Germans would try to do just this many times in the coming two years and he was doubtless correct in his caution but many of his subordinates and fellow officers chafed to get at the Germans. One of these younger officers was Roger Keyes. Keyes commanded the British submarine force. His ships had been sent, from the earliest days of the war, into the bight to gather intelligence on the German defenses and the patterns of the German patrollers. Keyes was able to glean enough evidence in the first weeks of August to convince him that the bight was sparsely defended and that the British could strike directly into the heart of German waters and destroy numerous German patrol craft. So Keyes proposed an attack into the bight with his submarines and the cruisers and destroyers of Commodore Reginald Tyrwhitt's Harwich Force. The plan was daring and risky and caught the attention of the First Lord of the Admiralty, Winston Churchill, who sanctioned it. It also played directly into the German war plan, to slowly whittle away at British naval superiority by attacking British ships off the German coastline. To alleviate some of the risk Jellicoe ordered the Battlecruiser Squadron, commanded by David Beatty, who was also eager to engage the Germans, to provide support, a move that would prove fortuitous.

On August 28, as the Battle of Tannenberg raged in East Prussia and German forces in the west were marching from one victory to another, Keyes and Tyrwhitt launched their operation. The plan was to use some of Keyes's submarines as bait to draw several of the patrolling German destroyers out of the bight and into the clutches of Tyrwhitt's light cruisers, which could outgun and outrun the smaller German vessels. Jellicoe, without informing Tyrwhitt or Keyes, sent Beatty south with five battle cruisers and a squadron of additional light cruisers to provide support. The weather on the 28th proved to be extremely foggy with low visibility and these factors would play a key role in the battle.[6]

The battle began when the German destroyer G-194 took Keyes's bait. Lookouts on the ship spotted the periscope of a British submarine and the Germans then gave chase. They pursued the British submarine right into the waiting arms of the British cruisers. When G-194's commander reported the presence of the British warships Hipper responded by ordering a number of German light cruisers to steam to the assistance of the German destroyer. What resulted were several running battles where opposing forces appeared out of the fog to engage one another only to then disappear again. German cruisers joined the battle piecemeal, engaging one at a time rather than forming into larger detachments because the Germans were unaware of the size of the force they were fighting. For a time the Germans appeared to have the best of the fighting, doing severe damage in particular to Tyrwhitt's flagship, the cruiser *Arethusa*, but the tide of battle changed severely when Beatty arrived with the battle cruisers. These ships far outclassed the smaller German warships, wielding in many cases powerful 12-inch guns against the 4-, 6-, or 8-inch guns mounted on the German ships. Furthermore they were nearly as fast as the German cruisers. The British battle cruisers easily overpowered the German forces and sank three German cruisers and a destroyer while seriously damaging three more cruisers. Three British destroyers and one cruiser were badly damaged but no British ship was lost. Hipper's own battle cruisers were unable to get to sea in time to assist their comrades because they had to wait for the tide to rise sufficiently to cover the sand bar outside the Jade estuary. This battle, the Battle of the Heligoland Bight, was a decisive British victory and the second missed opportunity for the Germans. Beatty placed five critically important warships in harm's way hundreds of kilometers from his bases and far from any support by the Grand Fleet. Had Hipper and Ingenohl been better prepared they might have been able to destroy Beatty's entire force. The loss of those battle cruisers would have deprived the Grand Fleet of its eyes and made Jellicoe's job much more difficult. Instead the British were able to penetrate right to the gates of the German fleet, inflict a major defeat, and leave with minimal losses.

The impact of the Battle of the Heligoland Bight went far beyond the number of ships the Germans lost. The battle shocked Kaiser Wilhelm II who promptly issued a crippling order that the dreadnoughts of the High Seas Fleet were not to be risked in battle without his express permission. In practice this meant that the most powerful units of the High Seas Fleet were immobilized. Ingenohl agreed with his sovereign's ruling because it served to provide cover for his own, very risk-averse, policies. It appears as if Ingenohl and many other German officers saw the outcome of the Battle of the Bight as confirmation of British naval superiority. Tirpitz on the other hand was angered by the Kaiser's order and by the reluctance of Ingenohl to use the fleet aggressively. He continually called for first Ingenohl and then his successors, Hugo von Pohl and Reinhard Scheer, to take the war to the British. His unwillingness to accept the Kaiser's position on the use of the High Seas Fleet led to Tirpitz being driven from power in 1916. The cautious Ingenohl only sent the battleships of the High Seas Fleet to sea once while he was in command. That sortie led to another missed opportunity.

In December 1914, with the war in the west stalemated and the promised short war rapidly turning into a long war, Hipper proposed a new plan for the High Seas Fleet; he suggested that the German battle cruisers bombard the British coastline in an attempt to draw Beatty's forces, and possibly part of the Grand Fleet, south. The High Seas Fleet would sortie out to Dogger Bank and wait to provide support to Hipper who would lead whatever British forces were pursuing him into the waiting arms of Ingenohl. This would allow the High Seas Fleet to destroy a portion of the Grand Fleet in detail and whittle away at Britain's superiority. The plan gave rise to what is known as the Scarborough raid of December 16, 1914, and it nearly resulted in disaster for both fleets. The action that took place that day came about because the Royal Navy was able to discover in advance just what the Germans intended.

Unbeknownst to the Germans, by December 1914 the British were able to decipher some of Germany's naval codes. The Admiralty was running a secret organization known as Room 40 (so named because of the room it was located in). The organization, headed by Captain Reginald Hall, was in charge of deciphering German codes and passing the information along to Jellicoe when it was deemed prudent to do so. This group of cryptanalysts would play a critical role in the defeat of the German navy.

The Germans made extensive use of radio transmissions to distribute orders to their fleets and, later, submarines. All of their messages were encoded and believed to be secure but over the course of late 1914, through a series of fortunate accidents, the British acquired the means

to decipher and read many of those codes. The first of these fortunate
accidents happened on August 11 when the Australians were able to seize
a copy of the German commercial code from a German merchant ship.
This was the code that the Germans used to communicate with their merchant ships.[7] The codebook was sent along to London and given to the
men of Room 40. Being able to read this code proved useful in the early
months of the war but its utility faded by the end of 1914 because the
German merchant marine had been swept from the seas. An event of
far greater importance took place in the Baltic on August 26 when the
German cruiser *Magdeburg* ran aground and was captured by the Russians.
On board the Russians discovered an intact copy of the codebook for the
High Seas Fleet. They sent the book to the Royal Navy where it became
the critical piece of evidence that allowed Hall's men to begin deciphering the main German naval codes. An additional stroke of luck came
in November when a copy of the codebook the Germans used to communicate with their overseas cruisers and their naval attaches was salvaged
from the wreck of a German destroyer. Using these codebooks the British
were able to read more and more of the German codes as the war went on
and since the Germans rarely changed their codes, because they were
confident that they were unbreakable, Room 40 was able to gain more
and more experience deciphering them. The intelligence that was discovered by Room 40 was used to great effect by the British at the Battle of
Dogger Bank and again at the Battle of Jutland but it became most critical
in the campaign against the German submarines in 1917. It was used for
the first time against Hipper in December 1914.

Knowing roughly where Hipper was going and when he would arrive,
the Royal Navy decided to lay a trap for the German battle cruisers. Hipper's ships would be allowed to bombard their target cities but they would
then be intercepted on their return to Germany by Beatty with his battle
cruisers and the most modern squadron of dreadnoughts. Even the best
intelligence though can sometimes be faulty and this was the case in this
instance. Room 40 did not discover that Ingenohl and the High Seas
Fleet were also at sea. They thought they were sending Beatty to trap
and destroy Hipper without knowing that they were also sending him into
the teeth of the entire High Seas Fleet. This was precisely the situation
the German admirals had dreamed of since the start of the war.

Early on December 16, all three forces set out, Hipper for the English
coast, and Ingenohl and Beatty for Dogger Bank. It was at Dogger Bank,
in the early morning hours of the 16th, that the destroyer van of Beatty's
force stumbled on the destroyers of Ingenohl's van. One of the decisive

moments of the war had arrived. Ingenohl could not know the size of the force he had encountered and he had to be mindful of the Kaiser's recent order not to risk the High Seas Fleet and those two facts, combined with his cautious nature, led him to assume that he was facing the entire Grand Fleet; accordingly he ordered the High Seas Fleet to turn for home, leaving Hipper and his battle cruisers to their fate. A more aggressive German commander who seized the moment might have been able to deal a devastating blow to the Royal Navy; instead the Germans missed another opportunity.

For his part, Hipper, unaware that he had been abandoned, carried out his mission and bombarded Scarborough and Hartlepool before turning for home. On their way home, his forces were spotted by the light cruisers of Beatty's force but due to poor signaling by the British, poor visibility, and fortunate decisions by Hipper, the Germans were able to escape the British trap and return to Germany. Neither side was happy with the outcome of the raid and both came to realize they had let a major opportunity pass through their hands.

The Germans had been surprised by Beatty's presence at Dogger Bank and believing that some of the fishing craft on the North Sea, in particular those around Dogger Bank, were sending intelligence on German movements to London, Ingenohl and Hipper decided to send Hipper's three battle cruisers (*Seydlitz*, *Moltke*, and *Derfflinger*) along with the heavy cruiser *Blücher*, back to Dogger Bank in January 1915. They hoped to capture any ships aiding the British and possibly to catch and destroy some patrolling British cruisers. They did not suspect that their codes had been compromised. Once again the British had advance warning through Room 40 of the German plan and once more Beatty was sent to sea to intercept the Germans on their way home. Beatty had five of his battle cruisers along with numerous cruisers and destroyers. This time Jellicoe also put to sea but stayed well to the north of Dogger Bank. Shortly after 7:00 AM on January 24, the scouting cruisers of Beatty's and Hipper's forces encountered and opened fire on each other. The Battle of Dogger Bank, the first clash between heavily armed modern battleships or battle cruisers, had begun.

The battle began with the Germans far to the east of the British forces. Both forces initially closed on each other but when it became apparent to Hipper that he had encountered a superior force he reversed course and turned for home at 7:30 AM. A chase developed in which Beatty had a significant advantage. Though Hipper had a significant head start in terms of distance, three of Beatty's battle cruisers were faster than all but one of Hipper's ships and were significantly faster than Hipper's slowest ship, *Blücher*. Hipper was reluctant to leave *Blücher* behind and therefore Beatty was able to gain rapidly on the German ships. The two forces opened fire on each other at a range of 20 kilometers and German gunnery proved to be superior to that of the British. Beatty's flagship, *Lion*, was brought under very heavy fire and was severely damaged. Once again, as in December, the British were plagued by signaling errors. Beatty tried to order his ships to engage their opposite number in the German battle line but his orders were not clearly transmitted by his flag officer and were not properly interpreted by all the captains of his other ships; as a result the German battle cruiser *Moltke* was not engaged by any of the British ships. Undisturbed *Moltke* could focus its efforts on the British flagship, *Lion*. The British did land several blows, in particular to Hipper's flagship, *Seydlitz*. One of the British shells struck one of its turrets and created an explosive flash that descended down the ammunition hoist toward the magazine and would have destroyed the ship had it not been for the quick thinking of a German officer who was able to close the door to the magazine in time. The German battle cruisers were badly battered above the waterline but they managed to avoid any damage to their propulsion systems. The same could not be said for the British flagship, *Lion*, which suffered significant engine damage and eventually ended up dead in the water. Beatty had to be transferred by destroyer to *Princess Royal*, which left the British force bereft of its commander for several critical moments. Beatty's final signal before his transfer had been an order to his other ships to engage the end of the German line. Beatty desired each of his ships continue to engage its opposite number among the German ships but the poorly worded signal resulted in all of the British ships concentrating their fire on the last ship in the German line, the slower and vastly less valuable armored cruiser *Blücher*. The smaller German ship was accordingly pummeled by shells from four British battle cruisers. Hipper, realizing that *Blücher* was doomed and hoping to save the rest of his squadron, used this respite to put distance between his and Beatty's force. While the superior British force destroyed the German heavy cruiser, Beatty waited in frustration for his transfer to an active ship. By the time the transfer was complete and Beatty could correct the earlier error, *Blücher* had been destroyed and the far more valuable German battle cruisers had managed to escape.

The Battle of Dogger Bank was another clear British victory to go with the Battle of the Heligoland Bight and it spelled the end of Friedrich von Ingenohl's command of the High Seas Fleet. On February 2, he was

replaced by Hugo von Pohl. The battle also confirmed the Kaiser's opinion that his ships could not be risked in open battle with the British fleet.
Some other means would have to be found to exert pressure on Great
Britain. In a surprising move Pohl would turn to a weapon that no one
before 1914 thought could play anything other than a secondary role in
naval warfare, the submarine.

The First Submarine Campaign 1915–1916

The first primitive submarines appeared during the American Civil
War; they were used by the Confederacy to attack blockading Union warships. They had very limited success. As the nineteenth century continued, naval engineers worked on new designs and slowly moved toward
the creation of modern submarines powered by diesel engines. France
led the way in this field and by the early-twentieth-century France had
31 submarines on order.[8] Eventually, under Admiral Fisher, the British
too began developing submarines. The Germans were late converts to
the submarine because of the cult of the battleship so assiduously pushed
by Tirpitz. When war came France possessed a fleet of 77 submarines,
Britain had 55, and Germany only had 28.[9]

The biggest question regarding the submarine was how it could best
be used. These early submarines were slow, especially when submerged,
unarmored, and weakly armed. Most had only a small deck gun and
carried three or four torpedoes, with only the newest submarines carrying as many as six. They did possess some advantages though, the most
important of which was their ability to submerge. Unfortunately they
could only do so for short periods. Second their low profile made them
hard to detect at a distance even when they were surfaced. However,
neither of these advantages would be of much use in a fleet action
where their slow speed and lack of armor would be fatal. Therefore
naval planners looked for another way to use these weapons. One
obvious choice, which was embraced by both sides in the war, was to
use them as coastal defense craft. Another, embraced in particular by
Sir Roger Keyes and the British, was to use them as advance reconnaissance craft. Ultimately though no one quite knew what to do with
them. The general conclusion on both sides of the North Sea at the
start of the war was that submarines would serve as auxiliaries to the
battle fleet, where they might be able to finish off damaged enemy warships, as reconnaissance craft, and for coastal defense. Few considered
that they might be useful as commerce raiders.

The first major success for the submarines of any nation came in early September 1914 when the German boat, the *U-9*, sank three old, slow British cruisers that were patrolling in the North Sea. These ships, *Aboukir*, *Cressy*, and *Hogue*, were sunk within an hour. The event shocked the Royal Navy and inspired the British to develop new antisubmarine measures. A resulting fear of submarines would lead Jellicoe to leave his main anchorage at Scapa Flow several times; it would also play a role in the Battle of Dogger Bank when Beatty ordered *Lion*, during the course of the running fight, to briefly turn away from the German fleet because a periscope had supposedly been spotted. However no German submarine ever repeated the success of *U-9*. The event, shocking as it was, turned out to be a fluke caused by the slow speed of the cruisers and the fact that the cruisers' captains had no idea how to deal with submarines. For example, the last of the cruisers was sunk while its engines were stopped and it was trying to rescue survivors from the other cruisers. That effort, while noble, made the cruiser a sitting duck for the submarine. The British learned their lessons from this event and though additional ships would be sunk by submarines in the coming months, with the most significant blow being the sinking of the battleship *Formidable* in January 1915, none of the ships that were sunk were frontline vessels. In fact, not one dreadnought-class ship was lost to a submarine in the entire war. In truth, the submarines of the First World War were too slow and weakly armed to be of much use against modern warships.

Hugo von Pohl, the new commander of the High Seas Fleet after Ingenohl's ouster, came to believe that the submarine, though ineffective against fleets, could be of use against merchant shipping. In November 1914 he began urging the German government to use the submarines to implement a blockade of the British Isles in response to the British blockade of Germany. The German government took the stance that the British blockade was illegal, both because it was not "effective" and because the British were seizing as contraband many goods that were not strictly military in their use, such as foodstuffs. Many of the German people agreed and there was a strong desire to hit back at the "perfidious" British. The submarine appeared to offer the only possibility of doing so. Both the Kaiser and the chancellor though dragged their feet over the implementation of a submarine blockade because there was no guarantee it would work. The submarines would encounter numerous problems if they were used as commerce raiders. While they could bypass the British defenses in the Channel and the North Sea to reach the heavy merchant traffic that plied the waters west of the British Isles, once they arrived they would have a difficult time acting in accordance with the accepted rules of cruiser warfare. These rules, which dated to the days of sail, required that any warship acting as a commerce raider had to stop merchant ships and search them for contraband before sinking them. Merchant ships could be destroyed once the search was complete but only after the crew of the warship had taken precautions to ensure that the crew of the merchant ship would survive. This meant in practice either allowing the crew to take to their lifeboats or taking them physically onto the raiding ship. In the case of the submarine the latter was not an option. The ships were too small and cramped as they were; there was no place to put captured sailors. That left the lifeboats, which were only of use if the encounter took place near land. Furthermore, stopping the merchant ship also meant stopping the submarine, which left the latter vessel a sitting duck for enemy forces and with the advent of ship's radios the German captains could never be sure that their targets had not sent out a call for help that might be answered at any moment. In addition, given their lack of armor, submarines were vulnerable to gunfire from even small caliber artillery. This meant that if the ship they stopped was armed they might well find themselves outgunned. The only way to avoid such a scenario was for the submarines to attack without warning, which went against the rules of international law.

Pohl and those who agreed with him, which eventually included Tirpitz, argued that those rules would simply need to be broken; that the needs of the war and the fact that the British had already broken those same rules with their own blockade meant that the Germans were justified in doing what was necessary to protect themselves. Those who were opposed to the use of what came to be known as "unrestricted submarine warfare," mainly Chancellor Theobald von Bethmann-Hollweg and the Foreign Office, warned that a campaign that violated the rules of war might drive other nations, in particular the United States, to join the ranks of Germany's enemies. The risk of that happening was, in their opinion, not worth the possible gains. In 1915 they were certainly correct; there were not enough German submarines to implement an effective blockade. In the end though Pohl and his supporters won over the Kaiser and in a conference on February 1, 1915, the Germans decided to turn their submarines loose against both enemy and neutral shipping. On February 15, the German government issued a press release stating that, as a result of the illegal blockade pursued by Great Britain, it (the German government) was obligated to retaliate; therefore the waters around Great Britain and Ireland would henceforth be considered a war zone in which every enemy merchant ship would be sunk without warning. Further-more, since the British government used neutral flags to disguise their ships, neutral vessels might also be sunk and they were therefore urged to stay out of the area. The campaign would commence on February 28.

The new campaign had limited success. Over the course of March and April 1915, the submarines sank a total of roughly 136,000 tons of shipping, barely making a dent in the total tonnage of British merchant shipping.[10] The numbers should not have been surprising; the Germans began the campaign with only 29 serviceable submarines, hardly more than they started the war with and far too few to create a true blockade.[11] Unsuccessful as it was the campaign did create concern in Great Britain where the Admiralty had little idea of how to deal with the new menace. Their focus was offensive: how could they find and destroy German submarines? They tried a wide array of gambits, none of which was effective and some of which were comical, such as trying to train seagulls to land on periscopes so that the attached submarine could be attacked.[12] In truth the biggest blow that was dealt to the submarine campaign was self-inflicted. On May 7, the British transatlantic passenger liner *Lusitania* was sunk off the coast of Ireland with the loss of nearly all on board. The death toll came to 1,198 people, 128 of whom were American. The sinking was hailed as a great victory in Germany because the liner was known to be transporting munitions at the time it was attacked. It was deemed barbaric in Britain and, more importantly, in the United States. The sinking of *Lusitania* led to a diplomatic crisis between Germany and the United States with the American president, Woodrow Wilson, sending a strongly worded warning to the German government to stop the sinking of passenger liners. The Kaiser eventually, against the protests of the Naval Staff, Tirpitz, and von Pohl, gave in to Wilson's demands and issued orders on June 5 that passenger liners were not to be sunk on sight. The damage however had been done. The U.S. government, which was angered by the British blockade and was the major reason why that blockade was not tighter, became increasingly anti-German, in particular when the sinking of passenger liners did not actually stop. In August another passenger liner, *Arabic*, was sunk, again off the Irish coastline. This time 40 people died, 3 of whom were American. Another strongly worded American protest followed on August 30 and once again the Kaiser intervened, this time to end the entire campaign. The first unrestricted submarine campaign came to a close on September 18. The submarines had sunk nearly 700,000 tons of shipping since February, not enough to make much of a dent in the British merchant marine. The British government was not even forced to institute rationing. In fact over the same span the British added 1.3 million tons of new shipping.[13] The British did however use the campaign to justify tightening their controls over neutral shipping, thereby strengthening the blockade. Germany was significantly worse off after the campaign than it were before.

The ending of the campaign was extremely unpopular with many of the leaders of the German navy. The man who took Pohl's place as head of the Naval Staff, Admiral Henning von Holtzendorff, conducted a study in late 1915 and concluded that the British could be forced to make peace within a year if the German submarines could sink 600,000 tons of shipping every month, a figure that was only slightly less than what they had sunk in the entirety of the first campaign. Holtzendorff, Tirpitz, and their supporters believed it could be done since Germany was building additional submarines. By the end of 1915 there were 54 German submarines in service.[14] Critically General von Falkenhayn threw his support behind the campaign as well. Falkenhayn was working on a new plan to win the war in 1916. He planned to "bleed the French army white" in a massive battle of attrition around the fortress complex of Verdun and believed that an unrestricted submarine campaign against Great Britain would help to drive the latter to the peace table once France was beaten. The Kaiser hesitated to grant permission because Bethmann-Hollweg continued to argue against the campaign out of fear that the United States would join the war. In the end Bethmann-Hollweg's protests were overridden and the submarine campaign was reinstituted in February 1916. The decisive argument was Falkenhayn's: that the war had to be won in 1916 if it was to be won at all because Germany's allies, Austria-Hungary, Bulgaria, and the Ottoman Empire, could not sustain another year of war. The Kaiser made one concession to Bethmann-Hollweg; he ordered that only armed freighters could be sunk without warning. This was ultimately a meaningless distinction since the submarine commanders and the Naval Staff were all aware that the British were using decoy ships, known as Q-ships, which carried concealed guns that would only be revealed when a submarine surfaced to attack. This meant that the submarine commanders had to assume that most freighters were armed. Even that small concession was too much for Tirpitz and he resigned in March 1916.

The new campaign was short-lived and ran into the same problem as its predecessor, the sinking of passenger liners. One month into the campaign the small liner *Sussex*, plying the waters of the Channel, was sunk. The U.S. government responded by demanding an end to the submarine

campaign. Failure to do so would result in the severing of diplomatic relations between the two countries. That led to the submarines being
ordered, once more, to obey prize rules. In the interim, von Pohl had been
replaced as head of the High Seas Fleet by Rear Admiral Reinhard
Scheer. Scheer, a strong supporter of the unrestricted submarine campaign, decided to withdraw all of the High Seas Fleet's submarines from
the commerce war in protest to the governments ruling. This left only
the submarines in the Mediterranean and those belonging to the Flanders
flotillas to carry on the commerce war. In the two months of the campaign the German submarines only sank 400,000 tons of enemy shipping,
not even close to the 600,000 Holtzendorff wanted them to sink each
month. The first two U-boat campaigns were, simply put, dismal failures.
The German fleet appeared to be utterly unable to aid the German war
effort. Reinhard Scheer disagreed.

Scheer had a far more aggressive mind-set than either of his predeces-
sors and he intended to use the High Seas Fleet to strike a blow at the
Grand Fleet. He returned to Ingenohl's idea of trying to separate and
destroy a portion of the Grand Fleet in detail. Scheer believed that he
could use the fleet's submarines and its airships to set a trap for the British.
He planned to send Hipper's battle cruisers out as bait and have them lure
Beatty and/or Jellicoe south over a line of submerged submarines that
would hopefully pick off several British vessels and weaken the main
force. Airships would provide reconnaissance for the High Seas Fleet so
that Scheer could avoid battle with a superior force but engage if the
enemy had been sufficiently weakened by the submarines. Scheer planned
to launch his operation in late May 1916. That operation resulted in the
climactic battle of the war at sea, the Battle of Jutland.

The Battle of Jutland[15]

Scheer intended to have Hipper and the German battle cruisers launch
another raid on the British coastline, this time at Sunderland, which was
just 100 miles from Beatty's base in the Firth of Forth. The hope was that
the insult of a German bombardment so close to a major British base
would lead Beatty to impulsively rush to sea. Hipper could then lead
Beatty over a line of German submarines and ultimately into contact
with the High Seas Fleet itself. The operation was initially planned for
May 17th and 16 submarines from the High Seas Fleet and another 6
from the Flanders flotillas were sent to take up their stations. Seven of
these were to wait off the entrance of the Firth of Forth to torpedo Beatty

as he left port; two were sent to the Pentland Firth near Scapa Flow to strike at the Grand Fleet if it left harbor; others were sent to lay mines off the Firth of Forth, Pentland Firth, and Moray Firth and the smaller ships of the Flanders flotillas were sent to Harwich to watch for a sortie by Tyrwhitt and his vessels. All of the submarines were to maintain radio silence except in urgent situations and were to remain on patrol as long as their fuel held out, which for most of them meant they would need to return to port on June 1. Scheer ended up postponing the operation twice, first from the 17th to the 23rd and then to the 30th because of boiler trouble with some of the High Seas Fleet's dreadnoughts. Unfortunately for Scheer as he waited the weather worsened and the zeppelins he was counting on for aerial reconnaissance ended up being grounded, which meant Scheer would sail without the ability to spot the Grand Fleet from afar if it took to sea. As a result of this development Scheer altered the operation; the attack on Sunderland was turned into a sortie to the north, in the direction of the Norwegian coast. Scheer still hoped to lure out Beatty but to do so in waters that were closer to the German bases rather than the British ones. The codebreakers of Room 40 intercepted and deciphered many of Scheer's signals and were well aware of the pending German operation. They dutifully informed Jellicoe who made plans to sortie with the entirety of the Grand Fleet in the hopes that he would be able to catch and annihilate the German fleet. Following one final delay that pushed the operation back another day the German and British fleets left their respective harbors on May 31, bound for the largest battle of the battleship age. Scheer's fleet included 16 dreadnoughts, 6 older and slower battleships that were brought along against his better judgment, 6 light cruisers, and 31 destroyers. Hipper's force consisted of 5 battle cruisers, 5 light cruisers, and 30 destroyers. These were opposed by the largest collection of naval power on the planet, the entire British Grand Fleet. Jellicoe sortied from Scapa Flow with 16 dreadnoughts, 3 battle cruisers, 4 older armored cruisers, 11 light cruisers, and 36 destroyers. Beatty left the Firth of Forth with 6 battle cruisers and the 4 largest and most powerful battleships in the world, the *Queen Elizabeth*–class super dreadnoughts (all of which also fought in the Second World War), along with 12 light cruisers, 27 destroyers, and a single seaplane carrier. Another 8 dreadnoughts, 4 armored cruisers, and 11 destroyers sailed from Cromarty and rendezvoused with Jellicoe.

Hipper's force left port first, shortly after midnight on May 31. He steamed north, 50 miles in advance of the High Seas Fleet. If he encountered British forces he was to lead them south into the waiting arms of the main German fleet, which left port at 5:00 AM. On the British side Beatty's force steamed nearly due east while Jellicoe's fleet, starting far to the north, would steam southeast to meet with Beatty roughly halfway between the coasts of Norway and Scotland. All four forces were on converging courses and the two British forces did indeed sail directly over the lines of waiting German submarines. Unfortunately for Scheer his trap failed, in spectacular fashion. Though some German submarines spotted the British forces they failed to damage a single ship, and, to make matters worse, they failed to warn Scheer that Jellicoe was at sea.[16]

The Battle of Jutland began at 2:20 PM on May 31 when cruisers in the advance screen of Hipper's force spotted cruisers from the advance screen of Beatty's force. The two forces engaged roughly 10 minutes later. As signals flew from the engaged cruisers, both commanders ordered their battle cruisers forward to give support. The British were steaming in an easterly direction and the Germans were steaming northwest. The relative positions of the two forces meant that the British were easier to see; they were, in effect, silhouetted by the sun while the German forces were more difficult to make out in the distance to the east. As a result Hipper spotted Beatty's force first, shortly before 3:30 PM. It appeared that the German plan had succeeded. Beatty's battle cruisers and a very powerful squadron of the Grand Fleet were at sea, apparently alone. Hipper now, according to plan, ordered his ships to turn onto a southern course, which would bring him toward Scheer and the High Seas Fleet. Beatty, unaware of Scheer's presence and seeing running before him the very ships that escaped him at Dogger Bank a year and a half earlier, gave chase. What followed is known as the "Run to the South."

Beatty's battle cruisers were faster than the German ships and began to gain ground on the latter while the super dreadnoughts, which were 10 miles to Beatty's rear, strove to catch up. Beatty's six battle cruisers commenced firing at Hipper's five battle cruisers at a range of 16,000 yards shortly after 3:45 PM. The Germans quickly returned fire. In the fighting that followed over roughly the next hour the Germans outperformed their foes. They were aided by several factors, the most critical of which was that they had superior range finders and centralized fire control mechanisms than the British did. This, combined with the British forces being silhouetted against the western horizon, made the German gunners' task much easier than it would have been otherwise. The wind was also on the German's side; it was blowing from the east, which meant that the British gunners had their own smoke blowing back into their faces. The superior German gunnery meant that the British suffered significantly more damage in this early fighting. At 4:00 PM Beatty nearly lost his flagship when a German shell struck one of the midships turrets on *Lion*. The hit killed nearly the entire gun crew instantly. The captain of the gun crew, though fatally injured, realized the great danger to his ship; the turret was connected through a series of hoists to its magazine below decks, a fire in the turret could spread down the shaft to the magazine and potentially destroy the entire ship. As his final act he called down the voice pipe to the magazine and ordered the magazine doors closed. As the doors below him closed, the powder in the turret ignited and a flash descended the shaft, instantly incinerating many of the crew but failing to reach the magazine through the closed door. A moment's hesitation would likely have resulted in the explosion of the entire ship and the death of nearly everyone on board, including Beatty. That very thing happened about 5 minutes later to the battle cruiser *Indefatigable*. *Indefatigable* was struck in one of its forward turrets and in this case the flash reached the magazine. The ship was wracked by a series of explosions, which caused it to first roll onto its side and then sink.

As the two forces continued to pummel one another the super dreadnoughts slowly came into action and at 4:10, at a range of 19,000 yards, the massive 15-inch guns of these four battle wagons opened fire. The last ship in the German line, the *Von der Tann*, suffered the worst of their wrath, taking multiple hits that led to massive flooding. Fortunately for its crew the German ships were designed to withstand massive punishment and possessed, in particular, excellent below decks compartmentalization, which allowed the crew to contain the damage and keep *Von der Tann* afloat. As the rear of the German line, *Von der Tann* and *Moltke*, began to feel the effects of the super dreadnoughts (*Barham*, *Malaya*, *Warspite*, and *Valiant*), at the front of the line the British continued to take a pounding. At 4:26 PM the battle cruiser *Queen Mary* was struck by three shells in the fore and midships turrets; another flash resulted and the British battle cruiser exploded. This prompted Beatty to turn to the captain of *Lion* and remark, "There's something wrong with our bloody ships today."[17]

Both forces continued to head south, pummeling one another as they went. As the battle wagons battered one another the smaller craft, the light cruisers, moved to the front of their respective forces. At 4:38 PM one of the British light cruisers, the *Southampton*, spotted, looming out of the south, the High Seas Fleet. The situation instantly changed as hunter became hunted. Scheer and Hipper could exult: they had done it; they had caught a portion of the Grand Fleet alone and vulnerable, or so they believed. Hipper now reversed course and took up his position in the van of the united High Seas Fleet. Beatty also quickly reversed course, ordering his four super dreadnoughts to form his rear guard. Around 5:00 PM the leading vessels of the High Seas Fleet, the most modern German dreadnoughts, opened fire on the four super dread-noughts. What ensued was another running duel, the "Run to the North" as Beatty now played the role Hipper had played earlier, trying to lead his foes into the waiting arms of Jellicoe and the Grand Fleet.

Over the course of the next 45 minutes the fleets continued to batter away at one another, until, at 5:50 PM, it was Hipper and Scheer's turn to be surprised when Hipper received word from one of his light cruisers that British dreadnoughts had been sighted just to the north. At 6:00 PM the High Seas Fleet emerged from a fog bank to see in front of it the massed force of the entire Grand Fleet, 16,000 yards away and closing.

Jellicoe quickly ordered the Grand Fleet to deploy into a battle line to port, which put his fleet on an easterly heading, which in turn allowed him to cross the German "T." Crossing the enemy's T meant that your bat-tle fleet was able to sail across the front face of the enemy's battle line. This allowed the crossing fleet to bring its broadside, the greatest number of its guns, to bear on the enemy while the enemy could only return fire with the forward guns of its leading ships. It meant one fleet could bring nearly all of its guns into action while the majority of the enemy's guns could not fire at all. It was the classic recipe for the annihilation of an enemy fleet. Jellicoe was able to swiftly bring this about and by 6:15 PM the van of the High Seas Fleet was being pounded by the mass of the Grand Fleet. Scheer had only moments to decide how to respond—to continue his course would likely mean the destruction of his fleet. Acting decisively he ordered his fleet to reverse its course, in place. Normally when a fleet turned it turned as a whole so that the leading ships would begin the turn and the others would then follow until they reached the point where the leading ship had turned, then they would turn as well. What Scheer ordered was a far more difficult maneuver that required all of his ships to turn at once, in place, so that his rearmost ship would now become the leading ship and vice versa. To make a normal turn into a crossed T would have brought every German ship, in turn, under the British guns and would likely have led to the loss of several of them. By executing this battle turn Scheer was able to quickly turn his fleet and retreat back into the mists, saving his fleet. The maneuver was completely unexpected by the British and resulted in what appeared to be the sudden disappearance of the German fleet. Scheer had, apparently, escaped destruction.

To this point the Germans had fought brilliantly. German gunnery had been outstanding, German vessels had proven they could take enormous damage and remain afloat, and the Germans had destroyed two British battle cruisers. Then, in the course of the initial fighting between the two battle fleets, the German battle cruisers claimed a third victim, the battle cruiser *Invincible*. *Invincible* suffered the same fate as *Indefatigable* and *Queen Mary*, a hit to a turret followed by a magazine explosion that destroyed the entire ship. All that remained of *Invincible* were the fore and aft sections of the ship, sticking up out of the relatively shallow water that she sank in. The British had clearly taken the worst of the fighting to this point but Scheer now faced an enormous problem. His fleet was to the west of the British fleet and his bases were to the east of the British fleet. In order to get home he would either have to go through or around the Grand Fleet. Knowing this Scheer decided to surprise Jellicoe and try to break through the British battle line. He ordered another battle turn at 6:55 PM putting his fleet back into its original formation and back onto its original path to the northeast. This was nearly disastrous.

For the British it was as if their quarry suddenly reappeared. To Jellicoe's surprise the Germans once again appeared out of the mists, heading directly toward his fleet, which was still in position to cross the German's T. The firing on both sides resumed with the Germans now suffering the heaviest damage. Only the 3 leading ships of the German line were able to return fire against 24 British battleships. As the German van was battered order in the German line began to break down. With his fleet slowly breaking up around him Scheer had no choice but to order a third battle turn. This time the British would likely expect the maneuver though so he ordered the battle cruisers, most of which by this point had most of their guns out of action and two of which were taking on enormous quantities of water, to sacrifice themselves in a suicidal charge at the British line. The hope was that the British forces would direct their attention to the battle cruisers, which would in turn allow the German battleships to escape once more. At the same time the German destroyers launched a torpedo attack on the Grand Fleet. They fired 31 torpedoes, which led Jellicoe to order his battleships to turn to the southeast, away from the torpedoes, in order to avoid them. As a result most of the torpedoes missed but Scheer was able once more to extricate the High Seas Fleet, including the battle cruisers, into the mist and the approaching darkness. The German fleet disappeared for a second time. Scheer's third battle turn, though it saved the High Seas Fleet from annihilation for a second time, did nothing to address his fundamental problem, that his enemy was between his now badly battered fleet and his bases.

As darkness fell on the North Sea both commanders faced critical decisions. The question both men had to answer was whether they should seek to engage the enemy under the cover of darkness or try to await the coming of dawn. The Germans were well trained in night fighting and in particular in the use of destroyers to launch torpedo attacks. Scheer could have chosen to turn his fleet around for a fourth time to move in for a renewed battle. He chose not to do so. He later claimed he chose not to risk a night battle because the Germans had already won the battle and he did not want to risk a night action, which could turn the tide. In truth he was well aware that the German fleet was in serious trouble. His sole ambition at this point was to get his fleet home in one piece. For his part Jellicoe, equally aware of the overall situation, saw no reason to hazard his fleet and his advantageous geographic position in a risky night battle where his dreadnoughts might be sunk by German torpedoes. So he too forewent a night battle. Instead he looked forward to the morning when, if he could find the German fleet once more, he could be all but certain of destroying it. All that was necessary was for him to determine how Scheer would try to get home and then position his fleet to intercept. Here Jellicoe was hampered by the failure of several of his ships, in particular his cruisers and Beatty's battle cruisers, to provide him with accurate information. However, he was aware just from the basic geography of the North Sea that Scheer had limited options open to him. The Germans could attempt to sail around Denmark and into the Baltic and return that way but the journey would have been long and many of the German ships had been badly battered in the fighting; they might not survive the passage so he rejected that option, wisely. As Jellicoe saw it, that left Scheer with only two options. Scheer would either have to race south and then east to try and beat the British to the German bases in the Ems and Jade estuaries or he would have to turn his ships southeast, which would lead them right back into contact with the Grand Fleet. Jellicoe assumed Scheer would take the safer approach and head directly south so he put the Grand Fleet on a southerly heading aiming to intercept the Germans at dawn.

Scheer understood his dilemma all too well. The safest route, the route to the north and east around Denmark, was out of the question for some of his ships, in particular *Lützow* and *Seydlitz*, had been very badly damaged and were taking on immense amounts of water. Therefore he had to take one of the shorter approaches. If he chose correctly his fleet might well survive; if he chose poorly his destruction was all but certain. He could choose the path that was safer in the short term, the route to the south or he could take the riskier path southeast, which might well bring him back into contact with the British. He chose the latter and the German fleet altered course. In the ensuing hours the German battle fleet passed to the stern of the Grand Fleet and ended up in several running battles with British destroyers, only one of which even attempted to alert Jellicoe that his enemy was passing behind him. Over the course of these skirmishes the British lost several destroyers while the Germans lost one of their pre-dreadnought battleships and a pair of light cruisers. Remarkably the Germans passed within 4,000 yards of several of the British dreadnoughts, none of which opened fire or bothered to report to Jellicoe what was taking place. The commanders of these ships seem to have assumed that if they knew what was happening the commander in chief must also know and that since they had not received any orders to engage the enemy they assumed that Jellicoe had other plans for the Germans. As a result of this inexplicable inaction on the part of these, often quite senior, British officers, Scheer was able to reverse his geographic position and get between Jellicoe and the German bases. By the time dawn came and Jellicoe realized what had happened it was too late. He ordered his fleet to alter course in an effort to cut off the Germans but by the time the British reached the area of the Horns Reef, where the German minefields began, the High Seas Fleet had passed through those minefields and into port. Scheer had escaped. A disappointed Grand Fleet turned for home. The greatest clash of battleships in history was over.

The Germans quickly claimed victory on the basis that they had sunk more British ships than they themselves had lost, which was true. They sank 14 British vessels and lost only 11 of their own. In particular, in terms of the ships that mattered most, battle cruisers and battleships, the Germans had destroyed three British battle cruisers and in the end lost only one of their own when the badly damaged *Lützow* was unable to make it back to port. It was scuttled by its crew late on June 1st. In addition the Germans killed nearly 7,000 British sailors compared to a loss of only 3,000 of their own. Both Scheer and Hipper were praised by the German papers and by the Kaiser who awarded them both Germany's highest military honor, the Ordre pour le Mérite. Both men were also promoted, Scheer to admiral and Hipper to vice admiral. The initial reaction in Britain was similar to that in Germany; the battle was viewed as a defeat. The British had anticipated another Trafalgar and instead they received an, at best, inconclusive outcome that left the enemy fleet basically intact. However, if one looked deeper, things appeared quite different. The surviving German ships were so badly mauled that many of them required extensive repairs; some were not ready to return to sea again for six months and the fleet as a whole was not ready for further action until August of 1916. The Grand Fleet on the other hand, unlike the British battle cruisers and the super dreadnoughts, was very lightly damaged and Jellicoe was ready for further action within 48 hours. Furthermore the British were left in possession of the field of battle and nothing substantive had changed in the war at sea. The British therefore quickly came to assert that it was they, in fact, who had won the Battle of Jutland. The question of victory in this battle has been debated by historians ever since as well. So just who did win the Battle of Jutland?

While one could argue that the Germans won a tactical victory by sinking more ships than they lost what mattered for the outcome of the war was the strategic situation after the battle and in that regard there is no question that the Germans lost the Battle of Jutland, and, what is more, it was a decisive defeat. British control of the seas was completely unaffected by the loss of ships at Jutland. New construction quickly replaced the British losses and the numerical superiority of the British fleet was soon increased. The blockade was completely unaffected. The ability of the Entente to send supplies and men wherever they were needed was completely unaffected. The results of the battle confirmed for Scheer and many of the other German leaders that the High Seas Fleet could not hope to win a decisive victory against the Grand Fleet. Only the submarines remained. If Germany was to win the war at sea they would have to unleash the submarines in a ruthless campaign of unrestricted submarine warfare, regardless of the diplomatic consequences. The outcome of Jutland led to the resurrection of Holtzendorff's claim that the submarines could win the war by sinking 600,000 tons of shipping every month for six months. After such heavy losses Britain would have no choice but to seek peace. Jutland, coupled with the defeats at Verdun and the Somme later that year, convinced the Kaiser and the new commanders of the German army, Generals Paul von Hindenburg and Erich Ludendorff, that Germany's only remaining hope for victory lay with the submarines. That view would lead to the playing of what they called "the last card" in February 1917, a gamble that would lead directly to the entry of the United States into the war and to Germany's defeat. To that end the Battle of Jutland was a decisive British victory. It meant that the Kaiser's precious fleet, which had done so much to bring Great Britain to the side of Germany's enemies, had suffered total defeat.

CHAPTER 5

The *Materialschlachten* of 1916

After their defeat in the Battle of the Marne the German armies on the Western Front and the Entente armies that opposed them engaged in the ultimately fruitless "race to the sea" in an effort to turn one another's flank. The end result of those 1914 campaigns was a series of trenches that ran quite literally from the coast of the English Channel and North Sea all the way to the border of Switzerland. The Western Front settled into stalemate.

The new head of the German General Staff, General Erich von Falkenhayn, looked at the German situation in late 1914 and realized that the kind of decisive victory that the Schlieffen-Moltke Plan was supposed to deliver was no longer feasible. Instead Germany would have to focus its efforts against just one of its foes in an effort to try and force that country to accept a separate peace. The strength of the defenses on the Western Front, the needs of his Austro-Hungarian ally, and the appeals of Generals Hindenburg and Ludendorff for additional men and materiel finally convinced a reluctant Falkenhayn that Germany should focus its efforts on the east in 1915. The result was a stunning series of victories that began with the Battle of Gorlice-Tarnow in May. That battle led to a series of successes that resulted in the Central Powers occupying all of Russian Poland, most of Lithuania, and parts of Latvia and White Russia, as well as parts of the Ukraine. The Russian army never completely recovered from the devastating blow that was dealt to it over these months. By the end of 1915 German forces were within 50 miles of Minsk and Riga.

The German victories in the east were matched by the failures of the British in the Middle East and at Gallipoli and the repeated failures of the French and British armies to make any headway against the German defenses in the west. This series of victories led to the entry of Bulgaria

into the war on the side of the Central Powers and with the aid of the
Bulgarians the Germans and Austro-Hungarians were able to overrun
Serbia in October 1915. However none of these victories, impressive as
they were, led to peace. The Russians remained in the war and significant
parts of the Serbian army escaped to Greece from where they would help
to bring about the ultimate defeat of the Central Powers. Therefore,
despite all the battlefield victories of 1915 the Germans found themselves
no closer to ultimate victory at the end of the year than they had been at
the start of it. Some other path would have to be found. Over the winter
of 1915 Falkenhayn concluded that the German army should begin to
substitute materiel, in particular high explosive shells, for manpower
and switch to a campaign of attrition. Over those same months the major
Entente commanders were coming to a similar conclusion. The combined
decisions of the two sides would result in the two most famous battles of
the war, battles that came to symbolize the futility of trench warfare:
the Battles of Verdun and the Somme. The Germans called them the
Materialschlachten, the battles of materiel, and they played a key role in
bringing on Germany's ultimate defeat.

Planning the Battles

The roots of the Battle of Verdun lay with General Falkenhayn. Following the failure of the victories in the east to bring about peace he
refocused his attention on what he had believed all along was the decisive theater of the war, the Western Front. He had become convinced,
as many Germans had, that Great Britain was the *Hauptfeind*, the main
enemy that Germany had to defeat if it was to win the war. The question was how to deal with Britain and here Falkenhayn believed he had
a two-pronged answer: the German navy would turn the submarines
loose on British and neutral shipping while the German army knocked
out Britain's primary ally, France. The latter was now to be achieved,
not by great sweeping encirclements as per the Schlieffen-Moltke plan,
but through attrition, the slow wearing away of the enemy's strength.[1]
This would be achieved by using heavy artillery to bombard the French
army's positions around the city and fortress complex of Verdun. Falkenhayn believed that the French would do everything they possibly
could to hold Verdun, a city of both historical and strategic importance, and that, therefore, his armies could "bleed the French white."
The capture of the city was a secondary goal; the primary goal was to
force the French to continually funnel fresh troops into Verdun where

they would be ground up by the meat grinder of the German heavy artillery. This would result, theoretically, in the breaking of France's will to continue the war. With the French army broken and their own commerce under dire threat from the submarines Britain would have little choice but to seek peace on German terms.

While the Battle of Verdun was born out of German frustration that their many tactical victories had not brought about strategic success, the Battle of the Somme was born out of the inability of the Anglo-French forces to win even tactical victories. The British and French armies had launched repeated and fruitless attacks against the German lines throughout 1915 in a vain effort to aid their Russian ally. They had suffered hundreds of thousands of casualties for no appreciable gain. On the Entente side as well planning over the winter of 1915–16 shifted toward attrition. Joffre realized that the Entente would have to wear down the German army and deplete its reserves before the Entente could win a decisive victory of its own and break the Western Front stalemate. This would be achieved with a series of well-coordinated offensives on every front. The planning for these simulta-neous offensives began at the Chantilly conference in December 1915. At this conference the British, French, and Italian commanders, along with representatives of the Russian commanders, agreed to launch nearly simultaneous attacks in the forthcoming summer. The hope was that a series of such strikes would prevent the Central Powers from using their interior lines to shuffle forces from quiet fronts to threat-ened ones and would, ideally, wear out the armies of Germany and Austria-Hungary. The Anglo-French contribution was to come at the Somme River.

By this time the "New Armies," the volunteer forces raised by Lord Kitchener over the course of 1914 and 1915, were arriving in France in large numbers. As a result the new British commander, Douglas Haig, was willing and able to play a far more significant role in this new offen-sive than the role British army had played in most of 1915. Despite his and his soldiers' eagerness however Joffre's plan called for the French armies to play the lead role in the offensive. The British would be given a supporting position. This offensive, like the German offensive at Ver-dun, was to rely very heavily on the use of artillery to pulverize the German defenses and, hopefully, kill the German forces manning those defenses. The Entente was forced to make significant and sudden changes in its planning though when, on February 21, the Germans launched their strike at Verdun.

Prologue to Armageddon

By February 1916 the French city and fortress system of Verdun formed a hinge in the French defensive line. The German lines extended around the northern and eastern edges of the city and then to the west and to the south, leaving the city and its fortifications facing German forces on three sides. Falkenhayn's plan was to use massive German artillery barrages to destroy the French defenders of the forts; he did not intend to take the city itself. German artillery would pour into the salient, creating an inferno of shrapnel and high explosives that would destroy the forts and their defenders. German artillery would also fire onto the roads behind the French positions and onto any French units that were sent up those roads and into the cauldron. Falkenhayn's plan was altered by Crown Prince Wilhelm though. The Kaiser's eldest son, who commanded the Fifth Army and was responsible for carrying out the attack, wanted the glory of capturing the city of Verdun, so he altered Falkenhayn's basic design to include the capture of Verdun itself. This change meant that the German army would not simply rely on its artillery to butcher French soldiers but that it would leave the protection of its trenches and assault the fortified French positions. It was a significant change; it altered the entire focus of the offensive and meant that the Germans would also take heavy casualties in the fighting.

The German offensive began with a massive barrage of more than 1,200 heavy guns raining death onto a sector of the front that covered only 8 miles.[2] This barrage continued for 9 hours and devastated the French front line. The German infantry launched their assault that afternoon and by the end of the first day some German units had penetrated as far as 2 miles into the French lines. The assault was aided by one of the deadly new weapons of the war, deadly to both the man wielding it and the enemy he aimed it at, the flamethrower. Over the course of the ensuing three days the German offensive drove the French lines back far enough that the Germans could begin assaulting the fortresses directly. On February 25, the first of these forts, Fort Douaumont, was captured. The fort quickly became a symbol to both sides and its capture was celebrated in Germany as a sign that the French army was breaking and that the war was soon going to be won. It was met in France with shock for the same reason, since it appeared to signal the imminent fall of Verdun. The French reaction was exactly what Falkenhayn had hoped for; the French committed themselves to holding Verdun, regardless of the cost. Verdun came to symbolize France itself.

Joffre quickly appointed a new commander, General Henri Philippe Pétain, to take charge of the defense of the threatened sector. Pétain's own determination stiffened the resolve of the French defenders. He began bringing up additional artillery and reserves along the roads behind the French lines, but his most important contribution was to rotate French units in and out of the battle rather than leaving exhausted units in the line for extended periods of time. This meant that by the time the battle ended 259 of 330 French regiments fought at Verdun.[3] This kept the troops somewhat fresh but also meant that every unit bled, prodigiously.

Over the course of the next several weeks as the French reserves and artillery moved in and the German barrages and assaults continued the struggle became a bloodbath. Over the course of March the fighting extended all the way around the Verdun sector as the French launched a series of counterattacks to try and recapture the territory the Germans had just seized. The German artillery inflicted massive damage on the French armies but the French did the same to the Germans as the battle escalated. The struggle raged on through March and April and the area around Verdun became a charnel house. One French soldier described it thus, "Everywhere there were distended bodies that your feet sank into. The stench of death hung over the jumble of decaying corpses like some hellish perfume."[4] As April wore on and the French defenses stiffened the German victories of February and March became distant memories and the battle settled into stalemate. By the end of April the Germans had lost 89,000 men and the French 133,000.[5]

Over the course of May the casualties continued to mount and German morale began to sink as it became increasingly clear that Verdun would not be captured. The last German victory came in May with the fall of another French fort, Fort Vaux, but by June the momentum of the German assault had been blunted and it was clear that Verdun would hold. Though the capture of the city had never been his goal Falkenhayn's grand plan became linked to the capture of the French city and when that clearly became impossible the plan was deemed a failure and Falkenhayn lost the favor of his subordinates and, most importantly, the Kaiser. As the slaughter raged on through June with no end in sight the first fruits were born of the Chantilly conference when the Russians, led by General Alexei Brusilov, launched an unexpected offensive against the Austro-Hungarian forces on the Eastern Front. The Russian attack enjoyed great initial successes and Falkenhayn was forced to shift several divisions from the Verdun sector to the east, a decision that marked, in effect, the end of the German offensive. That blow was followed by the beginning of a massive artillery barrage along the Somme sector in late June, a barrage that presaged the launching of the Entente's great western offensive of 1916. These blows drove the Germans onto the defensive in the west and marked the end of Falkenhayn's plan and, ultimately, his command.

In July, once the Anglo-French offensive at the Somme began, the French forces in the Verdun sector were able to go over to the offensive as well. Their counterattacks would continue all the way into December, making the Battle of Verdun the longest battle of the entire war. By the time the fighting on the Verdun sector ended in December 1916 the French had retaken forts Vaux and Douaumont and had driven the German army back to its original positions. After nearly 11 months of fighting, the lines were, essentially, back to where they were at the start of the offensive. The cost to achieve this stalemate was enormous, on both sides. The French lost 377,000 men and the Germans 330,000.[6] Verdun became a symbol of the futility of trench warfare. Though the French held Verdun and Falkenhayn eventually lost his job partly as a result of that fact, he did accomplish, at least in part, his main objective: the French army was very nearly bled white. It never completely recovered from the bloodletting at Verdun. In the spring of 1917 a series of mutinies took place in the French army. They were caused by the futility of the fighting. Though the French weathered that storm and ultimately prevailed in the First World War the shadow of Verdun would extend over the entire interwar period and would even have an impact in the Second World War when France's great hero of Verdun, General Pétain, would lead the French government into an armistice with Hitler's Germany, following the defeats of May and June 1940.

For the German army the price was simply too high. After the great successes of 1915 Verdun demonstrated that the Germans did not possess the same superiority in weapons, training, and effectiveness against the British and French as they did against the Russians and Serbians. Most importantly, rather than outgunning their enemies in artillery, as they did on the Eastern Front, in the west it was the Germans who were outgunned. That meant the Germans could not substitute men for materiel as effectively as their enemies could. Verdun was an initial introduction to this reality and it came as a shock to the German commanders and soldiers alike. What happened in the valley of the River Somme, starting in late June 1916, came as an even bigger shock.

Armageddon Unleashed

The German assault on Verdun, though not unexpected, did force the British and French commanders to alter their own plans for 1916. The initial conception for the Entente's assault had been for the French forces, led by Ferdinand Foch, to play the lead role and the British New Armies to play a supporting role. The British army was to wear down the German forces along the Somme sector with a series of heavy assaults that would pull in the German Western Front reserves. This was essentially the same concept that lay behind the German assault on Verdun. Then, when the German army had been sufficiently worn down by the British, the French would launch a massive assault on their own portion of the Somme sector, which would break through the German lines and win the war in 1916. The French losses at Verdun however forced the British to take on the major role in the offensive. In the new plan both British and French forces along the Somme would take part in the initial wearing down operations and then the British would break through the German lines and end the stalemate in the west.

The planning of the actual offensive fell to the new British commander, Douglas Haig. In some ways his plan resembled the German plan for Verdun: the basic concept was to substitute materiel for manpower and to make maximum use of heavy artillery to destroy the enemy. At that point the two plans diverged however. Rather than seeking to bleed the Germans white, Haig sought to annihilate them and clear the way for a major advance. To accomplish these goals the British prepared the largest artillery barrage ever seen, one that would dwarf the German barrage that launched the assault on Verdun and would shock the German generals with its intensity and its duration. The barrage was made possible by the mobilization of the British economy that had been accomplished under David Lloyd George's Ministry of Munitions. The British assembled 1,500 guns for the barrage and amassed more than 2 million shells. Unlike the German barrage, which lasted for several hours, the British barrage was to last for at least five days.[7]

The extensive barrage was necessary because the Entente forces were attacking one of the most strongly defended positions on the entire German front. The German position consisted of a series of three consecutive deep trenches dug into the chalky soil of the region, with several underground dugouts, some as far as 30 feet underground, where up to 25 men could shelter from artillery barrages.[8] The trenches were separated by roughly 200 yards with the front trench lightly held and the main forces based in the second trench with reserves in the third. In front of these trenches were barbed wire entanglements sometimes as much as 10 feet in depth.[9] The German defensive system was designed to expose as few men as possible to enemy artillery. They anticipated that the lightly held front trench would be lost if the Entente launched a massive offensive and that their forces in the second trench would then have to retake it in a series of counterattacks. In the counterattacks the Entente forces would be beyond the range of their own artillery and under fire by German artillery. This would make it very difficult if not impossible for the Entente to withstand the counterattacks and as a result the offensive would fail. The British hoped to deal with this by pulverizing the German front lines so that their attackers would take no or only minimal losses before being faced with the German counterattack. While the British forces advanced and took the initial German line, the Entente artillery would be brought further forward to range on the German second line.

The barrage began on June 24 and lasted, around the clock, for five days. In those five days the British expended over 1.5 million shells. Interspersed with the heavy artillery shells were a number of chlorine gas shells. The bombardment, devastating as it was, could have been much worse. Many of the British shells were duds and the majority were shrapnel, which had no effect on those German soldiers who were in dugouts below the lines. As a result the bombardment failed in its fundamental objective, it did not destroy the German frontline defenders. However, for those subjected to it the barrage was unending hell. One German soldier wrote "One's head is like a madman's. The tongue sticks to the mouth in terror. Continual bombardment and nothing to eat or drink and little sleep for five days and nights. How much longer can this go on?"[10] Many German soldiers went mad from the endless barrage.

In the early morning hours of July 1st the barrage intensified as the British honed in on key areas of the German lines, and then, at 7:20 AM, an enormous explosion shook the battlefield as the British detonated one of a series of 10 mines they had placed in tunnels that had been dug beneath the German lines. An observer wrote,

> The ground where I stood gave a mighty convulsion. It rocked and swayed . . . Then for all the world like a gigantic sponge, the earth rose high in the air to the height of hundreds of feet. Higher and higher it rose, and with horrible grinding roar the earth settles [sic] back upon itself, leaving in its place a mountain of smoke.[11]

Nine additional mines were also set off, signaling the onset of the British offensive. The surviving German soldiers now poured out of their dugouts and raced to their defensive positions as the British infantry, many of them from the relatively lightly trained New Armies, began leaving the safety of their own trenches and entering no-man's-land. These British forces were heavily weighed down with equipment and could only slowly move across the nearly 800 yards of open ground between their lines and the German positions, which were on high ground to the east. As a result they made excellent targets for the German gunners when the latter reached their machine guns. Furthermore the German artillery, which was behind the front lines, had mostly survived the barrage intact. Since those guns were pre-sited on no-man's-land and could now open fire the result was a slaughter, the single worst day in British military history. On this one single day 20,000 British soldiers were killed, with another 40,000 wounded or missing, which usually meant that they had been obliterated by an artillery shell and no remains were ever found. The New Armies were completely unprepared for what awaited them and the result was slaughter on an industrial scale.

The offensive had gotten off to a calamitous start, one that scarred the psyche of the British nation and continues to resonate to this day as a symbol for disaster and poor planning. It helped give rise to the notion that the British army were "lions led by donkeys" and that Haig and the other British generals were little more than butchers, throwing their men needlessly into the meat grinder. The tragedy was made even worse by the fact that many of the units consisted of what were called Pals' battalions, units of men who enlisted in 1915 when the British army, in order to encourage more volunteers, began promising that if you enlisted together you would serve together. As a result large groups of young men went off to enlist with their "pals." Some were coworkers; many, like a young J.R.R. Tolkien and several of his closest friends,[12] were young academics. Still others were friends who grew up together and went off to fight together, resulting in entire towns losing most or even all of their young men on this one devastating day. As a result of the disaster, much discussion of the Somme centers on the horrors of that first day. Doing so though skews our view of the battle. The battle did not end on that first day; it lasted for several more months and in the end it was a victory for the British, though not the kind of victory that the generals and the British people wanted.

Though July 1st was an unmitigated disaster for the British the more-experienced French troops had enjoyed success on that day, seizing all of their first-day objectives and advancing over 1 mile east in some places. By the end of that first day the Germans had suffered 10,000 of their own

casualties and their frontline positions had been reduced to ruins, with
even some second-line trenches having largely been destroyed. The British and French resumed their assault on the next day and over the course
of the ensuing two weeks they inflicted enormous casualties on the Germans. Over the course of early July the Entente forces captured roughly
20 square miles of ground. Falkenhayn insisted that his men launch
immediate counterattacks to retake each piece of lost terrain. No ground
was to be left in the hands of the enemy. This led to a series of heated and
desperate battles in and around the German first- and second-trench
lines. The Somme quickly became, as had Verdun, a massive killing
ground for the men of both sides.

On July 14th one of the "donkeys," General Henry Rawlinson, demonstrated that he had learned something over the previous weeks when he
launched a surprise night attack, preceded not by a heavy and long-
lasting artillery barrage but by a short, sudden, and accurate barrage, what
came to be known as a "hurricane barrage." This assault on the German
second line was a resounding success and resulted in the capture of
6,000 yards worth of territory. The offensive eventually ran out of
momentum and there was still no breakthrough, which led to further
recriminations against the British generals, but the Entente was beginning to wear down the German defenses and pull in and destroy their
reserves. The same thing that the Germans had done to the French at
Verdun was now being done to them. In fact, these offensives were what
finally ended the German assault at Verdun because Falkenhayn was
forced to send several reserve divisions from the Verdun sector to the
Somme front. The German plan to win the war in 1916 had failed.

The slaughter raged throughout July and August. The Germans took a
further 250,000 casualties over those two months,[13] and the morale of the
German army began to break as the individual German soldier could not
help but be impressed by the Entente's sheer superiority in numbers of
guns and shells. The mounting casualties, combined with the failure of
the offensive at Verdun and the Russian revival during the Brusilov
Offensive, convinced the Rumanian government that the time had come
to enter the war and on August 27th it declared war on Austria-Hungary,
opening a new front in the east. The German government responded by
declaring war on Rumania on August 28th. The Rumanian move was
the final straw for those, such as Chancellor Theobald von Bethmann-
Hollweg, who wanted to remove Falkenhayn. On August 29, Falkenhayn
was fired as head of the General Staff and was replaced by the hero of the
Battle of Tannenberg, Paul von Hindenburg. Falkenhayn was sent to the

Rumanian front to take charge of a new German force. He would lead that force in a victorious campaign that fall, which ended with the Central Powers occupying all of Rumania. For his part Hindenburg, accompanied by his aide, Erich Ludendorff, would quickly come to dominate not only the military side of the war but also the political and diplomatic sides. By the summer of 1917, he and Ludendorff would be de facto military dictators.

What the two men, who had long argued with Falkenhayn over whether the Eastern or Western Front was more important, quickly discovered was that Falkenhayn had been right: the Western Front was indeed the more critical of the two. The immediate problem they had to address was the growing disaster at the Somme where the constant pressure of the British and French offensive was slowly grinding away at the German army and pushing it east. While they considered their options the fighting continued and over the course of September the Germans suffered another 220,000 casualties on the Somme.[14] German morale took yet another blow when the British unveiled a new weapon, the tank, on September 15. The new weapon spread panic among the German soldiers when it first appeared. Fortunately for the Germans the British did not possess sufficient numbers of tanks or the reserves to follow them to fully sunder the German position; however, since the Germans did not have any tanks at all, this was further evidence to the German frontline soldier of the superior weaponry of his enemies. Hindenburg and Ludendorff had to do something, and quickly. Their response, and it was the only decision they could really make, was to abandon the very ground their men had been dying to defend over the last three months. In the short term the German soldiers would have to try and hold their ground while a new defensive position would be constructed along a shortened line between 15 and 20 miles to the rear of the current front. This was to be known as the Hindenburg Line, and when completed in early 1917, it shortened the German line considerably and freed several divisions from frontline duty. This allowed the general to create a new strategic reserve. Construction on the new position began in September 1916 and was completed in March 1917. In the interim the slaughter on the Somme and Verdun battlefields continued throughout October before finally grinding to a halt in November due to the inclement weather of fall and the mutual exhaustion of the armies.

The final casualty lists for 1916, for all three nations, were monstrous. In addition to the 330,000 men lost at Verdun, the Germans lost another 680,000 at the Somme, bringing the year's Western Front casualties to over 1 million men. Their enemies paid an enormous price of their own. The French lost 200,000 at the Somme to join the nearly 380,000 they had lost at Verdun and the British lost nearly 420,000 at the Somme.[15] As important and significant as the casualty figures are, the significance of these two battles runs much deeper.

The Impact of the *Materialschlacten*

To the general public and the governments of the Entente countries, the Battle of the Somme was not viewed as a victory. The hope that the battle would lead to a great breakthrough and the end of the war was shattered. Instead the battle was seen as little more than a calamitous loss of life. In particular, to a public that measured victory and defeat not in the slow erosion of the enemy's fighting strength but in the dramatic capture of territory, the achievements of the British and French armies at the Somme paled in comparison to the German overrunning of Rumania that fall. More professional observers knew better and understood that the battle had indeed been an Entente victory; in fact some referred to it as the turning point of the war. Perception, as it often does, trumped reality however, and as a result someone had to pay for what were seen as the failures of the Entente armies.

In France Joffre was replaced by Robert Nivelle, commander of the French Second Army at Verdun. Nivelle's men, in a series of counterattacks in the fall, recaptured much of the ground that had been lost to the Germans earlier in the year. His successes compared favorably in the public mind with the limited gains made at the Somme, though no one bothered to ask whether or not he would have had such success if the Germans had not had to send many of their reserves from Verdun to the Somme sector. Nonetheless Joffre was out and Nivelle was in. The shake-up was even greater in Britain where the losses at the Somme brought down the government of Herbert Henry Asquith and its replacement with a new government led by David Lloyd George. Surprisingly, Haig not only kept his command; he was promoted to field marshal. Haig remained convinced that the war would be decided in France and as a result he and Lloyd George would have serious disputes over strategy in 1917. The new prime minister was horrified by the losses of 1916 and was a committed "easterner" who wanted the British army to launch offensives in the Middle East against the Turks and to leave most of the heavy fighting on the continent to Britain's allies. The political and military changes brought about in the Entente nations by the losses of 1916, significant as they were, paled in comparison to the impact these battles had in Germany.

The Materialschlachten, in particular the Battle of the Somme, were disasters for the German army. In the German case, as with that of the Entente, the true results of the battle were hidden from ordinary observers by the relatively small amount of territory that was lost and the great victory that was won over Rumania. Those in the know however, such as the new commanders Hindenburg and Ludendorff, understood the true significance of what had happened. The German reserves had been seriously depleted and hundreds of thousands of experienced, well-trained men had been lost. These men could be "replaced"; the 1918 draft class was called to the colors early to make up for some of the losses, and the army went through those men who had previously been exempted from service for munitions work or other vital work on the home front and pulled some of them to the battlefront as well, but these replacements could not replace the experience, training, and esprit de corps of those who had been killed. Hindenburg was able to recreate a German reserve of more than 1 million men by the spring of 1917 but he could only do so by ordering a retreat to the Hindenburg Line, thereby shortening the front significantly. In short, the loss of manpower in these battles was critical.

The morale of the ordinary German soldier, civilian, and the new commanders alike was also severely damaged by the events of 1916. The hopes for victory that had been raised by the fall of Fort Douaumont had been dashed and a new sense of pessimism and depression set in both in the front lines and at home. On the part of both soldiers and civilians the hopes for an early victory were long gone by the winter of 1916–17 and they were replaced by a grim determination to hold out to the bitter end. Much of the turn in morale was due to the superiority of the British in particular in artillery and firepower. To counteract that superiority Hindenburg and Ludendorff concluded that German industry would have to drastically increase its output of munitions. That led to the creation of the Hindenburg Plan, an ultimately disastrous plan to rapidly expand Germany's supplies of munitions and guns.

Under the plan, which was unveiled on August 31, the output of munitions was to be doubled, from 6,000 tons per month to 12,000 tons per month by the spring of 1917. In addition the output of machine guns and artillery pieces was to be tripled. To accomplish this feat, new munitions factories were to be built. What Hindenburg hoped was that the increased production of munitions could be used to offset the manpower losses Germany had taken. The plan also called for a total mobilization of German society behind the war effort, similar to the mass mobilization undertaken by the French in the early wars of the French Revolution and to what Josef Goebbels would call for 26 years later. All German men were to be harnessed in some way for the war effort.

The plan was completely unrealistic. First of all, German industry had already been rationalized in 1914 under the War Raw Materials Department, which was led by Walther Rathenau. The *Kriegsrohstoffabteilung* (KRA) and German industry as a whole had two fundamental problems that were not addressed at all by the Hindenburg Plan; these were shortages of coal and manpower. These shortages could not be addressed without radical change, such as the large-scale recruitment of German women into the labor force. There was really no way for German industry to reach the numbers Hindenburg was aiming at.[16]

The latter part of the Hindenburg Plan led to the creation of the Patriotic Auxiliary Service Law. This law was motivated both by what the army saw as the needs of German industry and by the existence of a major problem that was wearing away at frontline morale. The problem was that wages for workers in war industry were rising and those men who remained home were getting better pay while the men at the front were suffering and dying. This was due to the shortage of skilled manpower and the willingness of the German government to pay whatever price German industrialists demanded for their goods. Those two factors created a situation in which German industrialists could pay larger wages and still make profits far above what they would have made in peacetime. That created fierce competition among the companies for skilled labor. German skilled workers naturally took advantage of the situation. As a result they were able to hold their own economically and have their wages keep pace with inflation while most Germans, including the soldiers and their families, saw the war erode their standards of living. This was a serious blow to morale. The Patriotic Auxiliary Service Law sought to deal with the problem by introducing compulsory labor for all men between the ages of 17 and 60. This would also prevent German skilled workers from leaving one job for another that paid better and would end the competition between German businesses for those workers. However, Ludendorff, the primary inspiration for the law, wanted the law passed by the Reichstag as a sign of national unity. According to the German constitution this was not necessary; the Bundestag was the law-making body. Ludendorff's decision meant that the Social Democratic Party, the largest political party in Germany and the dominant party in the Reichstag, would have a large say in whether or not the law passed. The party members were reluctant to give up a vital right of all laborers, the right to change their job, because of the power it would hand to the owners of industry. As a result they refused to pass the law unless some provision was included that would allow workers to leave their current job if they could attain higher wages at another position. Unable to get sufficient Socialist votes for the law without some kind of concession the government agreed to a compromise. Arbitration boards would be set up for German industry. These boards would have representatives from labor, industry, and the government. Any worker who received an offer of higher pay from a company other than one's own would be allowed to petition the board for the right to take the new job. The compromise was accepted and the law was passed. In practice though, the arbitration boards completely defeated this purpose of the law. They nearly always sided with labor and as a result very little changed.

The Hindenburg Plan also required that all suitable factories be converted to military use and that the labor and raw materials that were going to the production of civilian goods be transferred instead to military production. Going further it also required that smaller, less-efficient factories as well as nonessential businesses be shut down for the duration of the war in order to increase efficiency in production. Lastly Hindenburg also insisted that Belgians and Poles living under German control be conscripted into labor service. The latter demand resulted in the German army forcibly deporting Belgians into Germany at the rate of roughly 20,000 per week in October 1916.

To oversee the implementation of the Patriotic Auxiliary Service Law and to manage the Hindenburg Plan as a whole a new body was created, the War Office. It was placed under the command of General Wilhelm Groener, the man who had overseen the use of the German railways during the mobilization of 1914. The War Office was technically subordinate to the War Ministry and was given the power to command the deputy commanding generals in the German provinces. Groener was given control over: the War Raw Materials Department; the Labor and War Substitutions Department, which had been overseeing the creation and use of ersatz products; and the Arms and Munitions Procurement Bureau.[17]

The Hindenburg Plan did not succeed. It in fact unleashed further chaos on the already troubled German home front. The first major problem with the plan was that no thought was given to the economic realities of Germany in late 1916. The program was a conglomeration of contradictory ideas, any one of which would have been nearly impossible to achieve given the conditions of Germany by this point. As it was the plan called for using vast quantities of steel to build enormous new munitions factories so that munitions production could be expanded even further in 1918. This was despite the fact that many German munitions plants were running at less than full capacity due to a shortage of workers and coal. The new factories were completely unnecessary. What was worse was that they consumed the same stocks of steel that were being earmarked for the production of new machine guns and artillery pieces. The plan also created confusion on the German railways and led to an overworking of the already strained transportation system. Steel that could have been used to maintain the lines and engines of the rail network was instead used to build munitions factories that would never come into service. As a result of a corresponding lack of maintenance the German railway system began to erode and break down. Yet another problem stemmed from the army's efforts to call up workers from war industry. Many German coal miners were conscripted and sent to the front, which helped to cause the massive coal shortage of the winter of 1916. In the end many of them had to be sent back home from the front to try and increase coal production.[18] The end result was that production actually declined over the winter of 1916–17. For example in August 1916, before the implementation of the Hindenburg Plan, German industry produced 1.4 million tons of steel. In February 1917 it produced just under 1.2 million tons. The production of munitions went up slightly, from 6,000 tons per month in August 1916 to 6,400 tons per month in February 1917. Neither figure was close to its target.[19] By January 1917 a key element of the plan was already being abandoned when Groener's office decided to stop the construction of new munitions plants. The results of the plan were best summed up by the minister of the interior, Karl Helfferich:

> The program was decreed by the military without examining whether or not it could be carried out. Today there are everywhere half-finished and finished factories that cannot produce because there is no coal and because there are no workers available. Coal and iron were expended for these constructions and the result is that munitions production would be greater today if no monster program had been set up but rather production had been demanded according to the capacity of those factories already existing.[20]

Helfferich was no doubt correct but what he suggests as the wiser course was made untenable by the impact that the British superiority in munitions at the Battle of the Somme had on the new German commander in chief. Hindenburg's reaction to that British superiority was that German industry had to match the output of British industry; it simply had to, whether it could or not was immaterial. As a result the Battle of the Somme helped to cause even greater economic dislocation in Germany than was already being caused by the British blockade.

Though all of these effects of the battle certainly harmed or limited the German war effort the greatest impact of the *Materialschlachten* was the panic that they sowed in the minds of the new German commanders. Hindenburg and Ludendorff, who had been ensconced on the Eastern Front since 1914 and had been the beneficiaries of German superiority in training, leadership, artillery, and munitions against the Russians, had no real conception of the very different style of fighting that was taking place in the west and how much more-evenly matched or even overmatched Germany was against its western foes. They then arrived in the midst of the heaviest fighting of the war and their confidence was clearly shaken by what they experienced. As a result they became convinced that Germany could only win the war by defeating Great Britain and that Britain could not be defeated on the battlefields of France; it would have to be defeated in the waters around Great Britain. They threw their tremendous clout and support behind the German navy's campaign to resume unrestricted submarine warfare. At the Pless conference in January 1917 it was their support for the submarine campaign that tipped the balance against Chancellor Theobald von Bethmann-Hollweg and swayed the Kaiser to the side of the navy. That decision ultimately sealed Germany's fate and it was a decision they were driven to take by what happened over the summer and fall on the battlefields of the Somme. Bloody and awful as it was the Battle of the Somme was a critical victory for the Entente and a key component in its victory over Germany. The German official history of the war, *Der Weltkrieg*, summed it up best, "The Somme was the muddy grave of the German field army."[21]

CHAPTER 6

The Tightening Blockade and the Unrestricted Submarine Campaign of 1917–1918

By late 1916 Imperial Germany had reached a crossroads. Though the Schlieffen-Moltke Plan had not led to the destruction of the French army and a quick German victory, the successful advance of August 1914 had left the Germans in control of virtually all of Belgium and many of the richest provinces of France. When the Germans turned their focus to the east in 1915 in order to support their failing Austro-Hungarian ally they won further dramatic victories, driving the Russians out of Poland and nearly out of Lithuania. By the end of 1915 Serbia had been overrun, Bulgaria had joined the Central Powers, and the Entente had suffered a series of defeats in France and a serious setback against the Ottoman Empire in the Gallipoli operation. Optimism pervaded the Oberste Heeres Leitung (OHL), the German supreme command. Eight months later the picture was very different. In the early summer of 1916 the High Seas Fleet tried to inflict a decisive defeat on the British Grand Fleet. That effort culminated in the Battle of Jutland, which, despite German protestations to the contrary, was a decisive defeat that left the Royal Navy firmly in control of the seas. Most importantly the battle left the British blockade that was slowly strangling the German economy and starving the German people intact to continue its slow, grinding work. Coupled with the failure of the navy was the failure of General Erich von Falkenhayn's plan to destroy the French army at Verdun. Though the Germans certainly did "bleed the French Army white" they did the same to their own forces in a battle that took on a life of its own and helped to cause Falkenhayn's dismissal later in 1916. An even more serious blow was dealt to the Germans on the battlefields of the Somme where the British demonstrated a superiority in materiel that shocked the German commanders.

Though the British sustained enormous losses in the Battle of the Somme and the battle left the British psyche badly scarred it also badly scarred the psyche of the German high command. The Somme, Verdun, and the entry of Rumania into the war led to the firing of Falkenhayn and his replacement by Paul von Hindenburg and Erich Ludendorff, the heroes of Tannenberg. Those two men, in particular Ludendorff, were shocked by the vast number of guns and the prodigious amounts of munitions the British were able to deploy at the Somme. They knew that German industry, as it existed, could not possibly match British output and this in turn led them to create the Hindenburg Plan, which did more to harm than help German industrial output. The British superiority in munitions was not lost on the German soldiers either and it dealt a severe blow to German morale. Just as important was the sheer number of German casualties incurred in 1916. Those losses convinced Hindenburg and Ludendorff that Germany could not continue to hold all the ground it had taken from France in 1914. Therefore they decided to construct a new and stronger fortified line in France and Belgium, the so-called Hindenburg Line, which they pulled back to early in 1917. Things had even taken a turn for the worse on the Eastern Front where the Austro-Hungarian armies had been driven back by a major Russian offensive that was only stopped by the intervention of German troops; that success led to Rumania entering the war on the side of the Entente. Though Rumania was quickly overrun, briefly restoring some of the lost German morale, conditions at home soon eroded that optimism. The failure of the potato crop in the fall of 1916 brought on what was called the turnip winter, a winter of enormous suffering that led to the first strikes and protests against the continuation of the war. The German position, which looked strong from the outside, looked increasingly desperate to those running the country. To them, the chancellor, the new commanders, the naval leaders, and the Kaiser, defeat appeared to be inevitable unless Great Britain could be driven from the war. There appeared to be only one weapon capable of striking effectively at the British, the submarines.

Over the late summer and fall of 1916 the submarines had been held out to the German public as a potentially war-winning weapon, which the chancellor was not allowing the generals and admirals to use for fear of offending the United States. As the winter wore on and conditions worsened in Germany the question of whether or not the submarines should be turned loose against British shipping became increasingly urgent. By January 1917 this question consumed the German leadership. Men on both sides understood, correctly, that Germany's fate hung in the balance.

The Debate over Unrestricted Submarine Warfare

The debate over whether or not to resume unrestricted submarine warfare had raged in the background throughout much of 1916. The basic question at stake was whether or not the possibility of victory over Britain was worth the near certainty of war with the United States. That question led inevitably to others. Did Germany actually possess enough submarines to create an effective blockade? Could those submarines really sink so much shipping that Britain would be forced to come to the table and negotiate? Would resuming the submarine campaign lead to war with the United States? If it did would it matter as long as the submarines could defeat Great Britain? On one side in the debate stood Chancellor Theobald von Bethmann-Hollweg. Bethmann-Hollweg had no illusions regarding the position of the U.S. government on unrestricted submarine warfare. The two nations had already been through two severe diplomatic crises over this issue and the German ambassador in Washington, D.C., Count Johann von Bernstorff, kept him well informed of President Woodrow Wilson's views on the war as a whole and on submarine warfare specifically. Bernstorff made it abundantly clear to Bethmann-Hollweg that a renewal of unrestricted submarine warfare would mean war with the United States. Bethmann-Hollweg, unlike most of the German military men, had a healthy respect for American power, not only military but economic. It was American economic pressure that was keeping the blockade from being as tight and effective as the British wanted it to be and he was aware that this would change if the United States formally joined Germany's enemies. For that reason Bethmann-Hollweg was determined to do everything he could to keep the submarines working under prize rules.

Bethmann-Hollweg was opposed by Hindenburg and Ludendorff; both of them were convinced that the submarines had to be turned loose if Germany was to win the war. Hindenburg and Ludendorff were painfully aware of the weakness of Germany's military position, in particular with regard to Germany's allies. The Austro-Hungarians had performed terribly in the war, suffering defeat after defeat against the Russians, and would have been soundly defeated but for German support; as a result by late 1916 there was growing sentiment for peace in the Austro-Hungarian Empire. Further complicating matters was the death of the old emperor, Franz Joseph, in November 1916. His passing deprived the empire of its one major unifying force. Without him the multinational empire began to come apart at the seams. Conditions were not much better with Germany's other allies, Bulgaria and the Ottoman Empire. Hindenburg and Ludendorff doubted that Germany's allies could withstand another year of war. Both men were also aware that Germany itself was inferior to its Western Front foes in the production of munitions and by January 1917 it was slowly becoming clear that the Hindenburg Plan was not going to succeed. From their perspective the German position would only get worse as the war went on. The conclusion they drew was not that Germany should negotiate a compromise peace settlement from a position of strength, which would have been difficult, but that Germany had to employ this last possible war-winning weapon to defeat the British before it was too late. Neither man had much respect for the military potential of the United States. They knew the United States had a pitifully small army. It also had the third strongest fleet in the world but since the German battle fleet was already badly outclassed by the British, adding the American fleet into the equation would not fundamentally change matters. As for the economic perspective, as far as they were concerned the United States was effectively already a belligerent. They looked at the amount of money that the United States was loaning to the Entente and the quantity of American goods that were being purchased by the Entente and argued that the United States was already economically at war with Germany. In turn they discounted the pressure that the American government was putting on the British, pressure that was keeping open the neutrals loophole and preventing the blockade from being fully effective. As a result those men were willing to accept American entry into the war. They believed, based on what the navy told them, that the submarines would defeat the British before the United States could really bring its latent power to bear. Even if they proved to be wrong they felt they had little to lose. In Ludendorff's own words, "It has to be. We expect war with America and have made all preparations [for it]. *Things cannot get worse.*"[1]

The most critical figure in the debate was Admiral Henning von Holtzendorff. It was Holtzendorff who provided the answer as to whether or not the submarines could force Britain to make peace. In his mind there was no doubt: the answer was yes. Holtzendorff and his staff had undertaken an exhaustive study of British and neutral shipping and had compiled a 200-page report in which they argued, with mathematical precision, that the submarines would indeed force Britain to make peace within six months. Their report examined the amount of shipping available to Britain, the amount of cargo space in those ships, the relative prices of goods on the world markets, the costs of insurance on both ships and goods, and the degree to which Britain could supply itself internally. Their conclusion was that the British required 10.75 million tons of shipping, both British and neutral, in order to keep themselves supplied. The total amount of shipping available to Britain was estimated at 15.25 million tons. Holtzendorff, the author of the report, assumed that at least 1 million tons of neutral shipping would be frightened off the oceans once the Germans announced the resumption of unrestricted submarine warfare, leaving 14.25 million. That meant that, if the submarines could sink 600,000 tons of shipping every month, it would only take six months to reduce the available shipping below the magic number of 10.75 million tons. Holtzendorff argued that such a catastrophic loss of shipping would lead to such hardships in Great Britain that the British would be forced to make peace.[2]

The report that Holtzendorff was asking the government to stake the German fate on had numerous flaws, some of which should have been obvious and others that only appeared in hindsight. First of all the report ignored the fact that up to this point the British had not even been forced to begin a system of rationing. The German people had been suffering hardship and privation for over two years by late 1916 and continued to support the war. It was unrealistic and foolish to assume that the British people would immediately force their government to make peace if they suffered any inconvenience at all. Second, the report overestimated the amount of shipping that was necessary to supply Great Britain and the impact that unrestricted submarine warfare would have on neutral shipping. Third, the report failed to take into account the large number of German merchant ships that had been interred in neutral harbors, particularly in the United States, which would be seized and forced into Entente service if the United States entered the war. In effect Holtzendorff crafted a report that was designed not to present an accurate picture of the pros and cons of submarine warfare but to convince the Kaiser and the OHL that the submarines would certainly succeed. To that end he ignored any evidence that would cast any doubt on the ability of the submarines to achieve victory. Holtzendorff presented the submarine campaign as a certainty, a guarantee of Germany's salvation. It was a message that Hindenburg and Ludendorff, and the German people, badly wanted to hear. Bethmann-Hollweg, however, stubbornly refused to agree and, for a time, the Kaiser sided with him.

As fall turned to winter however and the German potato harvest failed, the pressure to act became overwhelming. Bethmann-Hollweg was eventually driven into a compromise. Seeing the direction things were heading the chancellor asked to be allowed to float a peace offer to the Entente and that while the peace offer was on the table the submarines would not be used. Hindenburg and Ludendorff agreed but extracted a promise from Bethmann-Hollweg that if the peace offer failed, and they were certain that it would, he would then withdraw his opposition to the submarine campaign. With the army's consent secured the German government sent a peace note to the Entente on December 12th. In the note they offered to begin negotiations aimed at ending the war. As the generals expected the peace feeler went nowhere; the Entente was utterly unwilling to talk peace while it believed it had the upper hand. Historians have debated ever since whether Bethmann-Hollweg was sincere in making this offer or whether it was a purely cynical ploy to demonstrate to the neutrals that the Germans had tried to make peace and that, since their enemies refused to talk, they now had no choice but to use all the means they possessed, including submarines, to defend themselves. For Hindenburg and Ludendorff the peace note was clearly the latter. For Bethmann-Hollweg it appears to have been a sincere attempt to save his nation from what he perceived as a looming disaster. Whichever it was, its failure cleared the decks for the resumption of unrestricted submarine warfare.

The chancellor was thrown a lifeline and given a final chance to avert what he was convinced would be disaster when the newly reelected American president, Woodrow Wilson, circulated his own peace note, asking the belligerent nations to list their war aims so that he could try to come up with a workable compromise that could end the war. Bethmann-Hollweg grasped at this chance but the very premise of it was rejected by the generals and the Kaiser. From their perspective any peace mediated by the American president would rob Germany of its justly won spoils and would make the sacrifices of the war meaningless. It was far better to continue the war and use the submarines to attain a German peace than to accept a compromise peace negotiated by the American president. As a result the German government sent a reply that reaffirmed its desire for peace but which refused to list any concrete war aims. This was a colossal failure of German diplomacy based on an overly optimistic reading of their position. Hindenburg and Ludendorff were so confident that the submarines would succeed that they refused to even consider the possibility of a negotiated peace. This would not be the last such error in judgment. Unfortunately for Bethmann-Hollweg and for Germany, the failure of the American president's initiative meant that the resumption of unrestricted submarine warfare was all but certain.

The final decision was made on January 8, 1917, at a meeting in Pless where Bethmann-Hollweg was presented with a united front of military and naval leaders, all determined to turn the submarines loose. By this time they had won the Kaiser to their side. Bethmann-Hollweg argued his case, warning of American intervention, only to have Holtzendorff give his word that the submarines would not only defeat the British, but would also prevent any Americans from ever reaching Europe (which was a remarkable claim considering that no German ship or submarine had to date prevented the shipping of a single British, Canadian, Australian, Indian, New Zealander, or French soldier). Eventually the chancellor accepted that he was beaten and acquiesced in the decision to resume unrestricted submarine warfare on February 1. It was the most fateful decision the German government had taken since the end of the Battle of the Marne. Even the men who most strongly supported the campaign called it "the last card," the final chance for Germany to attain a "German peace." With this decision they embarked on their second great gamble of the war; as with the implementation of the Schlieffen-Moltke Plan, this was an all-or-nothing throw of the dice. Either it would lead to a complete German victory or it would bring about conditions that would almost certainly lead to Germany's complete defeat.

The American Reaction

Bernstorff learned of the Pless decision on January 19th, while President Wilson was still hopeful that he could bring the two sides to the negotiating table. Bernstorff's pleas to his own government to postpone the campaign fell on deaf ears and on January 31 the ambassador presented notification to the U.S. government that unrestricted submarine warfare would resume on the following day. Wilson's reaction came very quickly. On February 3, the American president ordered an end to diplomatic relations with Germany, sending Bernstorff back to Germany and recalling the American ambassador, James Gerard. There was no immediate American declaration of war however. Even when American ships began being sunk by German submarines, the president was still reluctant to take the final step toward war. The final push that drove Wilson to ask for a declaration of war came from the German foreign ministry.

The ministry was under new leadership in early 1917; the previous minister, Gottlieb von Jagow, had resigned in November 1916 partly for health reasons and partly over the pressure to resume unrestricted submarine warfare, which he strongly opposed. He was replaced by Arthur Zimmermann, a powerful advocate for the submarine campaign. Following the Pless decision Zimmermann concocted a plan of his own to keep the Americans too busy on their side of the Atlantic to interfere in Europe. On January 16th he sent a telegram to the German ambassador to Mexico, instructing the ambassador to offer the Mexican government an alliance, proposing that, if the two nations defeated the United States, Mexico would receive Texas, Arizona, and New Mexico as its share of the spoils. The telegram, which became known as the Zimmermann Telegram, was decoded by Room 40 and kept under wraps by the British government until February 23rd when it was handed to the American ambassador in London. An outraged President Wilson released the note to the American press on February 28. There was some speculation that the telegram might have been concocted by the British government, speculation that was quickly dispelled when Zimmermann himself acknowledged his authorship on March 3. Large stretches of the country were outraged by the Zimmermann telegram but there were still areas, in particular in the Midwest, where there were significant German immigrant communities that did not want war with their former homeland. As a result of the divided country and his own divided mind Wilson continued to mull over his options before finally concluding, in late March, that the United States needed to enter the war. Accordingly on April 2, the president went to Congress and asked it to declare war on Germany. The Senate voted for war on April 4, with the House of Representatives following on April 6, and the United States entered the First World War. However Wilson refused to commit his nation to war for the aims of the Allied governments. He termed the United States an associated, not an Allied, power and proclaimed that the American war was to be a war to "make the world safe for democracy" and, later, that this war was to be "the war to end all wars." To that end the president would eventually craft a peace program of his own, known as the 14 Points, which he hoped to impose on all the warring nations, Central and Allied Powers alike.

To a degree Hindenburg, Ludendorff, Holtzendorff, and company were right to belittle American military capabilities. The U.S. army in 1917 was miniscule and it would take months before the country could field an army large enough and effective enough to impact the war in Europe. Nor was the country prepared for war industrially. Much of the equipment for the growing American army would have to come from the British and French. Though its immediate impact was slight, the specter of the growing American army would loom large in the distance as the war continued. American entry into the war meant that time was definitely not on the side of the Central Powers. For the Allied powers American entry meant that if they could just hang on long enough the United States would ensure Germany's defeat. For Germany and in particular its allies it meant that the war needed to be won quickly if it was to be won at all. In effect, it meant that everything now depended on the submarines. If Holtzendorff was right and if the submarines could sink 600,000 tons of shipping every month the war could still be won; if not it would certainly be lost.

Nigh Unto Victory: The Submarine War from February to July 1917

The Germans began their new gamble with far more submarines than they had in 1915; in February 1917 the Germans possessed 101 submarines of varying types; 23 of these vessels were based in the Mediterranean and the remainder were split between the High Seas Fleet and the Flanders flotillas.[3] Roughly one-third of them were at sea at any one time. Their main hunting ground was the region known as the Western Approaches, effectively the northern and southern entrances to the Irish Sea and the western end of the English Channel. Most British trade headed either toward Liverpool on the west coast of Britain or toward the Channel ports. The unprotected merchantmen on whom the outcome of the war now depended crowded into these waters and created a host of targets for the German submarines.

The general conception is that most submarine attacks were carried out by submerged submarines firing torpedoes; however, this was not the case. Even the largest of the German submarines only carried 16 torpedoes with many of the smaller UB-class submarines carrying as few as 4. The limited number of torpedoes meant that if a submarine was to do extensive damage without having to return to port constantly, it would have to make extensive use of its deck gun to sink enemy merchantmen. That meant in turn that the submarines would be most successful if they could do most of their hunting on the surface. The density of traffic in the Western Approaches, most of which was unprotected, made that area the perfect hunting ground and as a result the campaign got off to a stellar start in February with the sinking of over 520,000 tons of shipping.[4] Though short of the magic number of 600,000 the number of losses was alarming to the British and encouraging to the Germans. In March additional submarines came into service, bringing the total available to 107 and the amount of tonnage sunk increased to over 564,000 tons. In April the German submarines enjoyed their greatest success not only of the First World War but of both world wars. They sank an astounding 860,000 tons of merchant shipping, bringing the average for those three months to 648,000 per month, well over Holtzendorff's 600,000.[5] This created the worst crisis of the entire war for the British government. First Sea Lord John Jellicoe, who had been promoted from command of the Grand Fleet in late 1916, became convinced that the war would be lost if the loss of merchant shipping was not arrested somehow; the problem was that no one seemed to know what to do.

The Royal Navy was, quite simply, unprepared for the ferocity of the German onslaught. They had still not developed effective countermeasures or an effective doctrine for fighting submarines. The submarine threat presented two major problems for the Royal Navy: first of all, submarines were difficult to spot even when they were on the surface, and second, when they were submerged they were, for much of the war, all but impossible to attack. The first of these problems was never adequately dealt with in this war. The British tested many methods for the location of submarines, none of which were terribly effective until they hit upon the hydrophone. This was an underwater microphone used to pick up the sound of a submerged submarine's propeller. Though useful the hydrophone had one great failing: it could not be used by a moving ship because the sounds of the ship itself would drown out the quieter sound of submarine propellers. The second problem proved to be somewhat easier to tackle.

The Royal Navy developed depth charges in late 1916. These were essentially canisters of TNT that would be rolled off the back end of destroyers and set to explode at a particular depth of water. Though effective to a degree they were hampered by the fact that the destroyer had to get in front of a submerged submarine to use them. Speed was not the problem; destroyers were much faster than submerged submarines. What was problematical was finding the submerged submarine. In 1917 most destroyers only carried one or two depth charges, which meant that they could not blanket a wide area in the hopes of catching a hidden submarine. They had to have a good idea of just where the enemy submarine was. Therefore, even with depth charges it was difficult for Allied warships to effectively engage and destroy submerged submarines. Given the difficulty of finding enemy submarines and the additional difficulty of then engaging them it would have been logical for the Royal Navy to have employed a defensive doctrine against the submarines but this was not the case.

The Royal Navy's basic antisubmarine doctrine involved combining their destroyers into hunting packs. These packs would patrol the shipping lanes looking for and attacking submarines, much the way police officers patrolled neighborhoods. While it seemed sound the approach was fundamentally flawed for several reasons. First of all, it was much more difficult for destroyers to spot submarines than for the submarines to spot the destroyers. Therefore a submarine that spotted approaching British destroyers could usually submerge without being seen and then wait until the British forces had passed by before resurfacing. Since the hunting packs had no effective means of searching for submerged submarines they would often sail by completely unaware of the presence of the submerged submarine, which could then resume its own patrol once the British destroyers had moved on. Second, the British did not possess nearly enough destroyers to blanket the Western Approaches with hunting groups. They had roughly 260 destroyers in early 1917 and most of those were assigned to the Grand Fleet. Others were assigned to the forces operating out of Harwich and Dover and still others were escorting British and French forces on their way to and from the Mediterranean.[6] This left less than 100 destroyers for the critical antisubmarine patrols. It was simply an insufficient number. All of this meant that most of the time the submarines could hunt merchant shipping without interference from the Royal Navy. When a merchant ship was attacked it could send out a distress call but unless a hunting group was in the immediate vicinity the submarine would be gone by the time the destroyers arrived. The disaster of April 1917 clearly demonstrated that this approach was not working and that something else needed to be done.

A number of new ideas were proposed, some of which focused specifically on the submarine bases in Flanders. The Admiralty focused on Flanders because submarines using the bases in Zeebrugge, Ostend, and Brugges had a much shorter path back and forth to their hunting grounds. The Admiralty argued that depriving the Germans of those bases and blocking the English Channel to German submarines through the use of mines and extended patrols by the forces at Dover would force the Germans to take the longer and more hazardous journey around Scotland. That would leave the Germans with less time on station and would correspondingly reduce the effectiveness of the submarines. The best way to deprive the Germans of those bases, as far as Jellicoe was concerned, was to have the British army retake them. Pressure from the Admiralty planted the seed therefore of what would become the infamous Battle of Passchendaele. Haig and the British army would launch an offensive in late July that would, hopefully, begin pushing the Germans out of Flanders. That offensive was to be completed by an amphibious landing on the Flanders coast. In the end the offensive failed to make much headway and the amphibious landing never took place. The battle would become legendary for the horrific conditions endured by the British soldiers who fought it.

The second part of the plan to force the Germans to pass around Scotland, the closing of the English Channel via minefields, was implemented by the Dover Patrol. This force of destroyers began laying extensive minefields in the Channel that spring. The minefields also proved to be ineffective, for many reasons. First, the British did not possess enough mines to truly saturate the area; many of those they did possess were ineffective, and, second, their mine-laying efforts were periodically interrupted by German destroyers sortieing from either Germany or Flanders. The failure of both plans eventually led to a search for other means to deprive the Germans of the Flanders bases. Ultimately the effort to close those ports culminated in a plan, put together by Roger Keyes, to block the harbors of Zeebrugge and Ostend. Keyes proposed sending obsolete British cruisers into the canals that linked Zeebrugge and Ostend to the main German naval base in Flanders, the inland harbor of Brugges, and sinking them. The idea was that the German forces in Brugges would be trapped and Germany would no longer have the use of that harbor. The operation was carried out in April 1918, and though the cruisers were indeed sunk in the canals, it failed because the Germans were quickly able to dig channels around the wrecks. British forces only reclaimed the Flanders harbors in October 1918 in the course of the German retreat in the west. The British did finally manage to close the Channel with minefields in 1918 but by that point the submarines had already been defeated. What brought about that defeat was the decision to put Allied and neutral merchantmen into convoys that would be protected by British warships.

The practice of convoying involved gathering merchant ships into large groups that would sail together. These groups would be protected by Royal Navy warships, which would either deter German submarines from attacking the convoy at all or, if a submarine did attack, would engage and hopefully destroy it. This was not a new concept. The British had been using convoys for all of their military shipping since the beginning of the war, and by April 1917, not one ship in any British convoy had been lost to submarine attack. (That would remain the case for the rest of the war as well.) However both the Admiralty and the merchant captains themselves had resisted using convoys for merchant ships, for various reasons. The most important objection to convoying for merchant ships was that a convoy would simply be a large collection of helpless and unprotected ships and that if a convoy was spotted by a German submarine, the submarine would have a plethora of easy targets right in front of it. Furthermore, it was assumed that a convoy would be much easier to find than a single ship sailing on its own. After all a convoy of merchant ships would cover several miles of ocean while a single ship on its own covered merely a few hundred yards. Surely the former would be much easier to find. These assumptions, though they appeared to make good sense at first glance, were actually erroneous. First of all, though convoys were certainly large and, indeed, consisted mostly of unarmed ships, they were anything but unprotected. A convoy was similar to a herd of sheep protected by a number of sheepdogs; a wolf could certainly attack the herd but it would then be attacked in turn by the sheepdogs. Rather than being sitting ducks the ships in the convoy functioned more like bait in a trap. Second, though a convoy was undeniably much larger than a single ship, given the geography of the submarine war, with all the merchant ships coming into the congested waters of the Western Approaches, the difference in size was made far less consequential. To put it simply, it was so easy to find individual ships sailing alone in those waters that the greater size of the convoy did not matter.

Other objections were also raised. For example, there was great doubt on the part of both naval commanders and merchant captains as to whether or not the civilian crews of the merchant ships would possess sufficient discipline to keep to their station in a convoy. Failure to do so could cause collisions with other ships and mass chaos. Yet another objection was that it would take far more destroyers than the Entente possessed to keep a series of convoys safe and that an insufficiently protected convoy was worse than no convoy at all. Another concern was that British harbors would not be able to handle the extra congestion that would be caused by having a large group of ships all entering and exiting the harbors at one time. Perhaps most importantly though for much of the war there was an unspoken but understood view in the Royal Navy that convoy was too defensive and too passive, and that it was not the British way to wait for the enemy to come to them. Submarine hunting on the other hand, though less effective, maintained the offensive spirit of the fleet. For all of these reasons the Admiralty was long reluctant to employ convoys. It was only the crisis of April 1917 that led them to reconsider, basically out of desperation.

On April 27, Admiral Jellicoe, after a meeting with the new prime minister, David Lloyd George, finally agreed to set up a trial convoy. Just why Jellicoe finally came to this decision has been debated ever since. The prime minister later claimed the credit for the idea, asserting that he had in effect forced the Admiralty to adopt the convoy system. This seems unlikely. What seems to be the most likely reason was that Jellicoe quite simply had run out of other ideas and turned to convoy out of sheer desperation. Whether Jellicoe made the decision on his own or was forced into it by Lloyd-George the end result was the creation of a trial convoy, which left Gibraltar and sailed to Great Britain on May 10th.[7] To the great surprise of most everyone involved the merchant captains proved to be capable of keeping station and the convoy arrived in Great Britain without loss. Since the initial trial was a success other convoys began to be implemented, though the process was necessarily slow. It took another two weeks before the first transatlantic convoy sailed. That convoy lost only one ship, and that was because the ship could not maintain the requisite speed and was forced to drop out of the convoy. Surprisingly, convoy appeared to work.

The benefits of the convoy system were twofold: first of all German submarine commanders could not realistically hope to attack a convoy on the surface; therefore they were forced to expend valuable torpedoes when they attacked; second and the most important, even a successful submarine attack would claim only one or two victims before the escorting destroyers could attack the submarine and either force it to submerge or destroy it. In either case, the remaining ships of the convoy were free to continue sailing, and barring an encounter with a separate submarine, they would reach their destination. For these reasons the convoy system was a striking success. The Admiralty proceeded to spend the next several months expanding the system. By the end of 1917 most shipping to and from the British Isles would travel via convoy.

While the convoy system was being created, many ships continued to sail individually and remained rich targets for the German submarines. For that reason the Germans continued to enjoy great success for several more months. In May, German submarines sank 616,316 tons of shipping; well below April but still above Holtzendorff's monthly goal.[8] Also in May the submarine campaign finally began to hit home in Britain and the British government was forced to begin implementing some economic controls, including rationing, for the first time in the war. June saw the number of sinkings once again on the rise, with 696,725 tons of merchant shipping going to the bottom.[9] Despite all the successes though it was in June that the first signs of disquiet appeared in German military circles. The submarines had achieved Holtzendorff's goal; over the previous five months they had destroyed well over 3 million tons of Entente and neutral shipping, yet Britain had made no move to begin peace negotiations. More disquietingly still the Entente's shortage of destroyers was beginning to be alleviated by the arrival of American destroyers in British waters. This was yet another way in which the entry of the United States into the war, even without a large army, bore immediate dividends for the Entente and proved to be severely detrimental to the German cause. Eventually the entire American battle fleet would move to British waters, giving the Entente a better than 3:1 superiority in dreadnoughts over the German navy and providing the British with more than 70 desperately needed destroyers.[10]

July marked the sixth month of the submarine campaign, supposedly the final month before Britain would have to make peace, and the submarines continued to have great success though the amount of shipping destroyed dropped below 600,000 tons for the first time since March, with only 555,514 tons sunk.[11] Despite the continued successes though when the month ended and August began Britain remained in the war.

Conditions within Germany: American Entry and the Tightening Blockade

The resumption of unrestricted submarine warfare had been driven in part by the declining conditions within Germany during the winter of 1916–17. The turnip winter was devastating and those who survived it did not see much improvement in their conditions with the return of spring. In fact the government was forced to reduce rations even further in the spring of 1917. The sugar ration was reduced to 1.5 pounds per month and the meat ration was reduced to one-half pound per week. Germans were now limited to one egg per month and coffee disappeared completely from everything but the black market. The fodder ration was reduced to three pounds a day. The average German was allotted one ounce of butter every week. Overall the normal German (those not in the military or in war industry) was reduced to a diet of 1,100 calories a day.[12] These conditions continued to decline as the spring went on. In April the bread ration was cut by 15 percent throughout all of Germany, even though the bread was now filled largely with replacements such as potatoes or even, in some instances, oats and straw. As rations declined sales on the black market increased. In turn the government tried to crack down on black market sellers. In Berlin the police arrested thousands in the spring of 1917 and confiscated their food stocks. Unfortunately the food stocks were usually left in storage while the owner's case made its way through the courts, which, since the courts were clogged with cases, resulted in much of the food spoiling instead of being distributed to the people.[13] The government also cracked down on the practice of well-off city dwellers heading out to rural areas to buy food directly from the farmers. In Berlin police began stopping those returning from the countryside and confiscating the food they were bringing back. In Munich, in one day, police confiscated 5,000 eggs, 300 pounds of meat, and nearly 1 ton of cheese![14] Some German states, such as Bavaria, took even stronger measures, banning the export of food beyond their state borders. None of these measures proved to be particularly effective and most of them simply resulted in the government angering one group of citizens or another but any more substantial response was hampered by the position of the deputy commanding generals, most of whom worked to protect their area of the nation without regard for the other districts and who still could not be controlled effectively by the War Office. So Germany limped along toward another summer.

As the food situation continued to decline some Germans finally began to express their discontent openly and strikes became more common in the major German industrial areas. Between January and March 1917 there were a series of strikes throughout Germany with many employees demanding better food or higher wages so they could buy more food on the black market. Most of these strikes were settled by employers granting higher wages, which, in the end, only meant that black market prices went up even further because there was more money chasing the same low level of goods. In April 1917, when the government announced the cutting of the bread ration, a series of disturbances, not rising to the level of strikes, took place throughout the Ruhr and those disturbances in turn sparked major strikes in both Berlin and Leipzig on April 16. In Berlin 217,000 workers struck and held nonviolent protests throughout the city. The strike was settled quickly when the mayor of Berlin promised to create an advisory council to look into the food situation and to compensate for the lower bread ration with a higher meat ration. In Leipzig, however, the strike was far more political.[15]

The Leipzig strike was led from the beginning by a newly formed splinter section of the Social Democratic Party (SDP) known as the

Independent Social Democratic Party, or USPD. The USPD was formed in April 1917 when Hugo Haase, one of the more radical members of the SPD, left the party over the question of Germany's war aims. Haase and those who joined him espoused the ideal of the international socialist movement, a peace without annexations or indemnities. Furthermore they advocated international agreements limiting arms, courts of arbitration that could settle disputes between nations without resorting to war, and national borders determined by the right of national self-determination. For many Germans such a peace was still unacceptable in early 1917. Such a peace would have meant that all the sacrifices of the war would have been in vain. Even the main socialist party, the SDP, refused to ratify this program. That refusal led Haase and roughly one-third of the members of the SPD to leave and form the USPD. The new party decided that the time had come to end the *Burgfrieden* and to speak out against the war. One way to do that was to lead workers into the streets to protest the continuation of the war. They did just that in Leipzig.

The Leipzig strikers demanded that the government issue a statement expressing its willingness to sign a peace without annexations and indemnities. They further demanded an end to the Law of Siege and the Auxiliary Service Law, the release of all political prisoners, an end to press censorship and restrictions on meetings, and an end to the three-tiered system of suffrage in Prussia, according to which the population was divided into thirds on the basis of wealth. Each third of the electorate selected one-third of the Prussian Landtag, giving the votes of the wealthier Prussians greater weight. The demands of the Leipzig strikers inspired the Berlin strikers to return to the streets on April 18, just one day after agreeing to end their strike. The Berlin strikers now echoed the demands of the strikers in Leipzig. Even in Leipzig though the strikers were still driven mainly by economic concerns, which was demonstrated on the 19th when the employers of the striking workers in Leipzig agreed to reduce the workweek to 52 hours and increase employees' pay. The strike immediately ended. In Berlin the strikers remained out until April 23rd and were only persuaded to end the strike when the government threatened to militarize their factories and draft them into the army.

Though both strikes were ultimately ended without political change, the government did indeed take notice. Chancellor Theobald von Bethmann-Hollweg, even before the strikes, was beginning to fear defeat and the possible dissolution of the monarchy. By April 1917 he had become convinced that the Kaiser needed to take a dramatic step to renew the people's faith in the monarchy and their willingness to continue sacrificing for the war. Against the wishes of the military and many other members of the government Bethmann-Hollweg urged Kaiser Wilhelm to promise the Prussian people political reform, to be implemented once the war was successfully concluded. To that end the Kaiser issued a famous proclamation on April 7, 1917, in which he promised to end the three-tiered voting system in Prussia once the war was over. This so-called Easter Message did little to improve the morale of the German people. Only improved material conditions could do that, and those were not forthcoming. Instead the deprivations caused by the blockade and German economic mismanagement continued.

The civilian shortages continued to pile up as 1917 wore on. By the summer of 1917 the clothing shortage had become so acute that new clothing, even ersatz clothing, could only be ordered if the customer surrendered an already existing set of clothing when he or she placed the order. Most of the newer clothing was by this point made from various wood and paper by-products. Leather shoes were a thing of the past by the summer of 1917, being replaced by wooden soles with heavier paper products substituting for leather. Soap was also gone by the summer of 1917, having been replaced with ersatz soap made from either sand or clay. The coal shortage of the winter continued into the spring and summer, which meant a lack of coal not only for heating homes but also for heating water. As a result even hot showers had largely become a thing of the past by the summer of 1917. Public baths had to be shut down due to the coal shortages and store hours as well as the service hours of public transportation had to be cut back. When the fall returned and brought with it colder weather the government issued decrees that rooms could only be heated to the equivalent of 62 degrees Fahrenheit in order to conserve coal. Conditions became so brutal that summer that the breweries outside of Bavaria were ordered to shut down production in order to save fodder for the livestock and grains for bread. Only Bavaria was allowed to continue the manufacturing of beer.[16]

It was not only civilian industries that suffered shortages that year, so did vital defense industries. The institution of the Hindenburg Program at the end of 1916 threw German industry into chaos at a time when it could least afford it. That chaos led directly to decreases in production and shortages in vital sectors of the industrial economy. The most important of these was in the coal and railroad sectors, and the two problems aggravated each other. Already before the end of 1916 the German railways were deteriorating. Prior to that point the railways were in constant use, shipping men and materiel for the war effort; they could not be shut down for needed maintenance and as a result their condition continuously declined. Railway traffic was only reduced in the winter of 1916 and it was not so that work could be done on the tracks; it was because of the general lack of coal. The coal shortage that winter was so severe that from January 24 to February 5, all rail traffic beyond that which was militarily essential was stopped. The downtime could not be used to repair the railways though because so much of Germany's steel production was going to the construction of Hindenburg Plan factories that none was available to repair the railroads. The coal problem got worse as the months went by and by April Germany was no longer even producing enough coal to meet its military needs. The main problem was simply one of manpower; most of the miners had been drafted into the army. The manpower shortage had been compensated for to a degree by substituting machinery but that machinery could not be properly maintained without hampering production and hence was running down by 1917. Still a further problem stemmed from the food shortage. The strength of the remaining coal miners had been reduced by weakness and fatigue caused by lack of food. In order to address the problem the OHL was forced to send 50,000 soldiers home to work in the coal mines but even then production remained insufficient for Germany's industrial and civilian needs.[17] It would be another cold winter in Germany.

The shortage of coal was echoed by a shortage of metals, in particular copper. In order to find additional copper (mainly needed for shell casings) the German government turned to the churches of Germany and began seizing church bells so that they could be melted down and used for munitions; 18,000 church bells were seized in 1917, leaving a conspicuous silence in many German towns and villages that became another constant reminder of the war and the hardships it had brought to the country. Copper and silver coins became victims of this shortage also as they were confiscated and replaced with iron coins. The copper shortage was another reason for the shutting down of the breweries. If the breweries were shut down their copper vats could be seized and melted down along with the church bells.[18] Even steel production dropped, despite the German's control over the iron fields of Lorraine and northern France. In February 1917 Germany produced only 1,187,000 tons of steel, down from 1,417,000 in late 1916, before the implementation of the Hindenburg Program. The production of powder for ammunition was also down, to only 6,400 tons in February 1917.[19] These shortages were

another factor that helped to convince Hindenburg and Ludendorff to
order the retreat to the Hindenburg Line.

In the meantime strikes and disturbances continued throughout the
summer and fall. In June, bread stores in Dusseldorf were plundered by
hungry citizens; in Essen, potato stores were looted that same month. In
Dortmund, Halle, Merseburg, and Leipzig there were strikes later in the
year. Overall, over 650,000 German workers walked out at one point or
another in 1917.[20] The cultural consensus in favor of war was eroding.

These declining conditions internally meant that Germany became
even more dependent on the importation of goods from its neutral neighbors. Unfortunately, just as those imports were most needed the United
States entered the war.

The entry of the United States into the war meant not only that the
Entente would receive immediate naval reinforcements for the struggle
against the submarines and a badly needed boost to morale, but also
that it would be able to immediately tighten the economic noose
around Germany. As soon as the United States entered the war it
dropped all of its support for neutral rights and insisted on a dramatic
tightening of the blockade. From the summer of 1917 on, the neutral
"windpipe" into Germany would be constricted by American and British pressure. Nor would Germany's neutral neighbors be untouched by
the submarine campaign. The loss of their own shipping to German
submarines made them more amenable to American and British
demands that they reduce their shipments of goods to Germany. These
changes in the blockade, given the already dire internal conditions,
proved devastating to the German economy and to the German people
over the course of 1917 and 1918.

It did not take the U.S. government long to turn its economic power
against Germany. In June 1917 it created the War Trade Commission
and an exports council to prepare an embargo on exports to European
neutrals. The idea was to prevent any American products reaching Germany. This was followed very quickly by an embargo of corn, animal fodder, gasoline, coal, mineral oil, meat, iron, steel, and fertilizer.[21] In
October the embargo was extended to include all goods being shipped
not only to Germany but also to those neutrals that bordered on Germany. Some exceptions were made through the granting of export
licenses to some companies in the neutral nations but even in those
instances only very small and tightly regulated amounts were allowed
through. Table 6.1 shows the impact of the embargo on those neutrals
that were still conducting business with Germany.

Table 6.1   U.S. Trade to Northern European Neutrals

Nation	June 1915 to June 1916	June 1917 to June 1918
Denmark	55.9 million	5 million
Netherlands	97.5 million	6.4 million
Norway	53.6 million	25.2 million
Sweden	52 million	4.1 million
Switzerland	8 million	21.2 million[22]

This radical restriction of American imports forced these nations to rely far more extensively on their own supplies for their own survival, which made it far more difficult for them to continue exporting goods to Germany despite the deals, and threats, made by the German government. All of them, except for Switzerland, were forced to dramatically reduce their exports, especially of food products and fertilizer. Switzerland did the same, voluntarily. For example the value of Dutch trade with Germany was cut in half after the institution of the American embargo, from £25 million in 1917 to only £12.6 million in 1918. Norwegian trade was also cut almost in half, from £7.8 million to £4.4 million. Danish trade was reduced from £25.3 million to £15.9 million and Swiss trade dropped from £30 million to £17.8 million. Only Sweden continued a relatively strong export relationship with Germany, with its figures only dropping from £18.3 million in 1917 to £15.1 million in 1918.[23]

To make up for this reduced business in the neutral nations American companies increased their support for the Entente. In the three-year span 1914–1917 the Entente powers were able to purchase roughly $7 billion worth of American goods. Most of those purchases had to be paid for up front. A total of $1.6 billion worth were paid for with exports, another $1.1 billion were paid for with gold, $500 million came from liquidating American debts, and another $1.4 billion came from selling off American securities, most of them British owned. Only $2.4 billion were paid for with loans from American banks. After the United States officially entered the war on the side of the Entente American bankers became far more generous. Between April 1917 and the end of the war in November 1918, American companies sold another $10.3 billion worth of goods to the Entente and the vast majority of those goods, $7.1 billion worth, were paid for by new loans.[24] Those funds purchased, among other things: 926 million rounds of small arms ammunition; 31 million artillery shells; 1.2 million rifles; 569,000 tons of explosives; 42,000 trucks; 3,400 aircraft engines; and 866 airplanes.[25] In other words, American entry into the war provided a significant economic boost to the Entente and dealt a severe economic blow to the Central Powers at the same time. By the time American military forces arrived in Europe in force in 1918 the United States had already done serious harm to the German war effort.

By the summer of 1917 there was really only one thing that kept the German people hanging on, their belief that the unrestricted submarine campaign would break Great Britain and bring Germany peace. The government had trumpeted the submarine campaign as the key to victory all through the winter, spring, and early summer of 1917 and the German people were fed a steady diet of good news from the naval campaigns, news of sinking after sinking. Even the entry of the United States into the war in April did little to dim the belief in the inevitability of victory, thanks to the submarines. That belief was dealt a severe blow in July 1917.

The July Crisis of 1917

Holtzendorff's original prediction was that the unrestricted submarine campaign would force Britain to sue for peace within six months, pro-vided that the German submarines could sink 600,000 tons of shipping each month. The submarines were enormously successful, either coming very close or exceeding that figure in every month from February to June 1917, yet by July Great Britain showed no signs of surrendering. The reason was that Holtzendorff and the other naval planners had erred in a number of ways. They had overestimated the amount of neutral ship-ping that would be driven from the seas by fear; they had underestimated the amount of shipping the United States would be able to contribute to the Entente cause; they had underestimated the ability of the British government to handle the crisis caused by the submarine threat, and most importantly, they had underestimated the ability of the British people to withstand the same hardships that the German people had been enduring since 1914. Furthermore, though it was not apparent at the time, by July the submarine campaign had already reached its peak and the German threat was in the process of being contained by the convoy system. What this meant was that Germany's "last card," its final gamble to win the war, had failed. By the end of June this was apparent to the OHL, if not to the German people, who, because all war news was strictly censored, were told only what the government wanted them to know. For the most part, as July 1917 dawned, the German people remained quietly hopeful that the submarines would defeat Great Britain and bring a victorious end to the war before they were forced to endure another war winter. That quiet hope was shattered on July 6, 1917.

The hope for victory via submarine was destroyed by Matthias Erzberger. Erzberger was a member of the Catholic Center Party and had connections within the navy. Through those connections he had received intelligence regarding the true state of the submarine campaign, in particular, that sinkings by German submarines had been declining since April. Though the submarines were still near their mark of 600,000 tons every month, their commanders were finding it increasingly difficult to reach that figure as more and more merchant ships were brought into the convoy system. Armed with this information and convinced that the government had been lying to the people, Erzberger dropped a bombshell on July 6 when he stated, in a speech to the Reichstag, that victory by submarine was no longer attainable, which meant that victory itself was highly unlikely. He followed up by insisting that Germany seek a compromise peace and that the Reichstag issue a resolution declaring Germany's willingness to accept a peace of reconciliation. Erzberger's speech and the motion to issue a peace resolution sparked what became known as the July Crisis.

Up to this point in the war, the Reichstag, under the leadership of the SDP, had remained solidly behind the war effort. When the war began the party members had voted to fund the war and the Kaiser had responded by stating that from this day forward he no longer recognized political parties, only Germans. This political truce, which was called the Burgfrieden (the peace of the castle), had lasted all through the war. Erzberger's speech however marked an end to the Reichstag's quiet acceptance of the government's leadership. Chief among Erzberger's targets was the chancellor, von Bethmann-Hollweg. Erzberger concluded that Bethmann-Hollweg had to resign, for the good of the nation. By this point the chancellor was a deeply unpopular man. His unwillingness to accept the resumption of unrestricted submarine warfare earlier had made him enemies not only among the military but among the civilians in government as well, where the general conception was that the civilians needed to get out of the way and let the army handle the business of the war. The general view was that war was too important for the civilians to meddle in and Bethmann-Hollweg was seen as not only a meddler but also an obstructionist who prevented the generals and admirals from doing what was necessary to win the war. This view was very strongly held by Hindenburg and Ludendorff, who had concluded that Bethmann-

Hollweg could not provide the strong leadership that Germany needed to achieve victory and that he had to be replaced (in truth, they thought he was too sympathetic to the interests of the liberal and socialist elements in Germany). Bethmann-Hollweg's response to Erzberger only doomed him in the eyes of Hindenburg and Ludendorff.

The chancellor's response to Erzberger's speech was to urge the Kaiser to grant equal suffrage in Prussia immediately. He concluded that only the promise of major political reform could save the monarchy. For the Kaiser, and for Hindenburg and Ludendorff, this was defeatism and it could not be tolerated. The latter decided that the time had come to get rid of Bethmann-Hollweg. They approached the Kaiser and demanded the appointment of a "stronger" chancellor, which meant one that they could control. On July 13, beset on all sides, Bethmann-Hollweg resigned. The Kaiser named Georg Michaelis, an inoffensive bureaucrat who had helped oversee the food rationing program, as the new chancellor. Michaelis was approved by Hindenburg and Ludendorff and became in effect a rubber stamp for the OHL. His appointment inaugurated what one historian has called, the "Silent Dictatorship."[26] In effect, Hindenburg and Ludendorff became the civil as well as military leaders of Germany after July 1917. The fall of Bethmann-Hollweg removed the lone voice of moderation in the German government. Though he had been largely ineffective Bethmann-Hollweg had been one of the few members of the government to understand that war was the continuation of diplomacy by other means. His fall would ensure that for the remainder of the war diplomacy would be subordinated to military necessity.

In the short term the change in chancellors did not stop Erzberger and the Reichstag, which proceeded to pass their peace resolution on July 19. This resolution called upon the chancellor to negotiate a peace "without annexations or indemnities." Michaelis proceeded to famously accept the resolution, "as he understood it." In the end the introduction of the peace resolution had no real effect on German foreign policy; the German government remained committed to a peace of victory, not a peace of reconciliation. The war would go on until Germany either won it on its terms or collapsed from exhaustion. In the end the most important consequence of the peace resolution was the end of the Burgfrieden; from this point on the divisions within German society would become increasingly open.

This is one of the great what-if moments of the war. If the German government, in the midst of the great successes of the submarine campaign, had seriously proposed a peace of reconciliation, might it have been able to persuade the Entente to accept it? By July 1917 the tsar had fallen and Russia was run by a provisional government, which was about to face an attempted military coup; the French army was recovering from mutiny; and the British were still deeply concerned over the future of the submarine war. A serious proposal for a return to the status quo ante would have had great appeal to the people of Russia and France and even to some in Britain. Countering that appeal however was the looming presence of the United States. Would it be a better bet to hang on in the war in the hopes that the United States could help win it or would it be better to cut a deal that would leave no one satisfied? Obviously it is impossible to say; it seems unlikely but it is possible that the Germans may have missed an opportunity to escape from the war without losing it. Unfortunately for Germany and the people of Europe, it was not to be. Germany's military commanders still believed they could win the war, not just avoid losing it, and as a result the war would continue.

In the interim the divisions within Germany began to show in more serious ways. They appeared first in the navy in the summer of 1917. The navy's battleships, which had remained basically idle since the Battle of Jutland the previous year, became centers of discontent that summer. On June 6, there had been protests on the battleship *Prinzregent Luitpold* over the poor food given to the ratings as compared to their officers. Those protests were silenced but on July 5 a new series of food protests broke out, and, on July 19, the crew of the *Prinzregent Luitpold* announced the beginning of a hunger strike, with the strikers demanding better conditions and, in particular, better food. The response of the German officers was to crack down on the strikers. That led in turn to the strikers issuing demands that echoed the Reichstag peace resolution; they demanded a peace without annexations or indemnities. The disturbances continued into August before they were finally ended by minor concessions such as the granting of more shore leave and better food. The leaders of the movement however were arrested and two of them were shot as examples to the others. For now discipline was restored to the fleet.[27]

The OHL responded to this troubling news in several ways. First of all in August 1917 the deputy commanding generals were empowered to militarize some factories and were encouraged to take a more repressive approach toward the demands of German labor, including if necessary drafting troublesome workers into the army and sending them to the frontlines. The latter policy speaks volumes about how the German public was beginning to view the war. It was unpopular enough by the late summer of 1917 that military service was now held up as a possible punishment for troublemakers, many of whom were indeed sent to the front in 1918 and, ironically, helped to spread dissension into an army that was already growing weary of the war. To fight that war weariness in the summer of 1917 Hindenburg and Ludendorff ordered the institution of a program of patriotic instruction for the soldiers. This was an attempt to educate the German soldiers on the differences for Germany of a "Germanic peace," a victor's peace, or a "rotten peace," a peace along the lines of that proposed by the Reichstag.[28] Those sessions were led by members of a new German political party, the Fatherland Party.

The Fatherland Party was created on September 2, 1917 (Sedan Day, commemorating one of the great victories in the Franco-Prussian War of 1870–71), by the man who had overseen the construction of the German battle fleet in the years before the war, Alfred von Tirpitz. Tirpitz had backing from many of the leaders of the right in Germany, including many powerful industrialists. Together they created the Fatherland Party precisely in order to agitate for a "German peace." The OHL supported the creation of the party because it hoped the party would instill in the German people a greater willingness to hold out until victory had been achieved. The party grew quickly and by July 1918 it had over 1,250,000 members and was the second largest party in Germany, behind only the Social Democrats. The fragmentation of German political life that would culminate in revolution in November of that year was proceeding apace.

In yet another attempt to increase support for the war effort, in late 1917 the OHL gave its blessing to the creation of Universum Film AG (UFA), a semiprivate film company, in the hope that the new medium of the cinema could be used to bolster the morale of the German people. UFA, which became a dominant force in German cinema after the war, ultimately had little impact on the war.[29] What the German people needed were not films urging them to hold out; they needed more food, clothing, and coal, things that the OHL and the government were unable to give them.

Disputes between the Reichstag and the government continued throughout the fall of 1917. The Reichstag was unhappy with Michaelis as chancellor and when, in October, he made a speech to the Reichstag in which he referred to the USPD as traitors who threatened the very existence of Germany, a mass coalition formed against him, running from the Catholic Center Party though the SPD and the USPD. As a result he in turn was forced to resign on October 31, 1917.[30] He was replaced with the aging minister president of Bavaria, Georg von Hertling.

By the end of 1917 the situation in Germany was approaching disaster. Food was once again in extremely short supply during the winter and as a result the black market was once again rampant. Furthermore the Burgfrieden was clearly at an end and there were even some Germans who were being radicalized by the success of the Bolshevik revolution in Russia that November. German factories were competing with their own government in an attempt to acquire resources and also food for their employees. In fact some of the worst black market offenders were large German companies that could afford to pay black market prices in order to keep their workers fed and functioning. Nonetheless the declining food supply and the lack of raw materials continued to drive down the productivity of German workers, which led the factory owners to call for the army to release additional soldiers for work back home; yet those same soldiers were desperately needed on the frontlines where another 281,905 Germans had fallen over the course of 1917.[31] All hope now rested on the continuing submarine campaign.

Failure: The Defeat of the Submarines

At the beginning of August the outcome of the submarine campaign and the entire war hung in the balance. By the end of December the submarines had been defeated and so, for all intents and purposes, had Germany. The critical factors in the victory over the submarines were the slow but steady expansion of the convoy system and the continuing arrival of American destroyers to help escort the convoys.

The first serious setback for the submarine campaign came in August when the total amount of shipping destroyed dropped again, this time to just over 470,000 tons.[32] This was the lowest total of the entire campaign and it caused grave concern in Germany. It was clear to the German submarine commanders and to Holtzendorff what was happening. First of all it was becoming much harder for submarine commanders to find and attack merchant shipping. In practice convoys proved to be no easier to find than a single unescorted warship. In the words of one German submarine captain, "The oceans at once became bare and empty. For long periods at a time, the U-boats . . . would see nothing at all; and then suddenly up would loom a huge concourse of ships, thirty or fifty or more of them."[33] The submarines therefore spent a good deal of fuel and time patrolling empty waters, and then when they discovered the enemy, it was so well protected that it was difficult to sink more than one or two ships. Both that captain, Karl Dönitz, and Holtzendorff understood what the answer to this problem was; they would need to have multiple submarines attack a single convoy. In the interwar period Dönitz would refine this idea into the notion of the wolf pack, which the Germans would employ to great effect in the Second World War. That concept however revolved around nearly constant radio communications between the submarines and the naval headquarters, something that simply was not possible in 1917. The best the Germans could do at the time was to send submarines to sea in pairs so that they could coordinate and attack convoys in tandem. This was eventually done in October but in the interim the amount of tonnage sunk continued to decline, with the September total only reaching 353,602 tons.[34]

There was a brief resurgence for the campaign in October when 466,542 tons of shipping were destroyed. The increase was attributable in part to the pairing of submarines, which was limited, and mainly to the laying of a series of new minefields in the waters around Britain. Even with the upsurge however the numbers were well shy of the required target and the optimism that those improved numbers generated quickly evaporated in November, when the total amount of tonnage sunk dropped back to just over 300,000 tons.[35] By this point the convoy system was in full operation for all shipping except for that directly off the British coast. In December the German submarines would turn more heavily against that traffic and once again they destroyed more than 400,000 tons but by this point it was clear that the submarine campaign was not going to force Great Britain to make peace. The submarines would continue to destroy roughly 250,000–300,000 tons of shipping each month, every month, until September 1918, doing an enormous amount of damage to the world's merchant shipping, but they never came close to forcing the Entente to consider a "German peace."

Numerous scholars have analyzed why the German submarine campaign failed, pointing out the inadequacies of the submarines themselves, the insufficient number of submarines, or the tactical failures of German commanders. The truth of the matter is that the submarine crews themselves did exactly what they had been asked to do. Over six months they destroyed 3,813,798 tons of shipping, for an average of 635,633 tons per month. They accomplished exactly what Holtzendorff asked them to accomplish. The failure was not theirs; it was his and the government's. To put it simply Holtzendorff, Hindenburg, Ludendorff, Scheer, and the rest of the prosubmarine group underestimated their enemies. They assumed that the British people could not withstand the kind of hardships that the German people had been enduring for three years and that therefore the imposition of rationing and shortages of vital goods would lead the British people to demand peace at any price. Second, they underestimated the vast impact that the entry of the United States would have on the war. The morale impact of the addition of the United States to the Entente cause cannot be measured but it certainly appears to have been considerable. What can be measured were immediate benefits such as: the seizure and impressment into service for the Allied cause of the many German merchantmen and passenger liners that had been interned in American harbors; the addition of over 70 destroyers to the Entente cause; the arrival of the American dreadnoughts in European waters, which ensured naval supremacy and meant that construction on British dreadnoughts could be halted so that the materials that would have gone into those warships could instead be used to produce merchant ships; and the immediate tightening of the blockade that was brought about by American pressure on the European neutrals. With all of those factors in their favor and with the convoy system able to bring the amount of tonnage destroyed by the submarines down to acceptable levels there was simply no reason to seek peace. Holtzendorff and company had gambled their nation's future on a desperate throw of the dice and they, not the submarine crews, had failed. The price of that failure was the entry of the United States into the war and, ultimately, defeat. By November 1917 it was clear that Germany was out of options and nearly out of time. Until lightning struck in the east.

CHAPTER 7

The End of the Second Reich

By the end of 1917 the German army and people had endured three long years of war. The General Staff's plan for a quick victory in 1914 had failed, defeated by a combination of distance, exhaustion, and French tenacity. What resulted was a war unlike any the German government or people had envisioned, a long drawn out war of attrition that put both the German military and the home front to a severe test. The British naval blockade had long since cut the Central Powers off from any contact with the outside world and left them to rely only on themselves. Through a combination of the tightening blockade and the chaos of the German bureaucracy, where civilian agencies fought with the deputy commanding generals for scarce resources, conditions within Germany had steadily declined as the war went on. Further hopes for victory in 1916 had been dashed when the French managed not only to retain Verdun and stay in the war but to join the British in a massive offensive aimed at the German positions on the Somme. The defeats at Verdun and the Somme coupled with the failure of the German battle fleet to make any appreciable impact on the war to create an overwhelming pressure for the resumption of the unrestricted submarine campaign. That campaign was accordingly unleashed in February 1917 as the last card, the last desperate gamble to try and win the war before the army and nation became completely exhausted. Unfortunately the promised victory never materialized despite the fact that the submarine captains and crews managed to sink over 600,000 tons of shipping, on average, every month from February to July of 1917. Admiral Höltzendorff had promised that if they could sink that much shipping Britain would be forced to make peace, yet the British stubbornly refused to play their part and the war continued. By the end of the year the last card had clearly failed.

Making matters worse the submarine campaign had brought the United States into the war. Though the United States army was small and played no role in the war during 1917 the entry of the United States into the war led directly to a dramatic tightening of the blockade and a resulting sharp decline in the conditions within Germany. By the start of 1918 those conditions were catastrophic.

Disaster at Home: Germany in 1918

In the winter of 1917–1918 the cultural consensus in favor of the war, which had begun cracking in the summer of 1917, finally broke. The continuing, and increasing, shortages had finally begun to erode the population's belief in both the war and their own government. Over the course of that winter demands for an end to the "ridiculous" war were heard more frequently, in particular in Berlin.[1] As soldiers returned home for leave that winter and witnessed the terrible conditions that their families were enduring their own morale began to crack. There was even some speculation about what life would be like under British or French occupation and if it could be any worse than what they were currently experiencing.[2] By January 1918 the population of Berlin seemed to have lost all faith in their own government. Government communiqués were greeted with cynicism or apathy and more credence was given to rumors than to those official reports. Many Berliners began to wonder if their government had been lying to them all along.[3] A sense of fatalism began to set in as well. Resentment against merchants and anyone who could afford to buy goods on the black market was increasingly widespread, as were incidents of theft.[4] The cohesiveness of German domestic society was unraveling. Who could blame them? The shortages that had been plaguing them were getting steadily worse.

By that January the average German diet had dropped to 1,000 calories a day and it would decrease further as the year wore on. German grain production dropped to 16 million tons in 1918, from a peacetime norm of 30 million tons. Meat production was less than 1 million tons, down from 3 million tons in peacetime. As a result mortality rates were increasing and birth rates were declining. The birthrate fell from 6.1 per thousand before the war to less than 1 per thousand in 1918. Civilian mortality rates in 1917 were 32 percent higher than those of 1913 and in 1918 they were 37 percent higher than those of 1913. The mortality rate among children was 30 percent greater than it had been in peacetime. Incidents of disease became more common and those diseases became more deadly; for example, the number of cases of tuberculosis doubled between 1916 and 1918.[5] In addition to the food shortages Germany continued to suffer from the already documented shortage of clothing as well as a shortage of soap. The latter meant that most Germans, even on the rare occasions when they could bathe, were unable to get truly clean and that in turn led to an increase in incidences of skin diseases. In addition there was a shortage of housing in the areas around the munitions plants and a shortage of medical supplies such as disinfectants, bandages, petroleum jelly, cotton gauze, salves, and even corks to reseal bottles![6]

In addition to imposing severe material shortages on the German people the war also eroded the incomes and living standards of many Germans. Those hit the hardest by the war were civil servants and other white collar professionals. For the most part their salaries did not keep pace with the growth of inflation and they did not receive the same increases in pay that manufacturing workers did. Some saw their real income reduced by as much as 55 percent.[7] By comparison men working in the war industry saw their wages increase by 152 percent. Even those working in civilian industries saw significant wage increases, with their pay rising 81 percent over the course of the war.[8] With the working class enjoying greater wages and the professional classes seeing their incomes erode the latter began to feel that their status within German society was being threatened.

The increased wages for the working class were also contrasted with the fates of the men on the frontlines, who saw no increase in their pay over the course of the war. The disparity naturally led to great resentment as those who sacrificed the most for the nation received next to nothing and often saw their spouses trying to survive on state assistance while those who remained safe at home reaped enormous economic gains.

Even greater resentment was aimed at those who were, by far, the biggest economic winners in the war: the owners of the critical munitions plants. Many of these men came to be seen as nothing more than war profiteers. The increasing wealth and prosperity of these few Germans was not lost on the rest of the nation. In the winter of 1918 resentment against war profiteering, combined with the ever present shortages, the increasing weariness with the war, and decreasing faith in the ability and even the desire of the government to end the war, resulted in a massive outbreak of strikes.

The strikes began on January 1, with a wave of food riots in the Austro-Hungarian cities of Prague and Vienna.[9] In the ensuing days several

meetings of workers and politicians were held in the major cities of both
Germany and Austria-Hungary and many of those meetings resulted in
calls for an immediate end to the war and a peace without annexations
or indemnities. In Germany the Independent Social Democratic Party
(USPD) began distributing pamphlets on January 10, in which they
blamed the breakdown of peace talks with the Russian government
(which had begun in December at the Polish city of Brest-Litovsk) on
the annexationist demands of the German government. They called on
the workers of Germany to speak up for a peace of reconciliation.[10] In
Austria-Hungary those meetings were followed by work stoppages in
Budapest and Vienna, which ended only when the Austro-Hungarian
government pledged to seek peace and to consider democratic reforms
of the government. That success caused the antiwar movement to jump
from Austria-Hungary to Germany.

On the 28th of January, emulating what had happened in Austria-
Hungary, the USPD led German workers into the streets of Berlin. On
the ensuing day smaller sympathy strikes were held in other cities, such
as the major port cities of Kiel and Hamburg. Still others took place in
the major industrial centers of the Ruhr and in Bavaria. Roughly 4 million
strikers took to the streets over these several days.[11] The strikers
demanded a peace without annexations; that worker representatives be
allowed to take part in the peace negotiations with the Russians;
improvements in the food supply; an end to the law of siege; the release
of political prisoners; democratization and suffrage reform; and, finally,
promises that the factories would not be militarized.[12] The German
government however refused to deal with the strikers or to discuss political questions with them. In the end the government responded by banning worker's meetings as well as *Vorwärts*, the Socialist party's
newspaper, and by militarizing many of the largest munitions factories.
Once the factories were militarized many of the leaders of the strike were
drafted and sent to the frontlines, which proved to be an ultimately disastrous move. Once they arrived at the front these men proceeded to pros-
elytize and gain converts among the frontline soldiers. These moves did
break the strike and by February 4 the disturbances were over. For those
who were paying attention, however, the strike was further evidence that
German society was reaching its breaking point. Despite the suppression
of this strike additional strikes took place throughout the year. By the
end of 1918 Germany had experienced twice as many strikes as it did in
1917. Roughly 100,000 strikers missed work each month in 1918, up from
50,000 per month in 1917.[13] Simply put, the inability of the German

government to deal with the problems of the war or to win the war was eroding the German people's faith in and respect for the government. In the words of one German official from early 1918, "The authority of the state is collapsing."[14] It was clear to many observers that Germany could not withstand another winter of war; something had to give: either peace would have to be made or the war would have to be won in 1918. It was at this point that events in Russia appeared to give Germany one last chance at victory.

Grasping at Straws: The *Kaiserschlacht* and the False Hopes of 1918

On November 7 (October 25 O.S.) the Bolshevik Party of Vladimir Lenin seized control of the Russian capital city, Petrograd. In the ensuing days they also seized control of Moscow and proclaimed that the Provisional Government, which had ruled the country since the deposition of the Czar in March, had been replaced by a government of the Soviets, the worker's and soldier's councils that had also formed in March. Soon thereafter Russia collapsed into civil war. This series of developments seemed to offer the German government a reprieve; perhaps the submarines were not the last card after all. If the war in the east could be ended on terms favorable to Germany then the millions of German soldiers fighting on that front could be transferred to the west where they could be deployed in a new last card, a final grand offensive to defeat the British and French armies before the United States Army arrived in strength. The Bolsheviks, after first issuing a Decree on Peace to all the warring powers, which was ignored, proved to be amenable and Lenin's government, at his insistence, signed an armistice with the Central Powers in December. German and Russian representatives met in the Polish town of Brest-Litovsk to work out a final peace treaty for the Eastern Front. While those negotiations went on Ludendorff transferred over 1 million German soldiers from Russia to the west for a new offensive.

The Germans were now handed the opportunity to craft a peace treaty for the Eastern Front, a treaty that would embody their war aims and demonstrate to the western powers just what a German peace would look like. The discussions over the treaty revealed deep divisions within Germany and between Germany and Austria-Hungary. There were calls in the Reichstag for a peace of reconciliation, a peace without annexations, but the government, really led by this juncture by Ludendorff, insisted on taking this opportunity to ensure German domination of Eastern

Europe. In particular the Germans insisted on separating Poland, the regions of the future Baltic States, the Ukraine, and Finland from Russia. Accordingly they professed to support national separatist movements in those areas as well as in the Caucasus. What the German government decided to implement in the winter of 1917 was not a peace of reconciliation but a peace of victory. When the German demands were presented to the Russian delegation they balked at signing what was clearly a punitive treaty and the negotiations broke down. The reluctance of the Russian negotiators only hardened the German position. With the negotiations still stalled in January the German army began a new advance in the east. They met with little to no resistance and Lenin was eventually driven to force his government to accept the German demands. He feared that failure to do so would result in German armies marching into Petrograd and crushing his revolution in its cradle. The result was the Treaty of Brest-Litovsk. The treaty was signed on March 3 and it was, in every sense of the term, a *diktat*, a dictated peace. Russia lost Poland, Finland, Estonia, Latvia, Lithuania, Transcaucasia, and Ukraine. All were made into technically independent states but this was a fig leaf disguising German domination of all the regions but Transcaucasia, which was left in the Turkish sphere of influence. Russian lost more than 750,000 square kilometers, an area twice the size of Germany. The lost provinces contained 26 percent of the Russian population, 37 percent of Russia's arable land, 28 percent of Russian industry, 26 percent of all Russian railways, and 75 percent of Russia's coal and iron deposits.[15] In addition the people and businesses of the Central Powers were given free rein to own property in Russia (while Russian property was being nationalized by the Communist government) and freedom to conduct commercial and industrial activities without interference from Russian laws or the Russian state. In effect they were granted extraterritoriality. The Russians also agreed to completely demobilize their army and navy. The treaty marked the high point of success for the Second Reich. It also helped to seal its doom.

The Treaty of Brest-Litovsk was accompanied by the Treaty of Bucharest, which was signed with Rumania. Together the two treaties brought the war on the Eastern Front to a close and raised fresh hopes for victory in Germany. The end of the fighting in the east allowed Ludendorff to send German troops, soldiers who had enjoyed repeated successes and hence still had strong morale, to the Western Front. Just as importantly the signing of the treaties raised profound hopes among the German people that the worst of the food crisis was over. This was because, according to the Treaty of

Bucharest, the Central Powers gained control of Rumania's railways, oil fields, and, most significantly, its grain exports. Furthermore, the newly independent state of Ukraine, which was run by a strongly pro-German government, quickly signed a treaty with Germany that pledged the new state to ship supplies of Ukrainian grain to Germany starting in the fall of 1918. The promise of massive new imports of grain led the German government to pledge that there would be no reduction in the grain ration in 1918. Unfortunately in the actual event neither Rumania nor the Ukraine was able to provide anywhere near the amount of food that was necessary. Both areas had seen their production devastated by the war. Rumania had been invaded and overrun by the Central Powers and the Ukraine was quickly swept up into the civil war that soon consumed Russia. In addition both states had their own populations to feed. Furthermore, the Germans and Austro-Hungarians both desperately needed Rumanian and Ukrainian grain and in at least one famous instance the Austro-Hungarians seized grain that was bound for Germany. In the end the hopes that these new conquests would free the Central Powers from their deadly food shortages were misplaced and the ration of bread, along with all others, would indeed be cut once again in the summer of 1918.

The failure of the eastern treaties to provide the promised supplies left the Germans and their allies with only one final hope for victory, a great offensive to drive the British and French to the peace table before the Americans could arrive in sufficient numbers to make victory impossible. The end of the eastern campaign did indeed allow Ludendorff to shift over 1 million, high quality German troops from the east to the west; even though hundreds of thousands remained to police Germany's new conquests those that remained were second line units that would have been of minimal use on the Western Front. However, even with that additional million men the German army in the west was smaller in size than the combined armies of the Entente. After the transfer the Germans had roughly 3.5 million men in the west facing almost 4 million Entente soldiers, a figure that does *not* include the growing American force, which was at roughly 300,000 men by March 1918 and growing rapidly.[16] Ludendorff hoped to use this army, which was not even equal in size to that of its enemies, and which was severely outgunned not only in terms of artillery and shells but especially in terms of the newer weapons of war, the airplane and the tank, and which had been subsisting on a diet just slightly above starvation level for the last year, to force the British and French to accept a German peace, a peace that would clearly be harsh and punitive. The very idea was madness.

Much has been written about what has been called the *Kaiserschlacht*, or the Peace Offensive (which was actually a series of smaller offensives strung together), because they created an extremely dramatic final act to the war. However, the offensives never had a serious chance of success. They faced a myriad of problems. First of all, the Germans were outnumbered and outgunned. Second, Ludendorff had no overall strategic conception for the offensive. He simply planned to punch a hole in the enemy lines using new infiltration tactics and then hope that once the enemy lines were tactically broken strategic success would follow. Finally and most importantly, the American army continued to build in the background, which meant that there was little to no incentive for the Entente to consider a harsh Brest-Litovsk-style peace when they knew that millions of Americans were on their way to Europe. It is difficult to escape the impression that Ludendorff was simply grasping at straws in desperation. With the failure of the submarines there appeared to be no real path to victory but since defeat or even a compromise peace was unthinkable victory *had* to be possible and since there were no other options that meant a great offensive *had* to be able to win the war. It was circular reasoning born out of desperation and a refusal to admit that victory was all but impossible by this point.

What the entire episode of March to July 1918 represents is a snapshot of the single greatest German failing in the entire war; the Germans completely lost sight of the fact that war is a continuation of politics by other means and that war must serve a larger policy. The German conception that the war was too important to be left to the politicians and that the generals had to have carte blanche to fight it as they saw fit, which ruled the day after the ouster of Bethmann-Hollweg, led to disaster. There was no attempt after July 1917, and precious little before then, to make the military serve a larger political objective, partly because there was little idea of just what Germany was fighting for. The war began to support Austria-Hungary but then took on a life of its own and the German government never clarified precisely what its war aims were. Bethmann-Hollweg assembled what Fritz Fischer called the September Program[17] but it was never officially adopted as a list of aims. To a degree this reluctance to define just what Germany was fighting for was necessary in order to maintain the Burgfrieden, which would have been ripped apart by open debates over war aims, as it was in July 1917 but it was also caused by one of the great failings of the entire post-Bismarck epoch, a general inability to understand diplomacy. Under Wilhelm II's reign the German government specialized in disastrous diplomatic failures. The negotiations at Brest-Litovsk were the last of a series of disastrous foreign policy decisions that dated back to the failure to renew the Reinsurance Treaty in 1890. The Germans had an opportunity in the spring of 1918, not to impose a Germanic peace, but to at least avoid total defeat. Had the German government granted the Russians a peace of reconciliation at Brest-Litovsk they could then have launched a political offensive aimed at the war weary people of France and Great Britain timed to correspond to Ludendorff's military offensive. Such a move, offering a peace of reconciliation akin to the hypothetical one offered to the Russians, might have been enough, if coupled with a dramatic military victory, to convince the Entente governments to talk peace. It is impossible to say if it might have worked but it presented the only real opportunity remaining to the Germans and their allies. The idea of staying on the defensive through another winter of war was unthinkable to Germany's allies and to most of the German people; the war had to be ended in 1918, so an offensive had to be launched. It should have been accompanied by a diplomatic and political offensive but the actual Brest-Litovsk treaty closed off that opportunity. All that remained to Ludendorff and company then was a last, desperate throw of the dice.

What Ludendorff planned was a powerful strike at the British forces around the old battlefields of the Somme. He planned to use innovative new tactics, called stormtroop tactics, to end the stalemate in the west. The stormtroopers were small, mobile detachments of infantry that would penetrate through the enemy lines in a limited geographic area and then strike at the rear of the nearby enemy forces, creating confusion and allowing additional German troops to drive into the gap they created. By doing so they would end the stalemate and restore a war of movement. These tactics had worked brilliantly in Italy the previous year at the Battle of Caporetto and they would again prove their worth in this offensive. The operation, named Operation Michael, after the patron saint of Germany, began on March 21 and the stormtroopers did indeed break through, winning the most significant German victory on the Western Front since August 1914. They tore an 80-kilometer gap in the Entente lines and drove the British back 64 kilometers, inflicting 200,000 casualties in the process.[18] The victory was celebrated across Germany and the French government began making plans to evacuate Paris. In the heat of the crisis the military and political leaders of the Entente nations met to decide how to respond to the new German threat. The overall British and French commanders, Douglas Haig and Philippe Petain, could not agree on the best way to meet the German strike and each distrusted the other. Petain in particular became defeatist. As a result of the crisis the Entente's leaders decided on an unprecedented move; for the first time in the war all the Entente forces in France would be placed under a single commander. The Entente Supreme War Council turned to General Ferdinand Foch, who showed no inclination whatsoever toward peace. Foch likened the situation to that of 1914 and proposed to meet it the same way, by fighting to the end. However, by the time this decision was made the German offensive was already slackening. As dramatic as it was the German breakthrough did not cause the Entente lines to collapse, nor was it able to divide the British and French armies. After several days of fighting and after suffering heavy losses the German offensive ground to a halt. The victory had allowed them to recover most of the ground they had lost when they retreated to the Hindenburg Line in 1917 but it did not win the war. Instead the German lines now extended across the ruined battlefields of the Somme, an inhospitable area that would have to be traversed by German supply columns in order to keep the frontline forces ready to fight. In the meantime the Entente was able to bring up reinforcements. The victory was purely tactical, it did nothing to change Germany's overall situation, and it came at a high price. The Germans lost 239,000 irreplaceable men.

Unable and unwilling to admit defeat Ludendorff opted for another offensive, this time in Flanders. The same tactics were used and on April 9 the German army struck again. This offensive, code named Georgette, lasted until April 29 and was, once again, a tactical German victory. German forces advanced 19 kilometers but, as with Michael, the offensive only served to extend the German lines; it did not materially alter Germany's overall strategic situation. If anything, the victory made the German position worse because they lost another 100,000 irreplaceable troops. Though the Germans were gaining ground they were also losing men they could not afford to lose. In effect, in his chimerical pursuit of a desperate victory Ludendorff was bleeding the German army white.

Ludendorff tried again in late May, this time launching a strike toward Paris and the old battlefields of the Marne. Once more the Germans won an impressive tactical victory. This time they advanced all the way back to the Marne River; once again German soldiers were only 90 kilometers from Paris. However, this offensive also stalled. It turned out to be the last major German success of the war. A fourth offensive, launched further north on June 9, failed to achieve any notable gains. Ludendorff's final offensive had brought the German armies all the way back to where they had stood in 1914 but it had singularly failed to force the Entente to come to the negotiating table. The new last card had failed. In fact, with the exception of the brief moments in March when the Entente generals panicked, Ludendorff's offensive never came close to achieving the kind of strategic victory the Germans needed. In the process Ludendorff inflicted over 500,000 casualties on his own army, losses that were utterly irreplaceable at this juncture of the war. No one wanted to admit it yet, but the Germans had lost the war.

The End

When it came the end came suddenly. It began, poetically enough, at the same place where the Germans lost the most decisive battle of the war, on the Marne River. On July 15 the Germans launched what would be their final offensive of the war. This time Ludendorff hoped to break the Entente line in the Marne sector. Foch, through intelligence gathered partly from German deserters, had discovered where the next attack would take place and had prepared his defenses accordingly; therefore when the German attack began it fell on well-prepared enemy positions. As a result the Germans achieved only minimal gains and within two days the assault had stalled. What followed is known as the Second Battle of the Marne.

On July 18 the Entente struck back. French, British, and American forces now broke through the German lines, which were held by badly exhausted German soldiers who were far in advance of their supply centers and their elaborate defensive positions. The Entente armies won a stunning success and advanced 8 kilometers east on the first day. Between the 19th of July and the 3rd of August the German forces were forced to withdraw, surrendering much of the territory they had so recently conquered. Another 170,000 Germans were lost and the initiative in the war shifted, permanently, to the Entente.[19]

The Second Battle of the Marne was followed by a series of additional Entente offensives that drove the Germans further back. The period is referred to as the Hundred Days and it encompasses the final battles of the war. The first, and most significant, of this series of Entente attacks was launched on August 8 near Amiens. The British armies smashed through the German lines and advanced 13 kilometers while capturing 12,000 prisoners.[20] This was the first time in the war that large numbers of German soldiers surrendered and it so shocked Ludendorff that he labeled August 8 the "black day of the Germany army in this war." Throughout the remainder of August and into September the Entente forces slowly but inexorably pushed the Germans back toward their own borders. The morale of the German army was breaking under the pressure of the Entente's superiority in men and materiel. That morale had already been dealt a severe blow earlier in the year when German soldiers captured Entente positions during their own offensives and discovered that their enemies were far better supplied and fed than they were. The German soldiers had been told that the conditions of the Entente armies were as bad if not worse than their own because of the submarine campaign. When they captured those Entente positions they discovered irrefutable proof that the submarines were not actually starving their enemies into submission. Now those same men faced the likely prospect of another grim winter of starvation, illness, and death with no prospect of ultimate victory to make that sacrifice worthwhile. As a result of that breaking morale 110,000 German soldiers deserted in August.[21] Things were no better on the home front, where conditions already resembled those of the Turnip Winter.

By August the potato supply was all but exhausted and the government was forced to cut the bread ration down to 160 grams per day. In Vienna civilians were trying, and failing, to survive on a diet of only 760 calories a day.[22] By that point pork had all but disappeared and the only meat remaining to most Germans was horse meat. Even that was in such short supply that the government was forced to implement "meatless weeks" in August.[23] The failure of the great offensive and the dying of the last flickers of hope meant that all these sacrifices were for nothing. On the home front the food situation now took center stage and the last vestiges of the Burgfrieden collapsed. Despair became common for many of those hardest hit by the war, in particular white collar workers. Resentment of the wealthy and all those able to afford to eat on the black market swelled. Even the respect for the army began to collapse and soldiers returning from the front in many instances were no longer seen as heroes. Instead they were now just unpleasant reminders of the endless and futile war. Those same soldiers often gave in to despair themselves. In September the censors in the German army began seeing evidence in the letters of soldiers that the faith in an eventual victory was gone. Numerous letters referred to the Entente's superiority in artillery, aircraft, and, in particular, tanks. Many men were also becoming increasingly critical of their own officers, who were blamed for the horrible food situation and for lying to the men.[24] Hope was already fading fast when another lightning bolt struck.

In late September the Entente launched another series of major offensives, not only on the Western Front but in the Balkans as well. On

September 26 American forces attacked in the Meuse-Argonne sector, on the 27th the British launched an assault on Cambrai, and on the 28th British, Belgian, and French troops attacked on the Flanders front. On September 29 yet another British assault was launched, at St. Quentin against the Hindenburg Line. The decisive breakthrough came, however, in the same place the war started, the Balkans. On September 18 British, French, and, fittingly enough, Serbian forces attacked the Bulgarians. Bulgarian resistance evaporated and on September 26 the Bulgarian government asked for an armistice, which was granted and then signed on September 29. The armistice agreement required the Bulgarians not only to lay down their arms but to allow Entente forces access to Bulgarian territory. This opened the southern flank of the Central Powers position and exposed the tottering Austro-Hungarian Empire to invasion from the south. It also separated the Austro-Hungarians and the Germans from their remaining ally, the Ottoman Empire. Most importantly, it broke Ludendorff's morale. In panic he now concluded that the war was lost. He called on the civilian government to make peace, already arguing that it was the civilians, not the army, who had cost Germany the war. This attempt to whitewash his own failures would eventually bear poisonous fruit and give rise to the legend of the "stab in the back," according to which victory was stolen from the victorious German army by traitors at home. The chancellor, Georg von Hertling, refused to take up the charge of ending the war and resigned. He was replaced on October 3 by Prince Max of Baden, who, on the very next day, sent an appeal to President Woodrow Wilson, asking him to negotiate an armistice based on the president's famous 14 points.

The negotiations between the German and American governments took place over the first weeks of October while the German military situation continued to deteriorate, with the British in particular making extensive gains in Flanders. On October 17 they recaptured Ostend and on October 19 Zeebrugge. As the negotiations continued it became clear to Prince Max and then to Ludendorff that the Entente was not going to grant an armistice that would allow the Germans to resume the fighting later. The Entente was insisting, through Wilson, that the Germans abandon their conquered territory, end the submarine campaign, and turn over their artillery and machine guns as well as their submarines and the High Seas Fleet. When it became clear to Ludendorff that the Entente wanted Germany to surrender he changed his mind and argued that the Germans should reject Wilson's armistice demands and continue the war. In the middle of these negotiations Admiral Reinhard Scheer, who had been promoted to command of the entire High Seas Fleet earlier in the year, decided to act.

The war so far had demonstrated that the money that had been invested in the High Seas Fleet had basically been wasted. The German battleships had been unable to do anything to aid the German war effort and therefore the burden of actually fighting the war at sea fell to the submarines. With the war now nearing its end the commanders of the fleet feared that the utter failure of the battle fleet would endanger future funding for the navy, so they, in particular Reinhard Scheer, sought a dramatic means to recoup the honor of the fleet and position the navy for the postwar period. Scheer decided to send the High Seas Fleet on a final sortie into the North Sea. Once again submarines would be based off the British harbors and throughout the North Sea, waiting to attack the Grand Fleet, which would be lured out of its bases by a sortie from the entire High Seas Fleet. The hope was, as it had been in 1916, that the submarines would be able to damage the Grand Fleet before it arrived in battle so that the High Seas Fleet would have a better chance at destroying it. This time, however, the High Seas Fleet was ordered to seek and accept battle whatever the conditions. Ideally it might win a stunning victory that would turn the tide in the war; at the very least it was to die a *glorious* death and thereby sow the seeds for a new German navy to be created after the war. The orders were given to Hipper, now commander of the High Seas Fleet, on October 22, while Prince Max's government was in the middle of negotiations with President Wilson. Hipper was ordered to plan the operation. While he was doing so it became clear to the German government and the high command that President Wilson was not going to allow the Germans to simply gain a respite from the fighting. He was insisting on armistice terms that amounted to a surrender. Upon learning those terms, and having had time to recover his nerves, Ludendorff changed his mind and urged the Kaiser and the government to reject the president's demands and continue the war. When his demands were rejected he resigned his post in anger on October 26. With those events in mind, on the 27th Scheer approved Hipper's plan for the naval operation, without informing the Kaiser or the government of what he intended. Had the mission gone forward it would almost certainly have derailed the peace negotiations; it was stopped, however, by the sailors of the fleet.

Over the course of the 24th to the 28th of October rumors began to circulate within the High Seas Fleet that the officers were planning a *death ride*, a suicide mission designed to end the peace negotiations and prolong the war. Determined not to be the last to die in a lost war the crews on some of the battleships mutinied on October 29. The initial mutiny only lasted two days. It was suppressed on October 31 when the original mutineers were arrested. They had, however, achieved their immediate goal; there would be no death ride. Instead Hipper ordered the fleet dispersed. Many of the battleships were sent to the major port of Kiel in the Baltic, where they arrived on November 1. Unfortunately for the officers of the fleet the arrest of the original mutineers had not suppressed all mutinous opinion in the fleet and by dispersing the battleships Hipper also spread the mutiny to the ports. On November 3 several members of the crews from a number of German battleships took to the streets of Kiel to protest the arrest of the first mutineers. Those sailors were quickly joined in their march by large numbers of dockyard workers. Attempts to stop the protests led to fighting, which quickly marked the beginning of the German Revolution of 1918.

While these events took place in the fleet Germany lost her remaining allies. The Ottoman Empire agreed to an armistice on October 31 and Austria-Hungary, which was beginning to collapse into its component parts, quit the war on November 2. In Germany Prince Max's government had agreed in principle to all of Wilson's demands and plans were made to dispatch an armistice commission to France to officially end the war. Only one question remained: what would happen to the Kaiser?

Wilson had demonstrated a reluctance to make peace with the Kaiser's government and that led some members of the German government to conclude that they would receive more favorable peace terms if the Kaiser abdicated. Wilhelm refused to consider it and none of his officials had the heart or the will to insist upon it, until the events in Kiel began to spread to other German cities. The German people themselves, exhausted after more than four years of war and deprivation and with an end to the war in sight, refused to let the question of the Kaiser extend the war. By November 7 workers and soldiers councils were forming in German cities and behind the lines at the front. The Social Democratic Party was warning the government of the possibility of a Soviet-style revolution and urging the abdication of the Kaiser as the only means to prevent it. Prince Max was caught in the middle and tried to convince Wilhelm to step aside but the latter refused. Matters came to a head on November 9 when the Kaiser arrived at army headquarters and asked Ludendorff's successor, General Wilhelm Groener, if the army would follow him into Berlin to crush the Socialists and the revolution. When he was informed by Groener that it would not, Wilhelm was forced to realize that his reign was over. He fled the country for the Netherlands that same day. Also on that day the moderate Social Democrats, led by Friedrich Ebert, proclaimed the creation of a German Republic and the radical Socialists, led by Karl Liebknecht, proclaimed a radical German Republic. Order had broken down at home. The last act of the war followed two days later when the German armistice commission, led by Matthias Erzberger, signed the armistice agreement. At 11 am on November 11 the armistice went into effect and the guns fell silent for the first time in over four years. Germany had lost the Great War.

CHAPTER 8

Conclusion: Why the Germans Lost the First World War

In the aftermath of defeat the German nation was left reeling. During the war the government had closely censored all military news so for many Germans defeat came as a profound shock. They had been led to believe, repeatedly, that victory was just around the corner. Though conditions within Germany were disastrous by 1918 they had also been told that, because of the submarine campaign, conditions in the Entente countries were just as bad. When they looked at maps of the war they saw that the Central Powers occupied Serbia, Rumania, vast stretches of Russia, and even parts of Belgium and France yet in November 1918 they suddenly found themselves with a new government that immediately signed an armistice. The confusion provided fertile soil for what would come to be known as the "Dolchstoss Legende," the myth of the stab in the back. According to this idea, put forth by Ludendorff in November 1918, the army had been "stabbed in the back" by the revolutionaries who overthrew the Kaiser in early November. Ludendorff and those who agreed with him argued that the German army had never been defeated in the field and that victory could still have been won if the Socialists had not betrayed the Reich. The idea sounded all too plausible to many Germans and because of it the new government, the Weimar Republic, was blamed by many for the defeat of 1918. A series of Reichstag hearings looking into the reasons for Germany's defeat did little to dispel the myth and in the end the poisonous political atmosphere that resulted helped lay the groundwork for the rise of Nazism.

In reality there were many reasons why the Germans lost the First World War and none of them involved betrayal at home. Some of those reasons were objective factors beyond the control of the German government, such as the fact that the Central Powers were badly outnumbered by their enemies, but many others have to be laid at the feet of that government. Simply put it was the German leaders who failed their people, not the other way around. Germany's war effort was plagued, from the very start of the war, by a series of reckless gambles and poor decisions. Those decisions, combined with defeats in several key battles, brought down the Second Reich.

The poor decisions that ultimately brought down Imperial Germany predated the war. Kaiser Wilhelm II's assumption of the imperial throne brought about an end to the careful diplomacy of Otto von Bismarck. Bismarck had designed a system of alliances that was aimed at preserving the European peace and Germany's dominant position in Europe. The new Kaiser and the younger men that he brought in as advisors were not content with that position and they embarked on a new and ultimately disastrous foreign policy course. Their poor diplomatic decisions began with the Kaiser's refusal to renew the Reinsurance Treaty Bismarck had signed with Russia in 1887. That left an unattached Russia eager to sign an alliance with the equally unattached France, a deal which was completed in 1894. That created, as we have seen, an anti-German alliance that greatly outnumbered the German/Austro-Hungarian Dual Alliance. By 1914 the former alliance had a population of military age men that was double that of the German alliance. Wilhelm and his advisors made this problem much worse by then pursuing what they called Weltpolitik, a drive to create a powerful German empire and a fleet strong enough to protect it. The key figures in this move, Chancellor Bernhard von Bülow and Naval Secretary Alfred Tirpitz, were often openly anti-British and the German naval challenge in particular drove the British to tacitly join the Franco-Russian alliance. In 1904 Great Britain and France signed an agreement known as the Entente Cordiale and in 1907 a similar agreement between Great Britain and Russia turned that into the Triple Entente. That meant the anti-German coalition could now draw on the might of the British Empire as well. Hence the Dual Alliance was even more outnumbered. The changing diplomatic circumstances led the German government to believe it was being encircled by its enemies and that in turn led to disastrous foreign policy gambles, such as the one in Morocco, that, rather than disrupting the enemy coalition, made it even stronger. By 1914 the German government, through its diplomatic failings, had laid a noose around its own neck. Unable to grasp the subtleties of diplomacy the German regime was left to fall back on its military power and increasingly came to believe that it could only break the growing encirclement through military action, military action that ideally would come sooner rather than later since at least one of their enemies, Russia, was growing stronger as it became more industrialized and increased its railroad network. When Franz Ferdinand was assassinated in Sarajevo the resulting crisis presented an opportunity to possibly break that encirclement with a successful war. The first of many reckless gambles was taken on July 5, 1914, when the Kaiser and Chancellor Bethmann-Hollweg gave the Austro-Hungarian government the infamous blank check, promising they would support any Austro-Hungarian action against Serbia, even if it led to war. When war did indeed result the German government followed that first gamble with another; they implemented their only war plan, the Schlieffen-Moltke Plan.

Understanding that in a long war they would be at an enormous disadvantage the Germans crafted a military plan that was designed to win the war quickly. They would leave the Russian front relatively lightly defended and send the bulk of their army into France through Belgium in the hopes that they could force the French army into a decisive battle and destroy it, all within roughly six weeks of the start of mobilization. The plan left the eastern frontier of Germany largely undefended and Germany's Austro-Hungarian ally facing Russia effectively on its own. What was worse for Germany's long-term prospects was that the plan, by requiring that Germany invade Belgium, all but guaranteed that Britain would enter the war and enter it quickly. If all went according to plan that would not matter. The German army would defeat the French army and then be able to transfer most of its forces east for a longer war with the Russians. However, the plan required nearly superhuman efforts from the German soldiers and was never likely to succeed. In the actual course of events the German right wing pushing through Belgium did drive the French, Belgian, and British armies back, nearly all the way to Paris. However, the Germans were unable to destroy those enemy forces and as their own armies pressed further into France, suffering heavy casualties and leaving their supply centers further and further to the rear, the Germans grew progressively weaker. The French and British were able to regroup and stop the German advance at the Marne, eventually driving the Germans back away from Paris. The German defeat in the First Battle of the Marne marked the failure of the Schlieffen-Moltke Plan and meant that the war would now be a long and drawn out affair in which every advantage lay with Germany's enemies. The victories that the Germans won in the east at the same time could not offset the enormously important defeat at the Marne. The Marne was the most significant battle of the entire war and though it did not make German defeat inevitable it certainly set the course for the remainder of the war.

After both armies failed to turn each other's flank later in 1914 the war in the west settled into a stalemate. That allowed the Germans to turn their attentions to the east in 1915 in an effort to force the Russians to make peace. German armies won remarkable victories that year, starting with the Battle of Gorlice-Tarnow. They managed to drive the Russians completely out of Russian Poland and mostly out of Galicia and Lithuania. Additional victories were won in the south when the armies of the Central Powers overran Serbia late in 1915. None of these victories though changed the fundamental strategic reality of the war, which was that the war would ultimately be lost or won on the Western Front. Understanding that, in 1916 the German commander, Erich von Falkenhayn, switched the army's focus back to the Western Front. Falkenhayn hoped to knock the French out of the war by launching a battle of attrition around the French city of Verdun. He hoped to substitute materiel for manpower and use German artillery to slaughter the French defenders of the forts around Verdun in the belief that the German army could "bleed the French army white." The battle lasted from February until November 1916 and resulted in massive casualties on both sides. The Germans achieved small initial gains at Verdun but when the British and Russians launched offensives of their own that summer the Germans were forced to transfer substantial forces from the Verdun sector and go onto the defensive. That left the French to take the offensive themselves and by winter they had retaken all the land they had lost earlier in the year. The battle was a bloody and brutal failure. Though the Germans inflicted enormous damage on the French they were once again unable to force one of their enemies out of the war. The Battle of Verdun was the second major German defeat of the war. The third occurred nearly simultaneously.

In late June 1916 the British opened an artillery barrage of unprecedented intensity and duration against the German defenses along the Somme River. This presaged the beginning of the Entente's major western offensive of 1916, the Battle of the Somme. When the bombardment ended, British and French forces attacked on July 1. The British in particular suffered egregious casualties that day, with 20,000 men being killed and another 40,000 wounded or missing. The popular memory of the Somme is dominated by the terrible casualties of that first day but the battle was not a one-day affair, nor was it a British defeat. The British and French offensives continued all the way through the summer and well into the fall, only coming to an end out of exhaustion in November. Though the Entente forces failed to break through the German lines and win the war in 1916, as they had initially hoped, they inflicted massive damage on the German army. By the end of the battle the German reserves had been destroyed and the German army had nearly been bled white. In the midst of that battle Falkenhayn was replaced by Paul von Hindenburg and Erich Ludendorff. In order to make up for their own losses the new commanders ordered the German army to withdraw from much of the ground they had just fought so hard to hold. They pulled back to a newly constructed defensive position known as the Hindenburg Line. Doing so allowed them to shorten their lines and reduce the amount of ground they needed to defend, thus freeing up men who, when they were combined with the 1918 draft class, which was called up early, formed a new reserve.

The new German commanders, along with most other German generals and soldiers, were also shocked at the superiority in materiel the Entente armies demonstrated at the Somme. German industry at this point in the war was completely incapable of matching the Entente's prodigious output of shells and other munitions. Their shock at British superiority led Hindenburg and Ludendorff to institute the ultimately disastrous Hindenburg Plan. This was an attempt to push German industry to greater levels of production by, among other things, constructing new factories. However, by this point no plan could squeeze sufficient additional material out of German industry. It was being crippled by the British naval blockade.

These three critical battles, the Marne, Verdun, and the Somme, were major factors in bringing on Germany's defeat. Equally important was the utter failure of the German battle fleet. In the years before the war the German government had gone to great lengths to build a battle fleet that could rival that of Great Britain. They diverted funds that would have been better spent on the German army to the construction of what became known as the High Seas Fleet, in the process destroying what had long been a friendly relationship between Germany and Great Britain and driving the latter into friendship with the French and Russians. The British responded to the German challenge by expanding their own fleet and, unlike the Germans, they were not burdened by also having to maintain a large army. By the time war came in 1914 the British Grand Fleet outnumbered the German High Seas Fleet 21 to 13 in dreadnoughts and 26 to 16 in pre-dreadnought battleships. Due to their numerical disadvantage the German fleet opted for a defensive campaign and waited for the Grand Fleet to enter German waters to implement a naval blockade. The British, however, chose instead to implement a distant blockade by closing the entrances to the North Sea at Dover and between Norway and Scotland. The distant blockade managed to cut off German contact with much of the outside world without risking the Grand Fleet in unfavorable conditions. The High Seas Fleet had no answer. Its entire war plan had been premised on weakening the Grand Fleet through a series of torpedo-boat and submarine attacks when the former entered German waters to blockade the coast. Once the Grand Fleet had been sufficiently weakened the High Seas Fleet would then engage it in a decisive battle and destroy it. Because the British did not play their part in this German plan, the German admirals were left without options. Their hands were tied further after the British launched a successful raid into German waters with destroyers, cruisers, and battle cruisers on August 28, 1914. The raid led to the Battle of the Heligoland Bight, in which several German cruisers were destroyed with virtually no losses to the British. The Battle of the Bight led to Kaiser Wilhelm giving strict orders that his battle fleet was not to be risked unnecessarily, an order which handcuffed the German admirals. The Kaiser's order, combined with the natural timidity of the High Seas Fleet's first commander, Friedrich von Ingenohl, meant that the fleet did very little. For example, it made no effort whatsoever to interfere with the transportation of the British army to France. It did launch two operations and one of them resulted in the Battle of the Dogger Bank, a minor German defeat in which one German cruiser was destroyed. That defeat led to Ingenohl's ouster as commander. He was replaced by Hugo von Pohl, who fell ill and was replaced in turn by Reinhard Scheer. Scheer was a more aggressively minded commander who decided, despite the Kaiser's order, to risk the High Seas Fleet in a major operation to try and destroy part of the British Grand Fleet. This operation culminated in the decisive moment of the battleship war, the Battle of Jutland.

Late in the afternoon on May 31, 1916, the Grand Fleet and the High Seas Fleet met in the waters west of Denmark in the largest clash between battleship fleets in history. Over the course of several hours the two fleets battered one another with heavy gunfire and the German fleet did inflict more losses on the British than they received. However, the entire German fleet was nearly destroyed, twice, and was forced to flee from the battle. Over the course of the night of May 31/June 1 the Germans managed to sneak behind the British fleet and escape to their home ports.

Though they claimed victory on the basis of the number of ships they had sunk the Germans had once again suffered a decisive defeat. The Grand Fleet's strategic position was left untouched by the losses they suffered and the surviving British fleet was ready to return to sea within 48 hours while the High Seas Fleet was stuck in port undergoing massive repairs for months. Though it is not true that the High Seas Fleet stayed in port for the remainder of the war it is true that they were resoundingly defeated. They never again engaged the British in battle and the war at sea was left entirely to the German submarines. In the interim the British blockade was able to continue uninterrupted, with the only limitations on it coming from the British government's reluctance to anger the United States.

The triple defeats of 1916 combined with the tightening pressure of the British blockade and the disastrous Turnip Winter of 1916/1917 led the German government to launch a final reckless gamble. At the Pless Conference in January 1917 the German military was able to convince the Kaiser and the chancellor to launch a campaign of unrestricted submarine warfare in an attempt to starve the British into submission. The Germans had launched an initial campaign of unrestricted submarine warfare in 1915, at a time when they did not have enough submarines to inflict sufficient damage on the British. That initial campaign did destroy significant amounts of shipping but its most important consequence by far was that it drove the United States to become increasingly anti-German after German submarines sank a number of passenger liners, most famously the *Lusitania*. That initial campaign had been called off due to fears of war with the United States. By January 1917, however, the German military, out of desperation, decided that war with the United States had to be risked because only the submarines could defeat Great Britain. Accordingly the Germans launched their second unrestricted submarine campaign that February. The United States promptly severed diplomatic relations with Germany and then declared war on Germany in April. This last gamble brought the world's most powerful neutral into the war against Germany and immediately resulted in a dramatic tightening of the British blockade. When the British refused to make peace, despite the fact that the German submarines sank over 3.6 million tons of enemy shipping between February and August 1917, the Germans had effectively been defeated.

They were given a brief reprieve from imminent defeat when the Bolsheviks seized power in Russia and took that country out of the war in late 1917. This allowed Ludendorff to transfer substantial numbers of men from the east to the west and to launch one final series of offensives in the spring of 1918. The first of these offensives did succeed and sowed panic in the ranks of the Entente but the crisis was weathered and the German push was stopped. Ludendorff followed that strike with a number of succeeding ones but each offensive was less successful than its predecessor and by July 1918 the German army had exhausted itself. What followed was a successive series of Entente counterattacks that drove the Germans steadily back on the Western Front. The failure of their own offensives and the casualties they took in those battles caused the morale of the German army to begin to crumble. For the first time in the entire war German soldiers began surrendering in large numbers. At the same time Germany's allies began to collapse and by late September it was clear to the German High Command that the war was lost. The final collapse was not caused by revolution at home but by Ludendorff's own decision that the war was lost and that Germany needed to seek an armistice. A desperate attempt by the German navy to salvage its own reputation and destroy the peace negotiations with a desperate sortie of the High Seas Fleet resulted in mutiny, which turned to revolution. The revolution toppled the Kaiser and brought a new government to power, which signed an armistice ending the war on November 11, 1918. The war, however, was lost long before the revolution took place.

In the end the Germans lost the First World War for several reasons: first, they were fighting a coalition that greatly outnumbered them; second, that enemy coalition could rely on British naval power to cut the Germans and their allies off from the outside world while they themselves could draw on outside nations to supplement their own efforts; third, though they won many victories the Germans lost the most critical battles of the war. They were defeated at the Marne in the most decisive battle of the entire conflict. They were defeated in the massive battles of materiel in 1916. They were completely and utterly defeated at sea, first in the Battle of Jutland and then when the convoy system defeated the submarine campaign. The most significant factor by far though, because of its impact, both physical and moral, on the German home front and the military, was the British naval blockade. It is time to take a closer look at its impact.

Assessing the Impact of the Blockade

As we have seen Germany's ability to trade with the outside world was severely impacted by the institution and tightening of the British blockade as the war went on. That impact was, as Table 8.1 shows, disastrous.

Table 8.1   Value of German Imports and Exports, 1913–1918[1]

Year	Imports (billions of marks)	Exports (billions of marks)
1913	10.8	10.1
1914	10.6	9.0
1915	5.9	2.5
1916	6.4	2.9
1917	4.2	2.0
1918	4.2	2.8

By the end of 1914 the German merchant marine had been swept from the seas and Germany's ability to conduct overseas trade anywhere outside of the Baltic Sea had effectively ended. Take German exports to the United States as one example. In January 1914 Germany exported goods worth over US$16 million to the United States. By January 1916 that figure had been reduced to just over US$865,000. Even those exports had to be shuttled through Germany's neutral neighbors. In effect, Germany was left dependent on states such as Denmark and the Netherlands for its imports and exports. Of course, a simple decline in trade only tells one small part of the story; much more critical is how that decline in trade impacted the German economy as a whole. In order to understand that impact we will look first at German industry and then at the German food supply.

Table 8.2 tells part of the story.

Table 8.2 shows several things, first of all a significant decline in the production of both coal and steel upon the outbreak of the war. There are likely a number of factors driving that decline including the call up of men for the armed forces, the disruption of the economy as it transitioned from peace to war, and possibly the impact of the blockade.

Table 8.2   German Coal and Steel Production[2]

Year	Coal Produced (tons)	Steel Produced (tons)
1913	190,000,000	19,312,000
1914	161,000,000	14,408,000
1915	147,000,000	11,745,000
1916	159,000,000	13,293,000
1917	167,000,000	13,156,000
1918	158,000,000	11,864,000

In 1915 there was a further significant decline in production likely due once again to the disruptive effects of the war and the blockade. To a degree this decline was certainly due to the fractured nature of the German war economy and the inability of the German government to effectively orchestrate that economy during 1915. The increases seen in 1916 and 1917 are largely due to the greater centralization instituted by Walther Rathenau and the KRA as well as the release of men from the frontlines for use in the war industry under the Hindenburg Plan of late 1916. The 1918 decrease resulted from the general running down of German industry under the pressure of the continuing war. What impact did the British blockade play here? The blockade's impact was twofold. First of all the loss of imports such as Chilean nitrates certainly hampered Germany's ability to keep pace with its opponents and to produce its own internal supplies in sufficient quantities. More importantly though the existence of the blockade meant that Germany, unlike its opponents, could not supplement its own production by purchasing additional supplies overseas. The Germans, unlike the British and the other western nations in the Entente, did not have access to the major neutral market of the United States. The Entente, thanks to British naval mastery, was able to draw upon the industrial base of the United States to augment its own supplies. The blockade prevented Germany from doing the same and forced the Germans to rely on their own supplies. This forced the Germans into a much more difficult situation than that faced by David Lloyd George and the Ministry of Munitions in Britain. It also forced German industry and the German government into making several very hard choices, all of which led to a decline in the production of civilian good, which resulted in severe shortages of everything from coal to clothing.

In addition there were several goods that Germany simply could not produce in any measurable quantities on her own and the naval blockade cut Germany off, in some cases completely, from these critical imports. Cotton was one of these goods. After the British tightened the blockade in 1915 Germany was almost completely cut off from cotton imports. The result was a 90 percent decline in textile output by 1917, creating the clothing shortage that plagued Germany in the last years of the war. The Germans did produce wool but nothing near what was needed. In the entire course of the war they produced only 22,000 tons of wool. After creatively using flax, hemp, and even nettles, they were forced to turn to paper and create textiles out of paper fibers.[3]

Another good that was in extremely short supply was copper. Before the war Germany produced roughly 40,000 tons of copper annually but consumed nearly 220,000 tons. The vast majority of that additional 180,000 tons was imported from the United States. By January 1915 that supply was cut off since copper was widely recognized as contraband. This resulted in the German government requisitioning copper from German civilians, famously including church bells, but even that requisitioning, combined with increased internal production, left Germany 40 percent short of what she needed by 1916. By 1917 that shortfall had reached 50 percent. Creative attempts to substitute aluminum and zinc largely failed. Imports of nickel and tin were also nearly completely severed. Some small amounts came in through increased trade with the neutrals but when the United States entered the war in 1917 those imports ceased and Germany was completely cut off from those industrial metals.[4]

Rubber was yet another product that Germany could not produce internally. Prior to the war German industry imported 16,000 tons of rubber annually. That supply was completely severed by the blockade. This led German chemists to try to create synthetic rubber from coal and German industry to start recycling existing stocks of goods such as old tires. Even leather was imported before the war. As a result of the shortages of imported leather by 1917, 1,100 of the 1,600 German boot factories had closed and there was a serious shortage of footwear. What boots were produced of course went to the soldiers leaving the civilians with ersatz products made from paper and cardboard. In 1917 German industry produced only 12 million pairs of boots compared to the 120 million that were normally produced in peacetime.[5] Though the Germans were able to maintain coal and steel production at reasonable levels German industrial production overall had dropped to 57 percent of its prewar level by 1918.[6] The real disaster though was not in German industry but in German food production.

Table 8.3 helps to illustrate the collapse of the German food supply.

Table 8.3   Food Production in Germany, 1913–1918[7] (in thousands of metric tons)

Year	Wheat	Rye	Barley	Oats	Corn	Potatoes	Beets
1913	5094	12,222	3673	9714	621	54,121	18,540
1914	4343	10,427	3138	9038	–	45,570	16,919
1915	4235	9152	2484	5986	–	53,973	10,963
1916	3288	8937	2797	7025	–	25,074	10,145
1917	2484	7003	1865	3716	–	34,882	9967
1918	2528	6676	1850	4381	–	24,744	9884

Table 8.3 highlights several impacts of the war and the blockade on the German food supply. Most noticeable is the decline in the production of all grains and other staple goods. All of these goods were being produced at roughly half their peacetime level by the time the war ended. The decline in grain production took place immediately upon the outbreak of the war while potato production was able to remain somewhat level until the disastrous harvest of 1916, which it never recovered from. The single most important reason for the precipitous decline in food production was the shortage of fertilizer. The blockade cut Germany off from its imports of nitrates, in particular phosphoric and nitrogenous fertilizers, which were imported from South America. German fertilizer supplies fell precipitously as early as 1915. In peacetime German farmers had used 210,000 tons of nitrogenous fertilizers. By 1915 that figure had dropped to 73,000 tons; in 1916 it recovered slightly, to 80,000 tons thanks to the development of the Haber process. Phosphoric fertilizer supplies dropped from 630,000 tons in peacetime to 425,000 tons in 1915, 368,000 tons in 1916, and to 325,000 tons in 1917.[8] The decline in fertilizers forced German farmers to make greater use of livestock manure as fertilizer, which failed because, even though most German livestock populations (except pigs) remained stable throughout the war, those animals that survived were seriously malnourished by a lack of fodder, which meant in turn that they produced less manure, which meant in its own turn, less fertilizer and less food production, which led to less fodder and accordingly less manure in a vicious cycle that culminated in the near collapse of the German food supply by the end of the war.[9]

The collapse of the barley supply also led directly to the closure of many breweries and to a corresponding decline in beer production. Whereas in 1913 Germany produced over 69 million hectoliters of beer, by the end of the war that figure had been cut to just over 24 million hectoliters, a two thirds decline, and even the beer that was being produced was severely watered down and only available to the soldiers.[10] Further complicating the problem was the German rationing system, which sent one third of all food produced to the frontlines to feed the soldiers, leaving another third for all urban civilians and dividing the rest among the farmers for both their own food supply and seed grain for the next year's harvest. That meant that the largest segment of the population, the urban civilians, had the lowest level of supplies. By 1918 the daily ration for civilians was supplying 12 percent of the peacetime level of meat, 28 percent of the peacetime levels of butter, 15 percent in cheese, 7 percent in fats, 13 percent in eggs, 48 percent in bread (albeit mostly ersatz bread,

Table 8.4   German Food Imports during the War[11] (in metric tons)

Product	1916	1917	1918
Grains	20,063	3089	8322
Meat	5778	1848	504
Butter	7978	3513	2731
Vegetable Oils/Fats	791	148	56.2
Margarine	555	106	2.5
Cheese	6553	3187	2527
Fish	17,573	5416	4507

consisting of a mix of 55 percent rye, 35 percent wheat, and the rest various substitutes[12]), with only potatoes approximating their peacetime levels of consumption at 94 percent.[13]

What the earlier table does not show is the ability of the Germans to import additional supplies of food during the war. Table 8.4 illustrates those imports and shows very clearly the major impact of the American entry into the war in 1917.

Clearly German imports dropped disastrously in 1917. The major reason for the change was the entry of the United States into the war and the corresponding end to the American policies that had sought to limit the impact of the blockade. With American entry into the war the neutral loopholes that the United States had fought to maintain were closed by an American embargo on trade to the neutrals, such as the Netherlands, that had been reexporting goods to Germany. The American embargo forced these countries to reduce their exports to Germany. This resulted in an across-the-board decline in German imports, with the exception of grains in 1918. That exception stemmed from the defeat of Russia and Rumania and a resulting increase in trade between Germany and the newly independent Ukraine. Simply put, the blockade, in particular after the United States entered the war, devastated the German government's ability to feed its people. The story looks much the same when we look at the supply of German livestock (see Table 8.5).

Here too we see a decline, though with the exception of pigs that decline is not nearly as severe as the decline in grain and vegetable production. Indeed, on the surface the population of most German livestock remained remarkably stable. However, those animals that survived the war also suffered from the overall decline in grain production. For them it meant a decrease in their fodder supplies and this left most German livestock on a starvation diet by 1918. The major exception to the

Table 8.5   Amount of Livestock in Germany, 1913–1918[14] (1000s)

Year	Horses	Cows	Pigs	Sheep	Goats	Poultry
1913	4558	20,994	25,659	5521	3548	NA
1914	3435	21,829	25,341	5471	3538	NA
1915	3342	20,317	17,287	5073	3438	NA
1916	3304	20,874	17,002	4979	3940	65,178
1917	3324	20,095	11,052	4954	4315	58,995
1918	3425	17,650	10,271	5347	4321	51,305

generally stable population of German livestock was the pig population. This was directly due to the fact that pork was the meat of choice and therefore pigs supplied the majority of the meat on German tables. Furthermore the pig supply had been subjected to the *Schweinemord* of 1915, when many German farmers slaughtered their pigs out of fear that the government was going to requisition them. The porcine population never recovered. The decreasing supply of pork meant there was a great deal less meat in the German diet. That was also, of course, affected by the rationing policy of the government. In 1914 a German soldier received 285 grams of meat per day while the average civilian received 145 grams. By 1918 the corresponding figures were 127 grams for the soldier and 28 grams for the civilian.[15] Looking at both the livestock and grain figures, German food production in 1918 was at its lowest level since 1883.[16] By 1918 the average German diet consisted of less than 1,000 calories per day while that of the Entente nations remained near 2,000 per day. The British bread ration in 1918 was 415 grams, more than double that in Germany.[17] Only those Germans who could afford to access the black market were able to continue with even a marginal diet, and they were few in number.

Real wages in Germany dropped, across the board, by 34 percent during the course of the war.[18] Some groups survived better than others. Those employed in the munitions industries actually saw their pay keep pace with inflation while those in white collar jobs saw their pay collapse in comparison. Inflation was significant. For example, in July 1914 the average Berliner spent 23 marks on food every month. By October 1918, without going on the black market, the average Berliner was spending 65 marks every month, and getting much less in return.[19] Black market prices were much worse. For example, in 1914 one dozen eggs cost roughly 1 mark and by 1918 that same dozen eggs cost 17 marks on the black market. A half kilogram of butter that before the war would have cost roughly 1 mark cost 23 marks by 1918. A kilogram of meat that cost 3 marks before the war was going for 28 marks on the black market in 1917.[20] Simply put, these were prices very few Germans could pay. As a result the diet of the ordinary Germans was devastated and their ability to withstand the rigors of the war was correspondingly weakened.

The disastrous collapse of the German food supply resulted in many Germans losing between 20 and 33 percent of their weight during the course of the war.[21] That left the population much more susceptible to disease and over the course of the war German doctors reported a significant increase in the number of Germans suffering from rickets, scurvy, and dysentery; all of which are related to insufficient diets. In addition the lower diet and weakened immune systems of many Germans made them more susceptible to other diseases as well, the most notable of which were tuberculosis and influenza. Over the course of the war the number of tuberculosis-related deaths in Germany rose by 72 percent. The mortality rate rose overall throughout Germany over the course of the war, with the greatest increase, aside from soldiers, coming among women and young children. The mortality rate of German women in 1918 was 51 percent higher than it had been in 1913; that among children under the age of 5 was 50 percent higher than prewar levels and that of children aged 5 to 15 was 55 percent higher than it had been before the war.[22] One historian has estimated that the total German mortality rate, across all categories, increased by nearly one third over the course of the war.[23] Another historian has calculated that the German mortality rate increased from 9.5 percent in 1915 to 14.3 percent in 1916 and then to 32.2 percent and 37 percent in 1917 and 1918 respectively.[24] Those numbers do not distinguish between deaths from combat and deaths on the home front; the following ones do (See Table 8.6).

Table 8.6   German Civilian Deaths in Excess of Peacetime Figures[25]

Year	Excess Deaths
1914	42,369
1915	8871
1916	11,751
1917	68,598
1918	271,047
1919	71,449

The numbers clearly reflect the increasing mortality of German civilians as the hardships imposed by the war and the blockade ground on, with the peak coming, unsurprisingly, in the year of the great influenza outbreak, 1918. Another historian has tried to calculate how many of these deaths can be attributed directly to the British blockade and he estimates that total number as follows: 88,235 in 1915; 121,114 in 1916; 259,627 in 1917; and 293,760 in 1918 for a grand total of 732,736.[26] Combined with this increase in mortality was a corresponding decrease in births. The German birth rate of 1918 was 50 percent less than that of 1914, which meant roughly 3 million fewer births over the course of the war.[27] That meant, including the over 2 million battle deaths, that Germany lost nearly 6 million actual or potential people because of the war. It is likely we will never have a truly definitive set of figures for the damage wrought by the blockade but one thing is clear from the numbers we do have: the blockade wreaked havoc on German society and on the German's ability to prosecute the war.

In the final analysis the German government had good reason to fear a long war. At the end Great Britain's control of the seas allowed the Royal Navy, in particular once the United States had joined their side, to sever Germany's economic ties to the non-European world and thereby place enormous pressures on the German state and economy. Those pressures were echoed in the countries Germany was at war with, in particular during the submarine campaign of 1917, but they never reached the same level there that they did in Germany. The German government certainly did not respond to those pressures in the most efficient fashion; in particular, their ability to coordinate meaningful and effective responses to those pressures continued to be hampered throughout the war by the tremendous power given, on a local level, to the deputy commanding generals. The government's efforts to exert control over the food supply also ran into understandable resistance on the part of the German people themselves and the resulting inefficiencies and loopholes in the system were ruthlessly exploited by those who had the ability to do so, which meant that the pressures of war were not borne equally by German society and it was obvious to most Germans that this was the case. As the war continued and the sacrifices grew greater the social unity and cohesiveness of the early days of the war wore away and the cultural consensus in favor of the war broke down. By the Turnip Winter of 1916–17 it was only faith in the German military and the likelihood of eventual victory that kept the people going. When it became clear in the summer of 1917 that the submarines were not going to win the war for Germany and that their government had not been honest with them some segments of the population began demanding peace, a peace that their leaders were unwilling to accept, a peace without annexations. So the war and the suffering continued until it became clear to most Germans that even the great German army had been beaten and that it was necessary to end the war.

In the end British control of the seas and their naval blockade made two significant contributions to the Entente victory in the First World War. First of all it ensured that the Entente nations would be able to access the additional resources and industrial materials of the non-European world and that the Germans would not, thereby allowing the Entente to establish a critically important superiority in the production of munitions and newer weapons, such as the tank. Second, it allowed the Entente nations to shift their economies to a war footing while still having access to sufficient stocks of food and civilian goods, once again provided largely by the American economy. The Central Powers had to make that same shift without the benefit of American foodstuffs or imported fertilizers from South America and this meant agricultural disaster. The slow starvation of the German people sapped the will not only of the civilians but of the soldiers as well and made further resistance, once the army had been beaten in 1918, futile.

In the end the Germans lost the First World War because they had no answer to the problems caused by Britain's entry into the war. The German army won a remarkable series of victories over the course of the war but none of them could offset the geographical reality that Germany was cut off from the outside world by the Royal Navy. The victories of the German army could not offset the utter defeat of the German navy. In the final analysis Britain's control of the seas was the fundamental sine qua non to Entente victory. It was finally, in a desperate effort to disrupt that control, that the Germans made the decision that ultimately cost them the war, the decision to reinstitute unrestricted submarine warfare. When the submarines then failed to drive the British from the war and the United States joined them, Germany was doomed. The 1918 German offensive, dramatic as it was, could not have driven the Entente to accept a German peace. Only with a corresponding diplomatic initiative could the Germans have avoided defeat by that point. When that offensive was defeated the Central Powers lost all hope in victory and collapsed. That collapse started on the battlefields, not on the home front. The final blow came when Ludendorff admitted defeat in September 1918 and called for the government to negotiate an armistice. From that point there was no going back; the war was over.

Timeline of Major Events

June 28, 1914	Assassination of Archduke Franz Ferdinand in Sarajevo.
July 5, 1914	German government grants Austro-Hungarian government the blank check.
July 23, 1914	Austro-Hungarian government sends ultimatum to Serbia.
July 25, 1914	Austro-Hungarian government rejects Serbian response to ultimatum.
July 28, 1914	Austria-Hungary declares war on Serbia.
July 30, 1914	Russia mobilizes to support Serbia.
July 31, 1914	Germany demands that Russia cease mobilization or face war.
August 1, 1914	Germany declares war on Russia. German army mobilizes.
August 2, 1914	Germans occupy Luxembourg, send ultimatum to France.
August 3, 1914	Germany declares war on France. German army enters Belgium.
August 4, 1914	German assault on Liege begins. British ultimatum to Germany to leave Belgium. Britain declares war on Germany.
August 1914	Britain institutes naval blockade of Central Powers.
August 28, 1914	German navy defeated in the Battle of the Heligoland Bight.
September 5–9, 1914	German army defeated in the Battle of the Marne.
January 24, 1915	Germany navy defeated in the Battle of the Dogger Bank.

February to September 1915	First German unrestricted submarine campaign.
February to December 1916	German army defeated in the Battle of Verdun.
May 31, 1916	German navy defeated in the Battle of Jutland.
July to November 1916	German army defeated in the Battle of the Somme.
January 8, 1917	Pless Conference. German government decides on a new unrestricted submarine campaign.
February 1, 1917	Unrestricted submarine campaign begins.
April 4, 1917	United States declares war on Germany.
July 6–19, 1917	July Crisis in German government. Chancellor Bethmann-Hollweg forced out. Reichstag issues Peace Resolution.
November 1917	Bolsheviks seize power in Petrograd and Moscow, begin peace negotiations with German government.
March 3, 1918	Treaty of Brest-Litovsk signed.
March 21, 1918	Final German offensives begin.
July 18, 1918	German army defeated in the Second Battle of the Marne. Entente counteroffensives begin.
August 8, 1918	Black Day of the German army. First mass surrenders take place.
September 28, 1918	Bulgaria signs armistice with Entente. Ludendorff demands that the German government make peace.
October 3, 1918	Peace talks begin between the German government and President Wilson.
October 29, 1918	German High Seas Fleet mutinies.
October 31, 1918	Ottoman Empire signs armistice.
November 2, 1918	Austria-Hungary signs armistice.
November 9, 1918	Kaiser abdicates. German republic proclaimed.
November 11, 1918	Germany signs armistice ending First World War.

Major German Decision Makers of the First World War

Kaiser Wilhelm II	German Emperor, 1888–1918
Theobald von Bethmann-Hollweg	German Chancellor, 1909–1917
Helmuth von Moltke	Head of German General Staff, 1906–1914
Alfred von Tirpitz	Head of Imperial Navy Office, 1897–1916
Friedrich von Ingenohl	Head of High Seas Fleet, 1913–1915
Erich von Falkenhayn	War Minister, 1913–1914
	Head of German General Staff, 1914–1916
Hugo von Pohl	Head of the Naval Staff, 1913–1915
	Head of High Seas Fleet, 1915–1916
Reinhard Scheer	Head of High Seas Fleet, 1916–1918
	Head of Naval Staff, 1918
Henning von Holtzendorff	Head of Naval Staff, 1915–1918
Paul von Hindenburg	Commander of Eighth Army, 1914
	Head of German High Command in the east, 1914–1916
	Head of German General Staff, 1916–1918
Erich Ludendorff	Quartermaster General of Second Army, 1914
	Chief of Staff of Eighth Army, 1914
	Chief of Staff to High Command in the east, 1914–1916
	First Quartermaster General, 1916–1918

Notes

Introduction

1. This is precisely the argument made in Stephen Broadberry and Mark Harrison, eds., *The Economics of World War I* (New York: Cambridge University Press, 2005).

2. Though admittedly the chances of attaining a so-called German peace along of the lines of what the extreme nationalists, such as the Fatherland Party, were calling for were extremely slim. I do not see any way that the Germans could have achieved all of their war aims. The best discussion of those aims remains in Fritz Fischer, *Germany's Aims in the First World War* (New York: WW Norton, 1967).

3. Some however were long running and cannot be precisely placed into the chronology. I have decided to discuss those events roughly when they began.

4. This is traditionally referred to as the Schlieffen Plan. However, as recent research has shown the grandiose "Schlieffen Plan" was little more than an operational design that was adopted and developed by Schlieffen's successor, Helmuth von Moltke the Younger. Therefore, I have chosen here to refer to the plan by what I consider to be a more proper name, the Schlieffen-Moltke Plan.

Chapter 1

1. The literature on the origins of the war is incredibly vast and rich. There is no room here to delve into it in detail. A good introduction is James Joll, *The Origins of the First World War* (London: Longman, 1984). A series of new titles have come out in recent years, the most significant of which is Sean McMeekin's *The Russian Origins of the First World War* (Cambridge, MA: Belknap

Press, 2011). Others include McMeekin's *July 1914: Countdown to War* (New York: Basic Books, 2013); and Christopher Clark's, *The Sleepwalkers: How Europe Went to War in 1914* (New York: Harper Collins, 2013). The newer works confirm the essential status of Luigi Albertini's *The Origins of the War of 1914*, trans. Isabella M. Massey (London: Oxford University Press, 1952), which has recently been reprinted by Enigma Books. Older and important works include those by Sidney B. Fay, Bernadotte Schmidt, and A. J. P. Taylor. To delve more specifically into the older controversy over Germany's responsibility for the war, see Fritz Fischer, *War of Illusions: German Policies from 1911 to 1914*, trans. Marian Jackson (London: Chatto and Windus, 1975), and, for the other perspective, Gerhard Ritter, *The Sword and the Scepter: The Problem of Militarism in Germany* (Coral Gables, FL: University of Miami Press, 1969–73).

2. For excellent discussions of the arms races and how they helped to bring about war in 1914, see David Stevenson, *Armaments and the Coming of War: Europe, 1904–1914* (London: Oxford University Press, 1996), and David G. Herrmann, *The Arming of Europe and the Making of the First World War* (Princeton, NJ: Princeton University Press, 1996).

3. Niall Ferguson, *The Pity of War* (New York: Basic Books, 1999), 93. It should be pointed out however that these statistics are not exact. It is difficult to find sets of statistics for the period that do not disagree. For example Paul Kennedy in *The Rise and Fall of the Great Powers: Economic Change and Military Conflict from 1500 to 2000* (New York: Random House, 1987) lists 175.1 million for Russia, 39.7 million for France, 66.9 million for Germany, and 52.1 million for Austria-Hungary. I have chosen to use Ferguson's figures because they are taken from the German official history of the war, Reichsarchiv, *Der Weltkrieg 1914 bis 1918* (Berlin: E.S. Mittler und Sohn, 1925–1965).

4. Ferguson, *Pity*, 93.

5. For the number of men of military age, see B. R. Mitchell, *International Historical Statistics: Europe, 1750–1993*, 4th ed. (London: MacMillan, 1998), 13–47. For the number trained, see Ferguson, *Pity*, 93. Ferguson gives his own numbers for men of military age but does not explicitly list the years he is including.

6. Martin Gilbert, *Atlas of the First World War: The Complete History* (New York: Oxford University Press, 1994), 11.

7. Herrmann, *Arming of Europe*, 234.

8. Kennedy, *Great Powers*, 203. Herrmann only gives a number of around 700,000, which is too vague and seems far too low.

9. Ferguson, *Pity*, 92.

10. Kennedy, *Great Powers*, 203.

11. Ibid.

12. For a full discussion of these issues see Herrmann, *Arming of Europe*.

13. Mitchell, *Historical Statistics*, 426–431. All numbers in this table are taken from 1913.

14. Ibid., 452–453.

15. Ibid., 467.

16. Kennedy, *Great Powers*, 201.

17. Mitchell, *Historical Statistics*, 563.

18. Kennedy, *Great Powers*, 202.

19. Mitchell, *Historical Statistics*, 675.

20. Gilbert, *Atlas*, 141.

21. The key work on this topic is Samuel R. Williamson's *The Politics of Grand Strategy: Britain and France Prepare for War, 1904–1914* (Cambridge, MA: Harvard University Press, 1969).

22. Hew Strachan, *The First World War, Volume I: To Arms* (Oxford: Oxford University Press, 2001), 97.

23. The numbers for both Great Britain and the British Empire are taken from Ferguson, *Pity*, 93. Kennedy gives the British population as 45.6 million. Kennedy, *Great Powers*, 199.

24. Stephen Broadberry and Mark Harrison, eds., *The Economics of World War I* (New York: Cambridge University Press, 2005).

25. As with Table 1.2, the numbers of men of military age are taken from Mitchell, *Historical Statistics*, 13–47, and the number of men trained is taken from Ferguson, *Pity*, 93.

26. Kennedy, *Great Powers*, 203.

27. Gilbert, *Atlas*, 11.

28. Kennedy, *Great Powers*, 203. Ferguson's numbers are somewhat different with 1,268,000 tons for the Central Powers, 1,059,000 for France and Russia, and 2,205,000 for the British. Ferguson, *Pity*, 85.

29. Mitchell, *Historical Statistics*, 426–467. All figures are from 1913.

30. See in particular, Broadberry and Harrison, *Economics of World War I*.

31. Kennedy, *Great Powers*, 201.

32. Mitchell, *Historical Statistics*, 563.

33. Kennedy, *Great Powers*, 202.

Chapter 2

1. Mark Osborne Humphries and John Maker, eds., *Germany's Western Front: Translations from the German Official History of the Great War. Vol I: 1914* (Waterloo, Ontario: Wilfred Laurier Press, 2013), 39.

2. The Schlieffen Plan has been the subject of extensive debate amongst historians in the last several years beginning when Terence Zuber published an article, "The Schlieffen Plan Reconsidered" in *War in History* in 1999. His argument that there was no such thing as a Schlieffen Plan was further detailed in his book, *Inventing the Schlieffen Plan*, which was published by Oxford University Press in 2002. While there is no space here to lay out the intricacies of that debate and discussion, one of the effects of the research of Zuber and scholars

such as Annika Mombauer has been the relabeling of the plan as the Schlieffen-Moltke Plan.

3. Martin Gilbert, *Atlas of the First World War: The Complete History* (New York: Oxford University Press, 1994), 11.

4. The classic study of the Schlieffen Plan remains Gerhard Ritter, *Der Schlieffenplan: Kritik eines Mythos* (Oldenburg: Oldenburg Press, 1956). Translated into English as *The Schlieffen Plan: Critique of a Myth* (New York: O. Wolff, 1958). As was alluded to earlier, there is a lively debate within the scholarly community today regarding the Schlieffen Plan. This writer, though impressed by Zuber's research, is not yet convinced of his argument.

5. One of the areas where Zuber's argument is particularly compelling is that he calls into question the existence of the gigantic wheel around Paris, a move that makes very little operational sense in light of the rest of the plan. Had the Germans attempted such a move, their armies would have been separated by Paris as water flowing around a large rock and it would have made it far more difficult for them to achieve their aim of encircling the entire French army, something that surely Schlieffen would have been aware of, given that the Prussian army in the war of 1870–71 was forced to lay siege to Paris for several months.

6. The literature on the Schlieffen Plan is vast; consequently further details can be found in many places in addition to those cited earlier. For specific studies that informed this author, see in particular Hans Ehlert, Michael Epkenhans, and Gerhard Gross, eds., *Der Schlieffenplan: Analysen und Dokumente* (Paderborn: Ferdinand Schöningh, 2006); and Annika Mombauer, *Helmuth von Moltke and the Origins of the First World War* (Cambridge: Cambridge University Press, 2001); Peter Baldwin et al., eds., *New Studies in European History*. In addition there are the appropriate sections in the larger studies of Holger Herwig, *The First World War: Germany and Austria-Hungary 1914–1918*, 2nd ed. (London, UK: Bloomsbury, 2014); Hew Strachan, ed., *Modern Wars*; and Hew Strachan, *The First World War, Vol I: To Arms* (Oxford: Oxford University Press, 2003).

7. Holger Herwig, *The Marne 1914: The Opening of World War I and the Battle That Changed the World*. (New York: Random House, 2009), 42–45.

8. Bundesarchiv-Militärarchiv W-10/50276, "Die Militärpolitisches Lage Deutschlands," 72–73. Quoted in Mombauer, *Moltke*, 93.

9. Herwig, *Marne*, 36.

10. Ibid., 46–47.

11. These stats are taken from Herwig, *Marne*, 50–51.

12. David Stevenson, *Cataclysm: The First World War as Political Tragedy* (New York: Basic Books, 2004), 40.

13. Ibid., 40.

14. The following narrative draws, unless otherwise noted, most heavily from: Herwig, *Marne*; Humphries and Maker, *Western Front*; Strachan, *To Arms*; and Herwig, *First World War*.

15. Herwig, *Marne*, 145.

16. Ibid., 157.

17. Ibid., 244.

18. The participants themselves disagreed over whether or not Hentsch had been empowered to give orders in Moltke's name. In the aftermath of the defeat at the Marne, the army split into supporters of Moltke and Hentsch and supporters of Kluck. That debate raged into the postwar period and was reflected in the German official history of the war, *Der Weltkrieg*. It has never been resolved.

Chapter 3

1. Gerd Hardach, *The First World War 1914–1918*, History of the World Economy in the Twentieth Century, ed., Wolfram Fischer (Berkeley, CA: University of California Press, 1977), 56–57.

2. Otto Wilson, "Fertilizer Trade Development," *Industrial and Engineering Chemistry* 18, no.4 (1926): 401.

3. Avner Offer, *The First World War: An Agrarian Interpretation* (Oxford: Clarendon Press, 1989), 25.

4. B. R. Mitchell, *International Historical Statistics: Europe, 1750–1993*, 4th ed. (London: MacMillan, 1998), 259–317.

5. Ibid., 332–351.

6. Volker Berghahn, *Imperial Germany, 1871–1918: Economy, Society, Culture and Politics* (Providence, RI: Berghahn Books, 1994), 303.

7. Ibid., 305.

8. Ibid., 53–54.

9. Belinda Davis, *Home Fires Burning: Food, Politics and Everyday Life in World War I Berlin* (Chapel Hill, NC: University of North Carolina Press, 2000), 194.

10. Hardach, *First World War*, 200–204.

11. Gerald Feldmann, *Army, Industry and Labor in Germany 1914–1918* (Princeton, NJ: Princeton University Press, 1966), 52; Hardach, *First World War*, 57.

12. Feldmann, *Army*, 55.

13. Hardach, *First World War*, 59.

14. Offer, *First World War*, 27.

15. In fact, the Reichstag, the lower house, had surrendered its limited control over policy to the Bundesrat as part of the "Burgfrieden" established in August 1914. Feldmann, *Army*, 29.

16. Davis, *Home*, 28–31.

17. Feldmann, *Army*, 98–100.

18. Davis, *Home*, 28–31; Feldmann, *Army*, 101–102.

19. Hardach, *First World War*, 117–120.

20. Offer, *First World War*, 26; Hardach, *First World War*, 115–116.
21. Offer, *First World War*, 27.
22. Feldmann, *Army*, 45–47; Hardach, *First World War*, 57.
23. Hardach, *First World War*, 57.
24. Hardach, *First World War*, 57; Feldmann, *Army*, 47–49.
25. In the context of the First World War, this term refers to battleships and battle cruisers.
26. This issue is covered in detail in a number of works. A good starting point would be Paul G. Halpern, *A Naval History of the First World War*. A more detailed discussion can be found in what remains the master work on the Royal Navy during the war, Arthur J. Marder, *From the Dreadnought to Scapa Flow*. For the blockade specifically, the most recent work is Eric W. Osborne, *Britain's Economic Blockade of Germany, 1914–1919*. Naval Policy and History, no. 24, ed. Geoffrey Till (London: Frank Cass, 2004). The most useful older sources on the blockade include Archibald C. Bell, *A History of the Blockade of Germany and of the Countries Associated with Her in the Great War, Austria-Hungary, Bulgaria and Turkey* (London: HMSO, 1937); E. Keble Chatterton, *The Big Blockade* (London: Hurst and Blackett, 1932); Maurice Parmalee, *Blockade and Sea Power: The Blockade 1914–1919* (London: Thomas Crowell, 1924); Marion Siney, *The Allied Blockade of Germany 1914–1916* (Ann Arbor, MI: University of Michigan Press, 1957); and Paul Vincent, *The Politics of Hunger: The Allied Blockade of Germany 1915–1919* (Athens, OH: Ohio University Press, 1986). The following account is most indebted to Osborne's work and my own on the MarineKorps Flandern.
27. For further discussion of the idea of kleinkrieg, see Halpern's *Naval History*; or Holger Herwig's *"Luxury Fleet": The Imperial German Navy, 1888–1918*, 3rd ed. (New York: Routledge, 2014). More specific information can be found in my own history of the MarineKorps Flandern, Mark D. Karau, *Wielding the Dagger: The MarineKorps Flandern and the German War Effort, 1914–1918* (Westport, CT: Praeger, 2003).
28. Osborne, *Blockade*, 59.
29. Ibid., 60.
30. Ibid., 67.
31. Ibid., 75.
32. Sir Edward Grey, *Twenty-Five Years, 1892–1916*, 2 vols. (New York: Frederick A. Stokes, 1925), II: 107.
33. Osborne, *Blockade*, 76–77.
34. Ibid., 65.
35. Ibid., 73.
36. Hardach, *First World War*, 13.
37. Osborne, *Blockade*, 61.
38. Laurence Moyer, *Victory Must Be Ours: Germany in the Great War 1914–1918* (New York: Hippocrene Books, 1995), 127.

39. Moyer, *Victory*, 123–124.

40. Davis, *Home*, 50.

41. Offer, *First World War*, 26.

42. Moyer, *Victory*, 122–126.

43. Feldmann, *Army*, 102, 104. Germany was a federal state and it was the individual German states, Prussia, Bavaria, Baden, and others that enforced most of the decrees issued by the Reich government.

44. Davis, *Home*, 70.

45. Hardach, *First World War*, 200–204.

46. Davis, *Home*, 80–88.

47. Walther Rathenau, *Berliner Tageblatt*, December 25, 1915, cited in Moyer, *Victory*,135–136.

48. Moyer, *Victory*, 133.

49. Ibid., 136–137.

50. Ibid., 128.

51. Gold nails sold for FM 100, silver for DM 5, and iron for DM 1. *New York Times*, September 4, 1915.

52. Osborne, *Blockade*, 84–85.

53. Hardach, *First World War*, 18.

54. Osborne, *Blockade*, 85.

55. C. Paul Vincent, *The Politics of Hunger: The Allied Blockade of Germany, 1915–1919* (Athens, OH: Ohio University Press, 1985), 39.

56. Osborne, *Blockade*, 88.

57. Ibid., 103.

58. Osborne, *Blockade*, 93; Hardach, *First World War*, 20–27.

59. Osborne, *Blockade*, 125; Hardach, *First World War*, 27.

60. Osborne, *Blockade*, 125.

61. Ibid., 120–121.

62. Moyer, *Victory*, 156–160.

63. Ibid., 163.

64. Offer, *First World War*, 30.

65. Feldmann, *Army*, 108.

66. Moyer, *Victory*, 164.

67. Davis, *Home*, 137–159.

68. Hardach, *First World War*, 119.

69. Offer, *First World War*, 28.

70. Hardach, *First World War*, 118.

71. Offer, *First World War*, 45.

72. Hardach, *First World War*, 120.

73. Moyer, *Victory*, 161.

74. Davis, *Home*, 117–118.

75. Feldmann, *Army*, 128.

76. Davis, *Home*, 120.

77. The number of Germans on strike averaged 10,000/month in 1916, up from 1,000/month in 1915. Davis, *Home*, 120.

78. Moyer, *Victory*, 168–169.

79. Ibid., 173

80. Davis, *Home*, 180–184.

81. Ibid., 180–184.

82. German coal production in 1916 was 159 million tons, down from 190 million tons in 1915. Moyer, *Victory*, 175.

83. Moyer, *Victory*, 210.

Chapter 4

1. Gary E. Weir, *Building the Kaiser's Navy: The Imperial Naval Office and German Industry in the von Tirpitz Era, 1890–1919* (Annapolis, MD: US Naval Institute Press, 1992), 38.

2. Holger H. Herwig, *"Luxury" Fleet: The Imperial German Navy 1888–1918* rev. ed. (London: Allen and Unwin, 1980; London: Ashfield Press, 1987), 42.

3. Though all of these factors played a role in the divide between the two nations, the German fleet, which was clearly built against Great Britain, was the greatest problem between the two states. The best analysis of this growing divide remains Paul Kennedy, *The Rise of the Anglo-German Antagonism, 1860–1914* (London: Allen and Unwin, 1980). For the full British side of the story, see the five volume history by Arthur J. Marder, *From the Dreadnought to Scapa Flow* (Oxford: Oxford University Press, 1970).

4. Herwig, *"Luxury" Fleet*, 144.

5. Ibid., 144.

6. For a full discussion of the battle, see Eric W. Osborne, *The Battle of Heligoland Bight* (Bloomington, IN: Indiana University Press, 2006).

7. Tim Benbow, *Naval Warfare 1914–1918: From Coronel to the Atlantic and Zeebrugge. The History of World War I*, ed. Dennis Showalter (London: Amber Books, 2008), 67.

8. Benbow, *Naval Warfare*, 86.

9. Ibid., 88.

10. Mark D. Karau, *"Wielding the Dagger": The MarineKorps Flandern and the German War Effort, 1914–1918* (Westport, CT: Praeger, 2003), 53.

11. Herwig, *"Luxury" Fleet*, 163.

12. Ibid., 166.

13. Karau, *Dagger*, 53; Herwig, *"Luxury" Fleet*, 165.

14. Herwig, *"Luxury" Fleet*, 163.

15. The literature on the Battle of Jutland is vast. The best work is arguably Andrew Gordon's *The Rules of the Game: Jutland and British Naval Command* (Annapolis, MD: Naval Institute Press, 1996). Others that are outstanding

include the third volume of Arthur Marder's *Dreadnought to Scapa Flow*; and V.E. Tarrant's *Jutland: The German Perspective* (Annapolis, MD: Naval Institute Press, 1995).

16. Benbow, *Naval Warfare*, 146.

17. Robert K. Massie, *Castles of Steel: Britain, Germany and the Winning of the Great War at Sea* (New York: Random House, 2003), 596.

Chapter 5

1. For details on Falkenhayn's thinking on these issues, see Robert T. Foley, *German Strategy and the Path to Verdun: Erich von Falkenhayn and the Development of Attrition, 1870–1916* (Cambridge: Cambridge University Press, 2005).

2. Ian Passingham, *All the Kaiser's Men: The Life and Death of the German Army on the Western Front 1914–1918* (Gloucestershire: Sutton Publishing, 2003), 88.

3. Michael S. Neiberg, *The Western Front 1914–1916: From the Schlieffen Plan to Verdun and the Somme* (London: Amber Books, 2008)157.

4. Quoted in Passingham, *Kaiser's Men*, 92.

5. Neiberg, *Western Front*, 162.

6. Passingham, *Kaiser's Men*, 93.

7. Neiberg, *Western Front*, 170.

8. Ibid., 168.

9. For a full discussion of the German position, see William Philpott, *Three Armies on the Somme: The First Battle of the Twentieth Century* (New York: Alfred A. Knofp, 2009), 98–100.

10. Quoted in Passingham, *Kaiser's Men*, 107.

11. Quoted in Neiberg, *Western Front*, 171.

12. John Garth, *Tolkien and the Great War: The Threshold of Middle Earth* (New York: Houghton Mifflin, 2003).

13. Passingham, *Kaiser's Men*, 117.

14. Ibid., 121.

15. Ibid., 125–126.

16. Gerald Feldmann, *Army, Industry and Labor in Germany 1914–1918* (Princeton, NJ: Princeton University Press, 1966), 152–154. Feldmann's work remains the master work on this topic and it is vital for any understanding of the internal German situation during the war.

17. Gerd Hardach, *The First World War, 1914–1918* (Berkeley, CA: University of California Press, 1977), 63–69. Feldmann, *Army*, 192–194.

18. Hardach, *First World War*, 69–70.

19. Ibid., 70.

20. Quoted in Feldmann, *Army*, 272–273.

21. Quoted in Passingham, *Kaiser's Men*, 126.

Chapter 6

1. Cited in Holger Herwig, *The First World War: Germany and Austria-Hungary, 1914–1918* (Bloomsbury Academic, 1997), 314. The emphasis is this author's.

2. Robert K. Massie, *Castles of Steel: Britain, Germany, and the Winning of the War at Sea* (New York: Random House, 2003), 704.

3. Arno Spindler, *Der Handelskrieg mit U-Booten* (Berlin: E.S. Mittler, 1932–1966), IV:2–3.

4. Spindler, *Handelskrieg*, IV:194–195. Different sources list different numbers. I have chosen here to stick with the numbers presented by Spindler.

5. Spindler, *Handelskrieg*, IV:194–195.

6. Massie, *Castles*, 716.

7. For a full discussion of the implementation and expansion of the convoy system see Paul G. Halpern, *A Naval History of World War I* (Annapolis, MD: Naval Institute Press, 1994), 351–370.

8. Spindler, *Handelskrieg*, IV:194–195.

9. Ibid., 194–195.

10. Massie, *Castles*, 732.

11. Spindler, *Handelskrieg*, IV:194–195.

12. Lawrence Moyer, *Victory Must Be Ours: Germany in the Great War, 1914–1918* (New York: Hippocrene Books, 1995), 212.

13. Belinda Davis, *Home Fires Burning: Food, Politics, and Everyday Life in World War I Berlin* (Chapel Hill, NC: University of North Carolina Press, 2000), 190–200; Moyer, *Victory*, 215.

14. Moyer, *Victory*, 214.

15. Gerald Feldmann, *Army, Industry and Labor in Germany 1914–1918* (Princeton, NJ: Princeton University Press, 1966), 337–338.

16. Moyer, *Victory*, 205–6; Davis, *Home Fires*, 206.

17. Feldmann, *Army*, 254–266.

18. Moyer, *Victory*, 206–207.

19. Feldmann, *Army*, 270.

20. Moyer, *Victory*, 209. Gerd Hardach, *The First World War 1914–1918* (Berkeley, CA: University of California Press, 1977), 183–184.

21. Eric W. Osborne, *Britain's Economic Blockade of Germany, 1914–1918* (London: Frank Cass, 2004), 162–164; Paul C. Vincent, *The Politics of Hunger: The Allied Blockade of Germany, 1915–1919* (Athens, OH: Ohio University Press, 1985), 48.

22. Swiss trade increased for two reasons: first of all the French pressured the United States and Britain not to alienate the Swiss, and second, the Swiss themselves were willing to sign trade agreements that severely restricted what they would reexport to Germany.

23. Osborne, *Blockade*, 177–180.

24. Hardach, *First World War*, 147.

25. Ibid., 98–99.

26. Martin Kitchen, *The Silent Dictatorship: The Politics of the German High Command under Hindenburg and Ludendorff, 1916–1918* (New York: Croom and Helm, 1976).

27. Archibald C. Bell, *A History of the Blockade of Germany and of the Countries Associated with her in the Great War, Austria-Hungary, Bulgaria and Turkey, 1914–1918* (London: Her Majesty's Stationery Office, 1961), 680–682.

28. Feldmann, *Army*, 431.

29. Moyer, *Victory*, 226–227.

30. Herwig, *First World War*, 377.

31. Moyer, *Victory*, 200.

32. Spindler, *Handelskrieg*, IV:294–295.

33. Karl Dönitz, *Memoirs: Ten Years and Twenty Days* (Annapolis, MD: Naval Institute Press, 1959), cited in Massie, *Castles*, 733.

34. Spindler, *Handelskrieg*, IV:294–295.

35. Ibid., 294–295.

Chapter 7

1. Belinda Davis, *Home Fires Burning: Food, Politics, and Everyday Life in World War I Berlin* (Chapel Hill, NC: University of North Carolina Press, 2000), 224.

2. Davis, *Home*, 225.

3. David Stevenson, *Cataclysm: The First World War as Political Tragedy* (New York: Basic Books, 2004), 188.

4. Davis, *Home*, 219–222.

5. Paul C. Vincent, *The Politics of Hunger: The Allied Blockade of Germany, 1915–1919* (Athens, OH: Ohio University Press, 1985), 49–50, 81.

6. For the housing shortage see Gerald Feldmann, *Army, Industry and Labor in Germany 1914–1918* (Princeton, NJ: Princeton University Press, 1966), 459. For the shortage of medical supplies see Laurence Moyer, *Victory Must Be Ours: Germany in the Great War, 1914–1918* (New York: Hippocrene Books, 1995), 262.

7. Moyer, *Victory*, 265.

8. Feldmann, *Army*, 471.

9. Archibald C. Bell, *A History of the Blockade of Germany and of the Countries Associated with Her in the Great War: Austria-Hungary, Bulgaria and Turkey, 1914–1918* (London: Her Majesty's Stationery Office, 1961), 688.

10. Feldmann, *Army*, 447–450.

11. Davis, *Home*, 224; Feldmann, *Army*, 451.

12. Feldmann, *Army*, 449–451.

13. Gerd Hardach, *The First World War, 1914–1918* (Berkeley: University of California Press, 1977), 183–184.

14. Quoted in Moyer, *Victory*, 269.

15. Richard Pipes, *The Russian Revolution* (New York: Alfred A. Knopf, 1990), 595.

16. Robert K. Massie, *Castles of Steel: Britain, Germany, and the Winning of the War at Sea* (New York: Random House, 2003), 765.

17. Fritz Fischer, *Germany's Aims in the First World War* (New York: WW Norton and Company, 1967), 103–105.

18. Andrew Wiest, *The Western Front 1917–1918: From Vimy Ridge to Amiens and the Armistice* (London: Amber Books, 2008), 148.

19. Ibid., 163–164.

20. Ibid., 174–175.

21. Holger Herwig, *The First World War: Germany and Austria-Hungary 1914–1918* (New York: St. Martin's Press, 1997), 424.

22. Avner Offner, *The First World War: An Agrarian Interpretation* (Oxford: Clarendon Press, 1989), 71–72.

23. Moyer, *Victory*, 260.

24. Moyer, *Victory*, 276. In point of fact, by November even the German army was nearly out of food. The food reserve was down to roughly eight days. See Vincent, *Politics of Hunger*, 49–50.

Chapter 8

1. Albrecht Ritschl, "The Pity of Peace: Germany's Economy at War, 1914–1918 and Beyond." In *The Economics of World War I*, ed. Stephen Broadberry and Mark Harrison (New York: Cambridge University Press, 2005), 50.

2. Louis Guichard, *The Naval Blockade* (New York: D. Appleton and Company, 1930), 270–274.

3. Ibid., 262–266.

4. Ibid., 266–274.

5. Ibid., 277.

6. Paul Kennedy, *The Rise and Fall of the Great Powers: Economic Change and Military Conflict from 1500 to 2200* (New York: Random House, 1987), 272–273.

7. B.R. Mitchell, *International Historical Statistics: Europe 1750–1993*, 4th ed. (London: MacMillan, 1998), 259–317.

8. Guichard, *Naval Blockade*, 281–283.

9. Avner Offner, *The First World War: An Agrarian Interpretation* (Oxford: Clarendon Press, 1989), 61–63.

10. Mitchell, *Historical Statistics*, 555–557; Gerd Hardach, *The First World War, 1914–1918* (Berkeley: University of California Press, 1977), 114.

11. Ritschl, "Pity," 58.

12. Guichard, *Naval Blockade*, 285.

13. N.P. Howard, "The Social and Political Consequences of the Allied Food Blockade of Germany, 1918–19," *German History*, 11, 2 (1993), 163.

14. Mitchell, *Historical Statistics*, 332–351.

15. Howard, "Food Blockade," 164.

16. Eric W. Osborne, *Britain's Economic Blockade of Germany, 1914–1918* (London: Frank Cass, 2004), 182.

17. Offner, *First World War*, 379; Archibald C. Bell, *A History of the Blockade of Germany and of the Countries Associated with Her in the Great War: Austria-Hungary, Bulgaria and Turkey, 1914–1918* (London: Her Majesty's Stationery Office, 1961), 671–672.

18. Ritschl, "Pity," 54.

19. Belinda Davis, *Home Fires Burning: Food, Politics, and Everyday Life in World War I Berlin* (Chapel Hill, NC: University of North Carolina Press, 2000), 194.

20. Ibid., 194.

21. Offner, *First World War*, 33–38.

22. Holger Herwig, "Total Rhetoric, Limited War: Germany's U-Boat Campaign, 1917–1918." In *Great War, Total War: Combat and Mobilization on the Western Front, 1914–1918*, ed. Roger Chickering and Stig Förster (Cambridge: Cambridge University Press, 2000), 189; Paul C. Vincent, *The Politics of Hunger: The Allied Blockade of Germany, 1915–1919* (Athens, OH: Ohio University Press, 1985), 137.

23. Offner, *First World War*, 33–38.

24. Guichard, *Naval Blockade*, 300.

25. Howard, "Food Blockade," 166.

26. Bell, *Blockade*, 671–672.

27. Offner, *First World War*, 33–38.

Bibliography

The literature on the First World War could easily fill a library on its own. This bibliography is not a comprehensive one. The creation of this bibliography was guided by two principles: first, what works, in particular newer works, did this author find most useful in crafting this book and second, which sources are most accessible to the likely readers of this work, undergraduates and general audiences. For that reason, with the exception of some vitally important works, the bibliography is limited largely to newer English language works.

Afflerbach, Holger. "Planning Total War? Falkenhayn and the Battle of Verdun, 1916." In *Great War, Total War: Combat and Mobilization on the Western Front, 1914–1918*, ed. Roger Chickering and Stig Förster, 113–33. New York: Cambridge University Press, 2000.

Albertini, Luigi. *The Origins of the War of 1914*. 3 vols, trans. Isabella M. Massey. London: Oxford Press, 1952.

Asprey, Robert B. *The German High Command at War: Hindenburg and Ludendorff Conduct World War I*. New York: William Morrow, 1991.

Bell, Archibald C. *A History of the Blockade of Germany and of the Countries Associated with Her in the Great War, Austria-Hungary, Bulgaria and Turkey, 1914–1918*. London: Her Majesty's Stationary Office, 1937; published in 1961.

Benbow, Tim. *Naval Warfare 1914–1918: From Coronel to the Atlantic and Zeebrugge. The History of World War I*, ed. Dennis Showalter. London: Amber Books, 2008.

Berghahn, Volker. *Imperial Germany, 1871–1918: Economy, Society, Culture and Politics*. New York: Berghahn Books, 1994; reprinted, 2005.

Broadberry, Stephen, and Mark Harrison, eds. *The Economics of World War I*. New York: Cambridge University Press, 2005.

Brose, Eric Dorn. *A History of the Great War: World War One and the International Crisis of the Early Twentieth Century*. New York: Oxford University Press, 2010.

Buchholz, Arden. *Moltke, Schlieffen and Prussian War Planning*. Oxford: Berg, 1991.

Butler, Daniel Allen. *Distant Victory: The Battle of Jutland and the Allied Triumph in the First World War*. Westport, CT: Praeger, 2006.

Chatterton, E. Keble. *The Big Blockade*. London: Hutchinson and Company, 1932.

Chickering, Roger, *Imperial Germany and the Great War, 1914–1918*. 2nd ed. *New Approaches to European History*, ed. William Beik and T.C.W. Blanning. Cambridge: Cambridge University Press, 1998; reprint, 2004.

Chickering, Roger, and Stig Förster, eds. *Great War, Total War: Combat and Mobilization on the Western Front, 1914–1918*. New York: Cambridge University Press, 2000.

Citino, Robert M. *The German Way of War: From the Thirty Years War to the Third Reich*. Lawrence, KS: University Press of Kansas, 2005.

Clark, Christopher. *The Sleepwalkers: How Europe Went to War in 1914*. New York: HarperCollins, 2013.

Cornwall, Mark. "The Dissolution of Austria-Hungary." In *The Last Years of Austria-Hungary*, Exeter Studies in History, no. 27. ed. Jonathan Barry. Exeter: University of Exeter Press, 1990.

Cornwall, Mark. *The Undermining of Austria-Hungary: The Battle for Hearts and Minds*. New York: St. Martin's Press, 2000.

Davis, Belinda J. *Home Fires Burning: Food, Politics, and Everyday Life in World War I Berlin*. Chapel Hill: University of North Carolina Press, 2000.

Deist, Wilhelm. "The Military Collapse of the German Empire: The Reality behind the Stab in the Back Myth." *War in History* 3 (1996): 1–18.

Duffy, Christopher. *Through German Eyes: The British and the Somme 1916*. London: Weidenfeld and Nicolson, 2006.

Ehlert, Hans, Michael Epkenhans, and Gerhard P. Gross, eds. *Der SchlieffenPlan: Analysen und Dokumente*. Paderborn: Ferdinand Schöningh, 2006.

Feldmann, Gerald. *Army, Industry and Labor in Germany, 1914–1918*. Princeton: Princeton University Press, 1966.

Ferguson, Niall. *The Pity of War*. New York: Basic Books, 1999.

Fischer, Fritz. *Germany's Aims in the First World War*. New York: Norton, 1967.

Fischer, Fritz. *War of Illusions: German Policies from 1911 to 1914*. London: Chatto and Windus, 1975.

Foley, Robert T. *German Strategy and the Path to Verdun: Erich von Falkenhayn and the Development of Attrition, 1870–1916.* Cambridge: Cambridge University Press, 2005.

Garth, John. *Tolkien and the Great War: The Threshold of Middle Earth.* New York: Houghton Mifflin, 2003.

Germany. Marine-Archiv. *Der Krieg in der Nordsee.* 7 vols. Berlin: E.S Mittler, 1921–37.

Germany. Marine-Archiv. Reichsarchiv. *Der Weltkrieg 1914 bis 1918.* 14 vols. *Die militärischen Operationen zu Lande.* Berlin: E.S. Mittler, 1925–56.

Germany. Marine-Archiv. *Der Weltkrieg 1914 bis 1918. Kriegsrüstung und Kriegswirtschaft.* 2 vols. Berlin: E.S. Mittler, 1930.

Gilbert, Martin. *Atlas of the First World War: The Complete History.* New York: Oxford University Press, 1994.

Gilbert, Martin. *The First World War: A Complete History.* New York: Henry Holt, 1994.

Gordon, Andrew. *The Rules of the Game: Jutland and British Naval Command.* Annapolis, MD: Naval Institute Press, 1996.

Grey, Sir Edward. *Twenty-Five Years, 1892–1916.* 2 vols. New York: Frederick A. Stokes, 1925.

Guichard, Louis. *The Naval Blockade.* New York: D. Appleton and Company, 1930.

Halpern, Paul G. *A Naval History of World War I.* Annapolis, MD: Naval Institute Press, 1994.

Hardach, Gerd. *The First World War, 1914–1918.* History of the World Economy in the Twentieth Century, ed. Wolfram Fischer. Berkeley: University of California Press, 1977.

Herrmann, David G. *The Arming of Europe and the Making of the First World War.* Princeton: Princeton University Press, 1996.

Herwig, Holger. "The Dynamics of Necessity: German Military Policy during the First World War." In *Military Effectiveness: Volume I, The First World War.* Series on Defense and Foreign Policy, ed. Alan R. Millett and Williamson Murray, 80–116. Boston: Allen and Unwin, 1988.

Herwig, Holger. *The First World War: Germany and Austria-Hungary 1914–1918.* Modern Wars, ed. Hew Strachan. New York: St. Martin's Press, 1997.

Herwig, Holger. *"Luxury" Fleet: The Imperial Germany Navy 1888–1918.* London: Ashfield Press, 1987.

Herwig, Holger. *The Marne 1914: The Opening of World War I and the Battle That Changed the World.* New York: Random House, 2009.

Herwig, Holger. "Total Rhetoric, Limited War: Germany's U-Boat Campaign, 1917–1918." In *Great War, Total War: Combat and Mobilization on the*

Western Front, 1914–1918, ed. Roger Chickering and Stig Förster, 113–33. New York: Cambridge University Press, 2000.

Howard, N.P. "The Social and Political Consequences of the Allied Food Blockade of Germany, 1918–1919." *German History* 11:2 (1993): 161–88.

Humphries, Mark Osborne, and John Mayer, eds. *Germany's Western Front: Translations from the German Official History of the Great War, Volume 1: 1914*. Waterloo, OL: Wilfred Laurier Press, 2013.

Joll, James. *The Origins of the First World War*. London: Longman, 1984.

Karau, Mark D. *"Wielding the Dagger": The MarineKorps Flandern and the German War Effort, 1914–1918*. Contributions in Military Studies, Number 226. Westport, CT: Praeger, 2003.

Keegan, John. *The First World War*. New York: Alfred A. Knopf, 1999.

Kennedy, Paul. "Britain in the First World War." In *Military Effectiveness: Volume I, The First World War*. Series on Defense and Foreign Policy, ed. Alan R. Millett and Williamson Murray. 31–80. Boston: Allen and Unwin, 1988.

Kennedy, Paul. *The Rise and Fall of the Great Powers: Economic Change and Military Conflict from 1500 to 2000*. New York: Random House, 1987.

Kennedy, Paul. *The Rise of the Anglo-German Antagonism, 1860–1914*. New York: Allen and Unwin, 1980; reprinted, 1987.

Kitchen, Martin. *The Silent Dictatorship: The Politics of the German High Command under Hindenburg and Ludendorff, 1916–1918*. New York: Croom and Helm, 1976.

Marder, Arthur J. *From the Dreadnought to Scapa Flow: The Royal Navy in the Fisher Era*. 5 vols. London: Oxford University Press, 1961–70.

Massie, Robert K. *Castles of Steel: Britain, Germany and the Winning of the Great War at Sea*. New York: Random House, 2003.

McMeekin, Sean. *July 1914: Countdown to War*. New York: Basic Books, 2013.

McMeekin, Sean. *The Russian Origins of the First World War*. Cambridge, MA: Belknap, 2011.

Mendelssohn Bartholdy, Albrecht. *The War and German Society: The Testament of a Liberal*. New York: Howard Fertig, 1971.

Millett, Alan R., and Williamson Murray, eds. *Military Effectiveness: Volume I, The First World War*. Series on Defense and Foreign Policy, ed. Alan R. Millett and Williamson Murray. Boston: Allen and Unwin, 1988.

Mitchell, B.R. *International Historical Statistics: Europe 1750–1993*. 4th ed. London: MacMillan, 1998.

Mombauer, Annika. *Helmuth von Moltke and the Origins of the First World War*. New Studies in European History, ed. Peter Baldwin, et al. Cambridge: Cambridge University Press, 2001.

Mombauer, Annika, and Wilhelm Deist, eds. *The Kaiser: New Research on Wilhelm II's Role in Imperial Germany*. Cambridge: Cambridge University Press, 2003.

Moyer, Laurence. *Victory Must Be Ours: Germany in the Great War 1914–1918*. New York: Hippocrene Books, 1995.

Neiberg, Michael S. *The Western Front 1914–1916: From the Schlieffen Plan to Verdun and the Somme. The History of World War I*. ed. Dennis Showalter. London: Amber Books, 2008.

Neiberg, Michael S., ed. *The World War I Reader: Primary and Secondary Sources*. New York: New York University Press, 2007.

Offner, Avner. *The First World War: An Agrarian Interpretation*. Oxford: Clarendon Press, 1989.

Osborne, Eric W. *The Battle of Heligoland Bight*. Bloomington: Indiana University Press, 2006.

Osborne, Eric W. *Britain's Economic Blockade of Germany 1914–1919*. Naval Policy and History, no. 24, ed. Geoffrey Till. London: Frank Cass, 2004.

Parmalee, Maurice. *Blockade and Sea Power: The Blockade 1914–1919*. New York: Thomas Y. Crowell, 1924.

Passingham, Ian. *All the Kaiser's Men: The Life and Death of the German Army on the Western Front 1914–1918*. Gloucestershire: Sutton Publishing, 2003.

Philpott, William. *Three Armies on the Somme: The First Battle of the Twentieth Century*. New York: Alfred A. Knopf, 2009.

Pipes, Richard. *The Russian Revolution*. New York: Alfred A. Knopf, 1990.

Prior, Robin, and Trevor Wilson. *The Somme*. New Haven: Yale University Press, 2005.

Ritschl, Albrecht. "The Pity of Peace: Germany's Economy at War, 1914–1918 and Beyond." In *The Economics of World War I*, ed. Stephen Broadberry and Mark Harrison, 41–77. New York: Cambridge University Press, 2005.

Ritter, Gerhard. *The Schlieffen Plan: Critique of a Myth*. New York: Praeger, 1958.

Ritter, Gerhard. *The Sword and the Scepter: The Problem of Militarism in Germany*. Coral Gables, FL: University of Miami Press, 1969–73.

Schulze, Max Stephan. "Austria-Hungary's Economy in WWI." In *The Economics of World War I*, ed. Stephen Broadberry and Mark Harrison, 41–77. New York: Cambridge University Press, 2005.

Sheldon, Jack. *The German Army on the Somme 1914–1916*. South Yorkshire: Pen and Sword, 2005.

Siney, Marion. *The Allied Blockade of Germany 1915–1919*. Ann Arbor, MI: University of Michigan Press, 1957.

Spindler, Arno. *Der Handelskrieg mit U-Booten*. 5 vols. Berlin: E.S. Mittler, 1932–66.

Stephenson, Scott. *The Final Battle: Soldiers of the Western Front and the German Revolution of 1918*. New York: Cambridge University Press, 2009.

Stevenson, David. *Armaments and the Coming of War: Europe, 1904–1914*. London: Oxford University Press, 1996.

Stevenson, David. *Cataclysm: The First World War as Political Tragedy*. New York: Basic Books, 2004.

Stevenson, David. *With Our Backs to the Wall: Victory and Defeat in 1918*. Cambridge, MA: Belknap Press, 2011.

Strachan, Hew. *The First World War*. New York: Viking, 2003.

Strachan, Hew. *The First World War: Volume I: To Arms*. New York: Oxford University Press, 2001.

Strachan, Hew, ed. *World War I: A History*. Oxford: Oxford University Press, 1998.

Tarrant, V.E. *Jutland: The German Perspective*. Annapolis, MD: Naval Institute Press, 1995.

Van Creveld, Martin. *Supplying War: Logistics from Wallenstein to Patton*. Cambridge: Cambridge University Press, 2004.

Vincent, Paul C. *The Politics of Hunger: The Allied Blockade of Germany 1915–1919*. Athens, OH: Ohio University Press, 1985.

Weir, Gary E. *Building the Kaiser's Navy: The Imperial Naval Office and German Industry in the von Tirpitz Era, 1890–1919*. Annapolis, MD: Naval Institute Press, 1992.

Wiest, Andrew. *The Western Front 1917–1918: From Vimy Ridge to Amiens and the Armistice*. London: Amber Books, 2008.

Williamson, Samuel R. *The Politics of Grand Strategy: Britain and France Prepare for War, 1904–1914*. Cambridge, MA: Harvard University Press, 1969.

Wilson, Otto. "Fertilizer Trade Development." *Industrial and Engineering Chemistry*, 18:4 (1926): 401–4.

Winter, Jay, and Antoine Prost. *The Great War in History: Debates and Controversies, 1914 to the Present*. Cambridge: Cambridge University Press, 2005.

Winter, Jay, and Jean-Louis Robert, eds. *Capital Cities at War: Paris, London, Berlin 1914–1919*. Studies in the Social and Cultural History of Modern Warfare, ed. Jay Winter. Volume 2. Cambridge: Cambridge University Press, 1999.

Zuber, Terence. *Inventing the Schlieffen Plan: German War Planning, 1871–1914*. Oxford: Oxford University Press, 2002.

Index

About the Author

MARK D. KARAU is an associate professor of history at the University of Wisconsin-Sheboygan, where he teaches courses on the history of modern Germany and on the two world wars, including an interdisciplinary course on the First World War. He is the author of *"Wielding the Dagger": The MarineKorps Flandern and the German War Effort, 1914–1918* and "Twisting the Dragon's Tail: The Zeebrugge and Ostende Raids of 1918," which was selected for inclusion in an anthology of the best articles on twentieth-century naval history by Ashgate Press. He earned his PhD from Florida State University in 2000.